Anne Orthwood's Bastard

Anne Orthwood's Bastard

Sex and Law in Early Virginia

JOHN RUSTON PAGAN

OXFORD

UNIVERSITY PRESS

2003

OXFORD

UNIVERSITY PRESS

Oxford   New York

Auckland   Bangkok   Buenos Aires   Cape Town   Chennai
Dar es Salaam   Delhi   Hong Kong   Istanbul   Karachi   Kolkata
Kuala Lumpur   Madrid   Melbourne   Mexico City   Mumbai   Nairobi
São Paulo   Shanghai   Taipei   Tokyo   Toronto

Copyright ©2003 by John Ruston Pagan

Published by Oxford University Press, Inc.
198 Madison Avenue, New York, New York 10016

www.oup.com

Oxford is a registered trademark of Oxford University Press

Library of Congress Cataloging-in-Publication Data
Pagan, John Ruston.
Anne Orthwood's bastard : sex and law in early Virginia / John Ruston Pagan.
p.   cm.
Includes bibliographical references and index.
ISBN-13 978-0-19-514479-6

1. Sex and law — Virginia — History — 17th century. 2. Illegitimacy — Virginia —
History — 17th century. 3. Orthwood, Anne, 1639–1664 — Trials, litigation, etc.
4. Kendall, John, fl. 1663 — Trials, litigation, etc. I. Title.
KFV2967.S3 P34 2002
364.15'3 — dc21   2002025273

12   13   14   15   16   17   18   19

Printed in the United States of America
on acid-free paper

For
Clive Holmes

ACKNOWLEDGMENTS

This book began as a summer research project funded by the Mellon Fellowship program at the Virginia Historical Society. I am grateful for the Society's generous support and for the expert assistance of its library staff. I also appreciate the help I received from the staffs of the Bodleian Library at the University of Oxford; the Law Library of the University of Arkansas at Little Rock; the Muse Law Library at the University of Richmond; the clerk's offices of Northampton and Accomack Counties; and the Norfolk Record Office. Special thanks go to Branda and David Littleton, who computerized my data; to J. J. Tyzbir, my research assistant at the University of Richmond; to David Thomas Konig, Kris Marzolf, and Hamilton Bryson for their critiques of my manuscript; and to Susan Ferber, my editor at Oxford University Press, whose suggestions were invaluable.

Much of the credit for the book belongs to the wonderful teachers with whom I have had the pleasure of studying history and law. I shall always be indebted to Cam Walker, Boyd Coyner, and Thad Tate, my friends and mentors in the history department of the College of William and Mary, for inspiring my love of Virginia history; to Harold L. Fowler, professor of Tudor and Stuart history at William and Mary, Ivan Roots, my tutor at the University of Exeter, and John P. Cooper, my master's thesis supervisor at Oxford, for stimulating my interest in the seventeenth century; to the Harvard law faculty, for training me to analyze legal issues; to Roger Highfield and John Roberts, fellows of Merton College, Oxford, for encouraging me over the years; and especially to Clive Holmes, my doctoral supervisor at Oxford, for patiently guiding my research.

CONTENTS

Anne Orthwood's Bastard

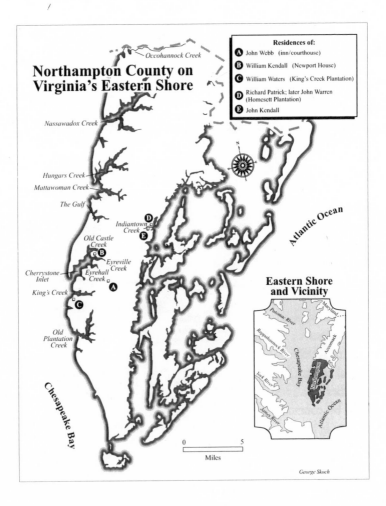

Northampton County on Virginia's Eastern Shore

Occohannock Creek

Residences of:

Ⓐ John Webb (inn/courthouse)

Ⓑ William Kendall (Newport House)

Ⓒ William Waters (King's Creek Plantation)

Ⓓ Richard Patrick; later John Warren (Homesett Plantation)

Ⓔ John Kendall

Nassawadox Creek

Hungars Creek
Mattawoman Creek
The Gulf

Indiantown Creek Ⓓ
Ⓔ

Old Castle Creek
Ⓑ
Eyreville Creek
Cherrystone Inlet *Eyrehall Creek* Ⓐ
King's Creek
Ⓒ

Old Plantation Creek

Atlantic Ocean

Eastern Shore and Vicinity

Potomac River
Maryland
Rappahannock River
Chesapeake Bay
Assateague
York River
Northampton
James River
Atlantic Ocean

Chesapeake Bay

0   5
Miles

George Skoch

INTRODUCTION

Anne Orthwood and John Kendall first had sex on Saturday night, November 28, 1663, at John Webb's inn near the site of modern-day Cheriton in Northampton County, on Virginia's Eastern Shore. They were intimate a second and possibly a third time later that weekend.[1] Anne was a single, white, 24-year-old indentured servant who had emigrated to Virginia from her home in Bristol, England, about a year earlier. John, a bachelor in his early twenties, was a free man from Norfolk, England, who lived with his uncle, Lieutenant Colonel William Kendall, one of the most powerful men on the Eastern Shore.

This was not a casual fling between strangers. Anne and John knew each other well and had probably been romantically involved for several months. They had been fellow residents of Newport House Plantation, Colonel Kendall's seat in lower Northampton County. Anne worked there as a serving woman, and John helped the colonel run his plantation and an extensive overseas trading business. Colonel Kendall evidently discovered their clandestine romance and grew worried over the possible outcome. Marriage to a lowly servant was out of the question, given Colonel Kendall's social aspirations for his young kinsman. An extramarital relationship was equally unacceptable on moral and economic grounds. As a head of household, Colonel Kendall had a religious obligation to prevent his family and servants from committing fornication; as a community leader, he owed a duty to protect his fellow colonists from the damaging financial effects of illicit pregnancy. Seventeenth-century Virginians considered bastardy "prejudiciall to the masters and mistresses of servants" because childbearing interfered with female servants' ability to work in the fields and perform domestic chores. Taxpayers wanted to deter out-of-wedlock births because they feared that parents might not support their illegitimate offspring, rendering the children "Chargable to the parish," which meant they had to be fed, clothed, and sheltered at public expense.[2] Since Colonel Kendall was a justice of the peace, church-warden, and member of the House of Burgesses, taxpayers looked to him for leadership in the war against illegitimacy. His honor and reputation would suffer if someone close to him committed a moral lapse. To shield John from temptation and obviate the manifold dangers of forbidden sex, Colonel Kendall decided to send Anne away from Newport House Plantation. He assigned her indenture (in other words, sold his contractual right to her services) to a fellow planter, Jacob Bishopp.

Anne and John were reunited as a result of the makeshift circumstances of early Virginia justice. Until 1665, when the first purpose-built courthouse went into use, the Northampton County Court sat in Webb's inn. The proprietor profited from the arrangement by providing food and lodging to people attending court and by charging the county a fee for allowing the justices to meet on his premises.[3] Anne and her new master stayed at Webb's inn during the weekend of November 28–29, 1663, because Bishopp had to attend the county court session on Monday, November 30. John went there with his uncle in order to enjoy the mixture of socializing and bargaining that gave court days the atmosphere of a country fair.[4]

We do not know what transpired between Anne and John prior to intercourse, but one imagines a scene not unlike that described in a 1654 case heard by the mayor of Portsmouth, England. A butcher asked a single woman to join him at the Queen's Head for a few pints of wine, after which "he lay on her for about three hours and had carnal knowledge of her body." He promised to "father the child if she was with child" and even said he would marry her. The butcher reneged, and the jilted — and now pregnant — woman sought help from the borough authorities. If he had kept his promise, she told the mayor, she would not have complained about the advances. Disgusted by her gullibility and the butcher's lies, the mayor committed both fornicators to prison.[5] Anne was foolish if, like the Portsmouth woman, she allowed herself to be seduced by false assurances of eventual matrimony. One can understand why she might have yielded, however. In the seventeenth century, many people thought it was justifiable for a couple to have sex after betrothal, despite the strictures of the church, and this view not only encouraged the widespread practice of prenuptial fornication but also made the promise of marriage a common ploy used by cads.[6] Having experienced the harsh realities of servitude in Virginia, Anne undoubtedly yearned for a fiancé who could afford to liberate her. To a woman in her position, John must have seemed the perfect catch. He was young, single, and from a prosperous, powerful family. For John, though, marriage to a servant was never a realistic possibility, notwithstanding a shortage of women on the Eastern Shore. He knew his family connections would enable him to capture a much better prize in the marriage market. As it turned out, events would prove him right; three and a half years later, he won the hand of a major heiress.

However their intimacy came about, the affair ended disastrously for Anne. She conceived twins and soon found herself engulfed in troubles. The first consequence of her illicit pregnancy was shame. The church taught that all fornication was sinful, and society reinforced the message by humiliating people caught transgressing sexual norms. The second consequence was punishment. Under Virginia law, fornicators were subject to a fine or whipping. Because she was an impoverished servant, Anne lacked the means to pay a fine and thus faced a much greater risk of flogging than did her affluent sex partner. The third consequence was economic.

Instead of being freed after four years of servitude, as provided in her original employment contract, Anne would have to serve her master an extra two years or pay him 2,000 pounds of tobacco to compensate him for the loss of her labor while she was incapacitated by pregnancy and childbirth. The fourth consequence pertained to her children's future. Anne herself had been born out of wedlock and therefore knew only too well the hardships and stigmatization her offspring would have to endure.

With these concerns weighing heavily on her mind, Anne concealed her condition as long as she could. Before her pregnancy became visible, Bishopp sold her indenture to Lieutenant Colonel William Waters, a justice of the peace and major landowner. Bishopp assured Waters that, so far as he knew, Anne was healthy and chaste. When the truth emerged that spring, Waters felt misled. Anne's pregnancy would prevent her from working as hard as he had expected, denying him the full benefit of his purchase. In June, Waters filed a breach-of-contract lawsuit against Bishopp in the Northampton County Court, attempting to cancel the sale and recover his down payment.

Waters v. Bishopp was the first of four legal actions resulting from Anne's pregnancy. The second, *Ex Parte Kendall,* involved John's civil liability for child support. As soon as the county magistrates learned that an illegitimate birth was imminent, they attempted to discover the father's identity so they could compel him to post a bond guaranteeing that he would support the child. Anne refused to cooperate, steadfastly refusing to name the man who had impregnated her. Perhaps John persuaded her to remain silent by reiterating a promise of marriage; maybe he offered to purchase her freedom and provide for her child if she would spare him the indignity of a paternity charge. Whatever the reason for her reticence, the justices gave up trying to extract the information themselves and turned to a midwife, Eleanor Gething, for help. They committed Anne to Gething's custody and ordered the midwife to interrogate her during delivery. While in labor on July 29, 1664, Anne identified John as the father and described the circumstances of conception. She gave birth to twins and died soon afterward, probably from an infection caused by unhygienic obstetrical procedures. One of the twins died in infancy; the other, a boy named Jasper, survived into adulthood. John denied paternity and disclaimed responsibility for raising Jasper. Knowing he was virtually certain to be sued by the parish churchwardens, John filed a petition in the county court in August 1664, seeking a judicial declaration of his innocence and exoneration of liability for child support.

The third case arising from the illicit sexual relations between Anne and John, *Rex v. Kendall,* was a criminal fornication charge lodged against John by the Northampton County grand jury in February 1665. In England, fornication was an ecclesiastical offense punished by the church courts. Because Virginia had no church courts, fornication came under the jurisdiction of the county courts. The statutory penalty in 1665 was a fine of 500 pounds of tobacco, payable to the parish in which the offender dwelled. For a high-status male defendant such as John Kendall, the worst aspect of a fornication charge was not the prospect of paying a relatively minor fine but the danger that a conviction might sully his family's hard-won reputation and stain his personal honor.

The fourth case, *Orthwood v. Warren,* arose a generation later and marked the final act of the Orthwood-Kendall drama. Anne's surviving child, Jasper, was bound into servitude as an infant. After he turned 21, on July 29, 1685, he asked his master, John Warren, to free him. Warren refused, invoking the English Poor Law of 1601,[7] which authorized churchwardens to bind out male bastards until the age of 24. Jasper hired a lawyer, Charles Holden, and sued Warren in the Northampton County Court in June 1686. Holden relied on a 1672 act of the Virginia Assembly that emancipated male bastards at 21.[8] The case presented a fascinating conflict-of-laws problem: Which statute controlled, the 1601 act of Parliament or the 1672 Virginia law? In other words, did Virginians consider themselves obligated to treat English statutes as supreme, or did they think colonial legislators had a right to disregard English laws if they did not suit American conditions? Besides raising an important point of law, Jasper's lawsuit revived memories of the community's most notorious scandal. This reminder of the circumstances of Jasper's birth embarrassed William Kendall, who recently had been elevated to the colony's highest elective office, the speakership of the House of Burgesses. Even in his hour of greatest glory, Kendall could not escape the effects of John and Anne's sexual encounters nearly a quarter-century earlier.

These four cases are worth examining because of the light they shed on the formative period of American law. Colonists brought English legal culture with them to the New World just as they transplanted the English language. Drawing on their heritage and innovating when necessary, settlers fashioned distinctive legal systems for each colony. The combination of traditional English doctrines with new rules tailored to local situations produced what the historian Lawrence M. Friedman has aptly termed "a creolized dialect of the English common law — the legal equivalent of pidgin English."[9] By analyzing the Orthwood-Kendall litigation, we can gain a clearer understanding of how the creole dialect of early Virginia law differed from the mother tongue. By viewing those differences in a broader political, social, and economic context, we can start to comprehend the complex forces that shaped law on the frontier of the English-speaking world.

Case studies are useful because they facilitate the exploration of large themes through specific examples. As the historian Alan Macfarlane has written, close examination of legal proceedings "allows us to enter the everyday world of that time," providing "a 'social drama' which, as anthropologists have argued, enables us to see into the heart of a society."[10] For the case-study technique to work, an author must be able to sketch fairly detailed portraits of the characters in the drama, depicting their family backgrounds, their socioeconomic status, their relationships with other characters, and various factors influencing their conduct. Such a portrayal is possible for the Orthwood-Kendall litigation because of the richness of the Eastern Shore archives. Northampton and its northern neighbor, Accomack County, possess the oldest continuous series of county court records in the United States. Unlike the records of most Virginia counties and the archives of the colony's central court, the judicial manuscripts of the Eastern Shore survived the ravages of the American Revolution and the Civil War.[11] They begin with an entry for January 7, 1633, and proceed, in a virtually unbroken sequence, to the present day.[12] These documents, augmented by English sources such as parish registers and lists of indentured servants, permit us to reconstruct the story of Anne Orthwood's bastard.

Since a story forms the core of this book, for the most part I have adopted a narrative rather than a topical structure. The narrative begins with Anne's birth, emigration to America, and entry into servitude; it ends with Jasper's emancipation suit and emergence as a free man. The characters encountered the colonial legal system at almost every turn. The system's response illuminates the emerging distinctiveness of early American law. Two interrelated themes appear throughout the book. First, the peculiar structure of Virginia's economy and labor system accounts for many of the differences between colonial and English law. Second, although less sophisticated technically than English law, the jurisprudence of early Virginia reflects colonial leaders' skillful manipulation of legal doctrines and institutions to enhance their social status and strengthen their political position. They did not achieve these aims by ruthlessly imposing their will. Most of the men who administered justice on the Eastern Shore in this period were insecure parvenus who lacked the authority of a traditional ruling class. By necessity, they governed through persuasion, always keeping a close eye on public opinion. If they did their utmost to steer the law in a direction that served their own interests, they succeeded largely because their interests coincided with those of the other property owners who made up the political community and because their decisions struck a socially acceptable balance between fairness and efficiency.

John Kendall and Anne Orthwood brought misery to their lives when they surrendered to their passions that weekend so long ago.

What this book is about.

Their affair produced embarrassment for him and death for her. For us, however, the well-documented consequences of their misadventure yield much that is valuable. John and Anne's story helps us appreciate the adaptability of English law and understand the process by which Virginians created their own legal identity just two generations after the first settlers landed.

ONE

ANNE ORTHWOOD,
INDENTURED SERVANT

Virginians knew the central figure in this story as Anne Orthwood, but her actual surname was Harwood or Horwood.[1] She was christened on August 12, 1639, in Worcester, England, a city a contemporary described as "pleasantly seated, exceedingly populous, and doubtless very rich." The city grew wealthy in the sixteenth and early seventeenth centuries from its highly organized textile industry. Despite a calamitous visitation of the plague in the summer of 1637, Worcester's population at the time of Anne's birth stood at roughly six or seven thousand.[2] Anne's baptism was performed at All Saints, an Anglican church close to the River Severn in the center of Worcester, by John Ricketts, the rector. Ricketts maintained the parish register himself, carefully noting each baptism, marriage, and burial in a clear hand. After every christening, he recorded the names of the child's parents. Of the 58 children Ricketts baptized in 1639, 57 had a married couple listed as the parents. The sole exception, Anne, was recorded with just the name of her mother, 19-year-old Mary Harwood. Lest anyone miss the significance of this aberrant entry, Ricketts placed an asterisk by Anne's name and added underneath, with a classical flourish, the word *notha* — Latin for "bastard."[3]

Labeling Anne a bastard implied that her mother had committed the sin of fornication, and this set in motion the church's disciplinary process. The ecclesiastical courts prosecuted fornicators and other sinners for the sake of their souls, to restore offenders to a healthy relationship with God and the Christian community. The typical sanction was penance, a public ritual of repentance and reconciliation. Dressed in a white sheet and carrying a white rod, the offender had to confess before the congregation during service time on Sunday or a holiday. Failure to perform the prescribed penance resulted in excommunication.[4] Mary Harwood's understandable desire to avoid the humiliation of penance probably prompted her decision to leave All Saints Parish shortly after Anne's baptism. She and her baby moved to the village of Alfrick, about five miles west of Worcester. The ecclesiastical authorities soon found her, however, and took steps to secure her appearance in court. During a Sunday service in August 1640, the curate of the church in Alfrick handed her a citation summoning her to appear before the chancellor of the diocese of Worcester the following month.[5] Instead of obeying, Mary moved again, this time to Bristol, the great port city near the mouth of the Severn, about 70 miles downriver from Worcester. Bristol was England's most important overseas commercial center outside London, trading primarily with the Iberian peninsula, France, Ireland, and, to a growing extent, North America. A relatively big city by seventeenth-century standards, Bristol had a population of about 15,000 when Mary and her infant daughter, Anne, arrived there, probably in the latter part of 1640.[6] Living in such a large, unfamiliar place, far from her family and friends, was not easy for Mary. She had to struggle to provide sufficient food, clothing, and shelter for Anne and herself. Her burdens grew even heavier when she conceived her second illegitimate child, a daughter named Mary, who was christened in the Church of St. Mary Le Port in Bristol in October 1642.[7]

Growing up as illegitimate children in Bristol during the 1640s and 1650s must have been difficult for Anne and her half-sister. Premarital sex was common (a quarter of all brides were pregnant on their wedding day), but illegitimacy was highly unusual in this period. Only 1–2 percent of births occurred out of wedlock, a much lower rate than in subsequent centuries.[8] "Bastard" remained a powerful term of opprobrium throughout the seventeenth century, reflecting popular resentment of illicit offspring as the living symbols of social irregularity.[9] As the legal commentator John Brydall observed in his 1703 treatise *Lex Spuriorum,* early modern Englishmen thought bastardy "staineth the Blood," causing children "Shame and Disgrace; for, though it be no fault for a Bastard to be such a one, yet it is a Dishonour derived from the Parents on the Child, and a thing easily subject to Contumely and Reproach." An illegitimate was *filius nullius* — the son of nobody — and therefore traditionally "of no reckoning, or esteem in Law." The law's harshness toward bastards had eased somewhat since the Middle Ages, but they still possessed fewer rights of inheritance and legal protections than legitimate children enjoyed. One of Brydall's purposes for writing his book detailing the legal handicaps of illegitimacy was "To let the People of this present Age see, what great Disadvantages Children born out of Holy Matrimony do lie under; which might (as he conceives) very much deter Men and Women from ever pursuing unlawful and exorbitant Embraces, of which this Nation, as well as foreign Countries, have been deeply guilty."[10]

Although illegitimacy made Anne's life especially hard, she also faced the same pressures as other members of her generation. Rapid population growth created a labor surplus, particularly among agricultural and textile workers and domestic servants. High prices, declining real wages, unemployment, rising rents, and land shortages combined to encourage many to leave home in search of better opportunities. People migrated to cities such as London and Bristol, and if they found no jobs there, sailed for the colonies, blissfully ignorant of the high mortality rates and harsh working conditions that awaited them. Around 112,000 people emigrated from Britain to the Americas in the 1650s and 1660s.[11] Approximately a third of those migrated to the Chesapeake Bay colonies of Virginia and Maryland, mainly from London.[12] Three-quarters went as indentured servants, paying for their transportation by contracting to work in the colonies for a certain number of years.[13]

The port of Bristol, from which Anne emigrated, required servants to record their indentures in the Tolzey Book, or *Register of Servants to Foreign Plantations*, which provides a detailed picture of migration from Bristol to America between 1654, when the *Register* begins, and 1686, when the last entries were recorded. The number of servants bound for Virginia from Bristol rose from a little over 100 in 1655 to a peak of around 500 in 1662. Roughly three-quarters were male and one-quarter female. Most were unmarried and in their early twenties. About half the men had agricultural backgrounds; others had craft or trade skills, and the rest were unskilled laborers. The *Register* rarely provides occupational information for women. Historians speculate that the average indentured female probably had fewer skills than her male counterpart and occupied a lower rung on the social ladder. Most male and female servants came from towns and villages in the west of England. Over 80 percent originated within 60 miles of Bristol.[14]

Anne's profile matched that of the typical Bristol emigrant. She turned 23 in August 1662, the high-water mark of emigration from Bristol to Virginia. She came from the Bristol area; she was single; she probably was unskilled. Like so many other young English men and women in this period, she felt pessimistic about her opportunities at home, particularly her chances of marrying and raising a family in an economically secure environment. Her outlook made her an easy target for pitchmen touting the virtues of life in the New World. Labor recruiters painted a rosy picture of maidservants' marriage prospects abroad, especially in the Chesapeake, where men greatly outnumbered women. The extravagant claims of the Virginia promoter William Bullock exemplify the kinds of promises that were directed at husband-hunting maidservants. If female servants "come of an honest stock and have a good repute," Bullock assured them, "they may pick and chuse their Husbands out of the better sort of people." Bullock, a London investor who owned an interest in a Virginia plantation, said he had "sent over many [maidservants], but never could keepe one at my Plantation three Moneths" because they found husbands so quickly. Even "a poore silly Wench, made for a Foile to set of[f] beautie" was snapped up by "a proper young Fellow" who paid Bullock a year of his own labor for the privilege of making her his wife.[15] The Eastern Shore court records contain numerous examples of the type of transaction Bullock described. Mark Hammon, for instance, bought the indenture of Thomas Powell's servant Anne Dennis so he could marry her. Thomas Church bound himself to Philip Taylor in order to obtain the early release of Nazareth Attcock, the maidservant he intended to marry. Richard Bundocke, desiring to marry John Foster's maidservant, promised Foster that he would replace her with "a sufficient man Servant, or a Boye of xiiii yeares or a Maydservant a sufficient hand to Serve in her stead to bee bought when shippinge came in."[16] Female emigrants' matrimonial hopes, then, were not entirely unfounded, but they left young women vulnerable to men who might use false promises of marriage as a means of seduction.

If emigration to the Chesapeake improved poor women's odds of marrying, seventeenth-century Virginia and Maryland also offered the prospect of an early death. Between 1607 and 1662, at least 35,000 people migrated to Virginia, but the population in 1662 stood at only 25,600. Had promoters fully informed prospective female emigrants about mortality along the tobacco coast, they might well have avoided the region or stayed home. The area's mortality rate improved after midcentury but still remained higher than in England or New England. Many immigrants died within a year of arrival, victims of diseases to which they lacked immunity. Between 40 percent and 60 percent of servants did not live to complete their service. Even if a woman did survive service and marry at, say, 25 (the mean age at marriage for female immigrants), she could expect to live only another 16 years. This was a much shorter life span than New England women enjoyed, due primarily to the risks of childbirth in an environment infested with malaria. Twenty-five-year-old male immigrants, by comparison, could expect to live another 21 years.[17] Short life expectancy, combined with delay in marriage because of servitude, adversely affected Chesapeake family life. Half of Chesapeake marriages were broken within seven years by the death of one of the partners, and the chances were just one in three that a marriage would last 10 years. Immigrant women typically bore only three or four children, half of whom died before reaching adulthood. This level of reproduction was barely adequate to replace parents in the population, let alone compensate for people who never had an opportunity to form families.[18]

Anne knew little or nothing about the hazards of colonial life. Her image of the New World came almost entirely from promoters' propaganda, which she found irresistible. Her old life had been harsh, demeaning, and precarious; a new life abroad seemed to offer the possibility of comfort, dignity, and security. Emigration would allow her to make a fresh start in a land where no one knew her origins, a place where she could escape the stigma of illegitimacy and become a respectable wife and mother. To finance her voyage, she needed to find someone who would underwrite the cost of her passage in return for a promise to repay the debt with her labor. The man she turned to was not a merchant with colonial trading interests, as one might expect, but a ship's surgeon from Bristol, Jasper Cross. Like other mariners, Cross sometimes took along one or two servants whose indentures he hoped to sell in the colonies at a profit.[19] Between 1656 and 1666, ten men and seven women were indentured to Cross for service in Virginia; two men for service on Nevis; and one man for service on Barbados.[20] Anne and Cross concluded their agreement in late July or early August 1662 and had it recorded in the Tolzey Book on August 8, a peak time for emigration.[21] Anne's indenture required her to work in Virginia for four years subject to "the usuall Conditions,"[22] which referred to a set of reciprocal obligations. She had to render faithful service, and her master had to pay her transportation costs, provide her with food, clothing, and shelter, treat her reasonably, and give her "freedom dues" (a customary allotment of corn and clothing) when her servitude ended.

Cross planned to sell Anne's indenture as soon as they reached Virginia, and he knew she would fetch a good price, thanks to the demand for labor created by the colony's burgeoning tobacco industry. The fortunes of the industry affected virtually every aspect of life in the Chesapeake, shaping its labor system, population growth, settlement patterns, wealth distribution, social classes, and political structure. Indeed, one scholar has argued that fluctuations in the tobacco market influenced the frequency of sexual relations.[23] The region possessed two physical assets that enabled it to become a great tobacco producer: a superb network of waterways that facilitated commercial intercourse over great distances, and an abundance of easily accessible virgin land, which could replace fields exhausted by tobacco cultivation after only a few seasons. These natural advantages, coupled with initially high prices, led to a rapidly growing volume of tobacco shipments during the trade's formative years. Within 25 years after the first barrels of Chesapeake tobacco reached London in 1614, Virginia leaf achieved a position of dominance in the English market and contributed to the rise of an important segment of London's commercial community. Virginia supplied London with over a million pounds of tobacco a year by the late 1630s, accounting for three-quarters of London's total tobacco imports.[24]

Such was the colony's success as a tobacco producer that she suffered from too much of a good thing. Output often grew faster than the English import and reexport markets could absorb, causing prices to fall. After declining in the 1620s, prices recovered in the mid-1630s and then plunged again in the late 1630s. Virginians sought to increase sales by trading with Dutch merchants, who received a boost when the English Civil War broke out in 1642, disrupting shipping between London and Virginia. The Dutch garnered a sizable share of the Virginia market during the 1640s and helped to stabilize prices for almost a decade.[25] Parliament passed a series of laws barring foreigners from trading with the colony, however, and in the 1660s largely succeeded in driving them out.[26] Despite the loss of direct trade with the Dutch and the establishment of an English monopoly, Virginia's tobacco industry continued expanding. Shipments exceeded seven million pounds in 1663 and reached 15 million pounds at the end of the decade. Tobacco prices and production fluctuated from year to year as the Chesapeake economy went through boom-and-bust cycles. Booms began when falling tobacco prices stimulated European demand. As demand rose, so did prices, triggering additional investment in land and labor. Planters cleared new fields and imported more servants in order to expand production. Invariably they overresponded to the price stimulus, and soon the supply of tobacco exceeded European demand. Prices fell again, and the resulting bust led planters to cut their intake of new laborers, causing a reduction in sales of livestock, grain, clothing, equipment, and other merchandise. Before long, though, the low tobacco prices boosted demand, and the cycle repeated itself.[27]

Anne Horwood emigrated to Virginia in 1662 during a "boomlet," a brief period of recovery in the middle of a decade-long decline in tobacco prices. In the early 1660s, a planter who was contemplating the acquisition of additional servants had good reason for cautious optimism. The price actually went up in 1662 for the first time in six years,[28] and on the basis of past cycles, prosperity seemed imminent. The boomlet explains why a planter would have wished to add male field workers in 1662, but what about female servants such as Anne? The conventional seventeenth-century view was that white women should not work in the tobacco fields. John Hammond, an ex-colonist who published the pamphlet *Leah and Rachel* in 1656, assured prospective female emigrants that they would be spared duty at the hoe:

> The Women are not (as is reported) put into the ground to worke, but occupie such domestique imployments and houswifery as in *England,* that is dressing victuals, righting up the house, milking, imployed about dayries, washing,

sowing, &c. and both men and women have times of recreations, as much or more than in any part of the world besides, yet som wenches that are nasty, beastly and not fit to be so imployed are put into the ground, for reason tells us, they must not at charge be transported and then maintained for nothing, but those that prove so aukward are rather burthensome then servants desirable or usefull.[29]

Notwithstanding these assurances, white female servants did, in fact, work in the tobacco fields until the eighteenth century, when slaves came to predominate the work force.[30] Even if Hammond's description of women's work had been accurate, rising tobacco prices still would have created a need for additional female servants. Higher prices meant more field workers and increased demand for those who carried out "domestique imployments" such as milking, cooking, cleaning, washing, and sewing. Jasper Cross therefore expected to find a ready market for Anne's services in Virginia.

The ship bearing Anne and Cross left Bristol in September 1662, probably sailing south to Madeira and then southwest toward the West Indies, where they caught the prevailing winds that carried them northwest to the Chesapeake Bay. Ships laden with servants generally sailed in late summer or early autumn so as to arrive two or three months later, after the pestilential Chesapeake summer, which was especially hazardous to newcomers. Shipmasters liked to be within the capes of the Chesapeake Bay by November in order to avoid the winter westerlies, which brought gale damage and sometimes blocked entry into the Bay for weeks. A late autumn arrival also offered the advantage of coinciding with the seasonal rhythms of tobacco production. Growers finished transplanting the young plants by the end of May, harvested the mature crop by mid-September, and cured the leaves during the winter. After discharging their passengers, mariners spent the winter assembling return cargoes of tobacco and then left for England in the spring, hastening to avoid the summer, when fevers attacked crews and the voracious teredo worm bored holes in ships' hulls.[31]

Anne doubtless experienced great discomfort during the Atlantic crossing. Passengers on seventeenth-century vessels occupied makeshift quarters, usually little more than temporary partitions of wood and canvas, with cots and hammocks jammed into whatever space was available. Crowded together in dank and fetid conditions on a rolling ocean, nearly every emigrant suffered from seasickness, producing a ceaseless stench of vomit. Violent storms inflicted terror and injury; typhus, dysentery, and smallpox occasionally ravaged a ship's company. The lack of fresh vegetables and vitamin C in the shipboard diet caused scurvy, whose symptoms included aching joints, bleeding gums, and extreme weakness. Some passengers were so disabled by the disease that they could not carry their baggage ashore.[32] Even if Anne's crossing was not as horrible as Lord Culpeper's voyage in 1680 — "a most tedious passage of eleven weeks and two days, full of death, scurvy and calentures [fevers]"[33] — she must have given thanks for her deliverance when the lookout spied land.

Around November 1662, Anne's ship passed between Cape Henry and Cape Charles and turned northward into the Chesapeake Bay, making landfall somewhere on the lower part of Virginia's Eastern Shore. The Shore is a peninsula about 75 miles long and six to eight miles wide bounded on the east by marshes, a chain of islands, and the Atlantic Ocean and on the west by the Bay, which separates the Shore from Virginia's mainland. English colonists first settled on the Eastern Shore in 1614 or 1615. Moving northward from the initial settlement sites along the southwest coast, colonists obtained government land grants (patents) to most of the lower half of the peninsula by 1655.[34] The English population grew from 17 people in 1616 to about 1,500 in 1662.[35] In 1634, the Virginia Assembly divided the colony into eight shires and named the Eastern Shore the county of "Accawmack" after the tribe of friendly Indians who lived there. The legislature renamed the county "Northampton" in 1643, probably because Obedience

Robins, a prominent Eastern Shore colonist, came from North-amptonshire. In 1663, shortly after Anne's arrival, the Assembly subdivided the Shore, with the southern part retaining the name "Northampton" and the northern part becoming "Accomack" County.[36]

The Shore's planters welcomed the arrival of fresh workers and clamored to hire them. To sell Anne's indenture, Cross took advantage of his ties to community leaders such as Captain William Jones, a Northampton justice of the peace with whom he co-witnessed a land transaction and attended a county court session in late December.[37] Cross's networking brought him into contact with another of Northampton County's leading citizens, Lieutenant Colonel William Kendall. As a large-scale planter and merchant, Kendall needed additional workers, both male and female. Cross saw an opportunity to sell Anne's indenture to Kendall, and a bargain was struck. Kendall gained not only an extra servant but also a bonus of 50 acres of land. Under Virginia's headright system, the provincial government awarded 50 acres to anyone who financed an immigrant's passage. This was signified by a headright certificate, a transferrable document that the holder could redeem for a patent conferring title to a specific tract. Cross assigned Anne's headright to Kendall along with her indenture, and on December 29 Kendall obtained a certificate that he later used to obtain land as a reward for her immigration.[38]

The transaction between Cross and Kendall was the first of three sales involving Anne's indenture. Multiple transfers were common on the Eastern Shore and in the rest of Virginia. Going through the court records, one often comes across a reference to a servant who "was assigned over to two or three severall men" before his present master bought him.[39] Contemporary English observers thought Virginians' practice of trading servants like chattels and even using them as gambling stakes smacked of slavery.[40] From a technical legal standpoint, of course, Anne was not conveyed as a piece of property. Cross simply assigned his contractual right to her services and delegated his duties as her master. The distinction between the sale of a human being and the transfer of contractual rights and duties seems clear enough now, but to seventeenth-century eyes, servant assignments looked uncomfortably similar to livestock sales. This created a potentially serious obstacle to servant recruitment. Colonial promoters such as William Bullock tried to counter rumors about enslavement with reassuring words. "Malitious tongues ha's impaired it [Virginia] much," Bullock complained,

> For it hath beene a constant report amongst the ordinarie sort of people, that all those servants who are sent to *Virginia,* are sold as slaves: whereas the truth is, that the Merchants who send servants, and have no Plantations of their owne, doe onely transferre their Time over to others, but the servants serve no longer then the time they themselves agreed for in *England:* and this is an ordinarie course in *England,* and no prejudice or hurt to the servant.[41]

Bullock's reference to English practice is misleading. English common law did not permit a master to "transferre [a servant's] Time over to others" unless the servant consented.[42] The consent requirement recognized that people create employment relationships with each other's personal qualities in mind. A servant might be willing to work for a master who was kind and generous but not for one who was cruel or niggardly. Just as workers did not consider employers fungible, English law regarded each employment contract as a unique arrangement that neither party could alter unilaterally. If an employer tried to transfer a servant to a different master without the servant's consent, the action would amount to a discharge, which English law forbade unless the master persuaded a justice of the peace that the servant had committed misconduct warranting dismissal.[43] What English law did allow was a novation, that is, a replacement of the original contract between the servant and master A with a new contract between the servant and master B, an arrangement requiring the assent of everyone involved.[44]

Virginia practice conflicted with the English rule.[45] It is true that Virginians occasionally consulted their servants before transferring them to another master. For example, when the Northampton County planter John Foster was asked whether he would part with his manservant and maidservant, "hee answered yes (if they were willing)."[46] Before finalizing the sale of his servant to John Johnson, Daniel Wayne "demanded of the servant if hee was willinge to serve the said John Johnson," and the servant "answered that hee was willinge."[47] Edward Robins had to "gett the good will" of Elizabeth Charlton's three servants and agree to a one-year reduction in their service obligations before she would assign him their indentures.[48] But these cases plainly were exceptional. They stemmed either from extraordinary kindheartedness or a pragmatic recognition that a contented servant made a more productive worker. They did not reflect a legal requirement. Far more typical were the numerous Virginia bills of sale and assignments that said nothing about servants' having a role in the decision.[49]

There is also evidence of transfers made in spite of servants' vehement objections. When John Chaundler assigned Robert Warder's indenture to William Burdett, breaking an earlier promise to release Warder in return for the payment of six pounds, Warder

> taxed the said Mr. Chaundler saying it was very ill done of you to saye one thinge and doe another, Whereupon the said Chaundler replyed saying I thinke I have bine a Freind unto you in gieving you a yeare of your tyme For I might have sold you for Fower yeares and I have sold you but For three yeares.[50]

Virginia law was on Chaundler's side. Warder, having no choice in the matter, served Burdett for three years.[51] Thomas Mountford, another Northampton master, evinced a similar disregard for his servant's wishes. When the servant, Mary Arms, expressed unwillingness to serve her proposed new master, Thomas Leatherberry,

"Mountford answered her you shall" and took her over the creek to Leatherberry's house. Because of the servant's recalcitrance, however, Mountford offered her to Leatherberry and his wife on a week's approval. The maid, who was subject to fits, became ill, and Mrs. Leatherberry tried to cure her by "sweating" her in a chamber heated by an herbal bath. The maid became thirsty during the treatment, so Mrs. Leatherberry offered her a dram of liquor. The servant drank half a bottle and then died. Leatherberry refused to pay the purchase price, claiming he never intended to keep the servant. Mountford sued, but the court ruled in Leatherberry's favor, holding that "noe Lawfull sale" had been proven.[52]

Virginia deviated from the English rule that a servant could not be transferred to a new master without the servant's consent because in Virginia, unlike England, indentured servitude was a credit system as well as an employment relationship.[53] An English farm worker was hired on a year-to-year basis;[54] he worked for present wages, not in order to repay an antecedent debt. A colonial indentured servant, on the other hand, had to be retained for at least four or five years since he entered employment heavily indebted to his master. That initial master, usually an English merchant or mariner such as Jasper Cross, acted as a temporary creditor. He advanced the funds the servant needed to emigrate, intending to recover his capital outlay fairly quickly by transferring the loan, and the servant who secured it, to a Virginian who would serve as the permanent lender. The servant amortized the loan with his labor over a period of several years, and the permanent lender bore the risk of loan default if the servant died or ran away. The temporary lender, for his role as intermediary, received reimbursement of his costs, his profit (the "interest" on the short-term loan), and an additional premium that compensated him for running the risk that the servant might have died before the permanent lender took over the loan. Had Virginia followed the English approach and given the servant veto power over the choice of a transferee, the temporary lender would have demanded an additional premium for risking a possibly lengthy delay in recovering his investment.

The added premium would have increased planters' labor costs, a particularly unwelcome development, given the downward trend in tobacco prices. To maintain a free-flowing labor market, unimpeded by the troublesome matter of worker preferences, Virginia departed from the English employment-contract model.

Because of this legal innovation, Anne probably was not consulted during the negotiations over her future. Cross and Kendall simply arrived at a mutually agreeable price and then informed Anne that she would spend most of the next four years at Kendall's plantation on Cherrystone Inlet. Anne ended up staying with Kendall less than a year, but that was long enough to transform her life.

TWO

WILLIAM KENDALL,
PARVENU

The rise of William Kendall, Anne Orthwood's second employer and the uncle of her lover, John Kendall, is a remarkable seventeenth-century success story. He began his career in Virginia as an indentured servant and ended it as speaker of the House of Burgesses, senior justice of the Northampton County Court, colonel in the militia, and one of the wealthiest men on the Eastern Shore. Kendall's career illustrates the permeability of social strata in the early decades of settlement. For men with talent, ambition, and luck, Virginia offered a chance to transcend humble beginnings and achieve a preeminence that few servants could have dreamed of attaining in England.

Kendall was born in Brinton, Norfolk, in 1621,[1] the seventh child of John Kendall, a tailor, and his wife, Anne Pleasance Kendall. The family consisted primarily of farmers and craftsmen—blacksmiths, carpenters, and the like.[2] Some members of the Kendall and Pleasance families owned land, and a few held minor offices, such as churchwarden. William, therefore, grew up belonging to the social group historians term the "middling sort." He came from respectable stock but did not possess a pedigree that would automatically entitle him to deference. Unlike men born into the gentry, he could not claim power as his birthright.

When Kendall reached adulthood, in the early 1640s, he moved from the tiny village of Brinton to the seaside Norfolk town of

Yarmouth in search of better economic opportunities. Judging from the commercial skills he displayed later in his career, he probably found employment at a mercantile concern, perhaps as a clerk. In Yarmouth he met his first wife, Ruth, a widow whom he married in 1644. They had a son, William, who died in infancy in 1647.[3] Kendall remained in Yarmouth through 1648,[4] but his circumstances soon changed dramatically. His wife died, probably in 1649, and he began thinking about starting a new life elsewhere. For the same reasons as countless other Englishmen, he found himself drawn westward by glowing tales of the prosperity that awaited him in America. Almost 30, Kendall was older than the typical indentured servant, almost three-quarters of whom were under 25.[5] Nevertheless, since he lacked the means to emigrate as a free man, servitude offered his only avenue to advancement. Resolving to make the best of his situation, Kendall bade farewell to his family, indentured himself for five years, and boarded a ship for Virginia.

Kendall probably sailed in late summer 1650 on the *Peter and John* with his new master, Edward Drew, and a fellow servant. Drew, an Eastern Shore planter, had gone to England in early 1650 to conduct business and acquire additional workers, the asset Virginians regarded as "more advantageous . . . then any other Commodityes."[6] He and his wife, Mary, residents of the Shore since 1625, operated a plantation on Eyrehall Neck, a peninsula abutting Cherrystone Inlet on the Bay side of the Shore. Despite his illiteracy, Drew served as one of the leaders of the frontier community, holding a variety of offices, including the important post of sheriff.[7] A hard-driving and contentious man, Drew was not the kindest and most generous of masters. In 1636, Edward Morrish sued Drew "for clothes in the tyme of his service."[8] The court ruled in Morrish's favor, but a year later Morrish had to sue Drew again because he refused to pay the customary freedom dues—five barrels of corn and a new suit of clothes—that Morrish was entitled to upon completing his term of service. In 1638, another of Drew's ex-servants, William Carter, successfully sued him for clothes due by custom. Yet another servant, John Evans, won a judgment against Drew for clothes in 1643. Relations between the Drews and their servant Mary Jones became so sour that Jones struck her mistress and ran away. The court ordered Jones to receive 10 lashes for her offense. One of the magistrates, Obedience Robins, objected to the punishment, perhaps a sign that he thought the Drews' harsh usage of the servant had provoked her misconduct.[9]

In November 1650, shortly after he and Kendall reached the Eastern Shore, Drew fell gravely ill. His conscience troubled him, and he did not wish to die without having made amends for his uncharitable conduct toward his servants. He granted one servant her freedom and shortened the terms of Kendall and another male servant by one year.[10] Soon afterward he died, bequeathing to his wife, Mary, a life estate in his house on Eyrehall Neck, a life estate in one-third of his land, and one-third of his other property, including Kendall's service obligation. The rest went to the children of a friend.[11] In July 1652, Mary married William Strangridge, a mariner from Boston, Massachusetts, and the couple took up residence on Eyrehall Neck.[12] Strangridge's commercial activities included carrying tobacco from the Shore to Manhattan and Boston and bringing back rum, brandy, sugar, and other goods to sell in Virginia. He recognized Kendall's mercantile talents and quickly made him an integral part of his business operations, appointing Kendall his agent to collect debts and look after his affairs while he undertook his periodic voyages up the eastern seaboard.[13]

Kendall completed his service obligation and gained his freedom in July 1654.[14] For an ordinary servant, emancipation meant a chance to work for wages or as a tenant farmer until he accumulated enough capital to acquire land and establish his own plantation. Thanks to Strangridge's patronage, however, Kendall had access to the wider commercial world, where one could strive for wealth far beyond the hopes of the average freedman. In August 1654, Kendall succeeded Strangridge as the agent for William Payne, a New England merchant, and brought suit on Payne's behalf for 370 pounds sterling against Lieutenant Colonel Edmund Scarburgh II, a magistrate, former speaker, and major landowner.[15]

That Payne entrusted litigation of that magnitude to Kendall indicates a high level of confidence in the ex-servant's abilities. Kendall received an even greater financial boost in November 1654, when Strangridge died and left half his estate to his "Loveing Freind" Kendall. He bequeathed the other half to his wife, Mary.[16]

Strangridge's bequest to Mary, together with the property she had inherited from Drew, left her well off and a prime candidate for remarriage. Kendall quickly seized the opportunity, and by April 1655 they were wed. Although they were relatively far apart in age — Mary was 47, Kendall 33 — and formerly had occupied different social stations, marriage offered benefits to each of them. Kendall gained control of Mary's property, giving him additional working capital; Mary obtained protection and security; both derived comfort from the companionship of a trusted friend. Lest anyone doubt her status, Mary continued to remind the community of her affluence by arraying herself in knit silk gloves and other finery.[17]

The county court records show a burst of commercial activity by Kendall following his marriage to Mary. He sold liquor and other goods locally and traded butter and an ox to a man in New Amsterdam. In November 1656, he and his partner, Captain William Whittington, an Eastern Shore planter and magistrate, shipped to Amsterdam between 80 and 100 hogsheads, containing roughly 500–600 pounds of tobacco apiece. Six months later, he and Whittington contracted with Jacob Lavoris van Sloot, a Dutch mariner, to ship tobacco to Manhattan. Soon Kendall expanded his business enterprises from buying and transporting his neighbors' tobacco to owning at least one of the ships that carried it. In July 1659, Abraham Johnson of Amsterdam sold to Kendall, Whittington, and John Michael a ship called the *Christina Regina,* which the new owners renamed the *Sheppard.* Kendall bought out Michael's share in December 1660 for 200 pounds sterling. Kendall's ability to afford such a large capital expenditure only a half-dozen years after his emancipation illustrates the magnitude of the economic success he enjoyed as a result of Strangridge's bequest, an advantageous marriage, and his own business acumen.[18] Another indicator of Kendall's expanding commercial network was the number of nonresident traders who designated him as their representative on the Eastern Shore. Merchants and mariners from England, New England, and the Virginia mainland frequently called on him to collect their debts and guarantee their obligations.[19]

Kendall's mercantile success called attention to his skills and positioned him for political advancement. The Eastern Shore justices recommended that the governor and Council appoint him to the county court, and in April 1656 he acquired a seat on the bench after undergoing an accelerated version of the usual apprenticeship, which entailed such minor but essential governmental functions as examining disputed accounts, appraising decedents' estates, and serving as a juror. He remained an active justice for the next 30 years, attending court 405 days, more than any other Eastern Shore magistrate in the seventeenth century.[20] He also held office at the provincial level, serving by popular election as one of the Shore's representatives in the House of Burgesses in 1658 and from 1663 to 1686.[21] His status as a burgess and magistrate probably helped him win a commission from the governor and Assembly as a lieutenant colonel in the militia in April 1658.[22] Having risen from humble origins, he took great pride in his military rank, regarding his martial title as a sign of public confidence and esteem.[23]

Like other Englishmen of his time who succeeded in trade, Kendall sought to enhance his social standing and enlarge his wealth by acquiring property. He made his first major purchase in August 1657 when he bought Newport House and 600 acres from the heirs of Edward Robins, a deceased merchant. The tract occupied much of what is now called Eyreville Neck, a peninsula on the Bay side of the Shore bounded on the north by Old Castle Creek, on the west by Cherrystone Inlet, and on the south by Eyreville Creek, called Newport Creek in the seventeenth century. Across Eyreville Creek lay Eyrehall Neck, Mary Drew Strangridge Kendall's property where Kendall had worked as a servant. Together the two necks of land gave Kendall an ample base of operations, affording ready access to the Bay and the Atlantic Ocean beyond.[24]

Kendall acquired substantial amounts of land for his own mercantile and agricultural purposes, but he obtained the bulk of his property in order to lease it out or resell it at a profit. He amassed land in two principal ways. The first involved the use of headright certificates, some of which he earned by importing servants and slaves, and some of which he bought from his neighbors and visiting mariners. He redeemed the certificates by presenting them to the provincial government at Jamestown and received patents to specific acreage in return. The second method of acquisition was to purchase land directly from an owner and then to record the sale in the county deed books. Using both techniques, Kendall gained title to over 7,500 acres during the 1660s, three-quarters of which he eventually sold. He added more than 15,000 acres in the 1670s and over 3,000 acres in the 1680s. Although he parted with much of this land during his lifetime, selling some and giving vast tracts to his children, he still owned thousands of acres at his death in 1686.[25]

Kendall's wife, Mary, died in 1658, and in December of that year he married his third wife, Susanna Baker Eyre Pott. Kendall was Susanna's third husband. Her first husband, Thomas Eyre, a surgeon, died in 1657, leaving Susanna only a life estate in a 200-acre plantation. Her second husband, Francis Pott, the brother and heir of the former governor John Pott, made her wealthy. They had been married less than a year when Pott died and left her 2,550 acres, a bequest that no doubt enhanced Susanna's attractiveness to Kendall and sped their union.[26] Kendall's household expanded considerably as a result of his marriage to Susanna, reaching around 20 people in the early 1660s. Roughly half were family members and the rest servants and slaves. Susanna's three sons by Thomas Eyre resided with the couple at Newport House, and soon they were joined by the colonel's own offspring. In 1661, Susanna gave birth to a daughter, Mary, followed by a son, William II, around 1664.[27] Two more relatives also lived with them: Susanna's brother,

Daniel Baker, and William's nephew, John Kendall. The son of one of William's older brothers, John grew up in England, at Taverham, a village six miles northwest of Norwich, the cathedral city and administrative center of Norfolk.[28] He probably emigrated to Virginia around 1662 when he was in his early twenties. William treated John as a surrogate son, providing for him and, later, his family with much the same protective generosity that he would display toward his own progeny. The remainder of the household consisted of two slaves (a boy and a woman); a free black male servant who bought his freedom from Kendall in 1660 and continued working for him until 1665 to pay off the purchase price; two or more white male servants; and several white female servants, including, from late 1662 to sometime around the middle of 1663, Anne Orthwood.[29]

Colonel Kendall's household was a patriarchal institution whose organization and ideology were based on the family as the basic unit of society, with the father as its divinely appointed head. A father's power extended over the whole of his family, including his servants as well as his relatives, all of whom owed him a duty of obedience. In return, he owed them support, protection, guidance, and example. Collectively, the heads of families formed the political community, and the monarch symbolically functioned as the father of all families. The government regulated society primarily by controlling the behavior of male heads of household, and they, in turn, were expected to govern the women and male dependents in their families. This resulted in a blurring of the lines between family and community interests. In early America, as in England, the community intruded deeply into the inner workings of family life.[30] New Englanders took an especially active approach to maintaining social order, regularly intervening in households whose patriarchs had failed to provide adequate supervision of subordinates. Although many Chesapeake families were too truncated, anomalous, and unstable to perform traditional regulatory functions, a few households, such as Kendall's, fit the classic model closely enough to create community expectations of patriarchal oversight.[31]

Chief among these community expectations was a demand that patriarchs prevent their dependents from engaging in conduct offensive to God and threatening to the neighborhood. The supervisory obligations of patriarchs received influential exposition in the theologian Richard Allestree's devotional manual *The Whole Duty of Man*,[32] a book that enjoyed great popularity in colonial Virginia.[33] Allestree stressed patriarchs' responsibility to correct wayward subordinates, especially if they committed faults against God, "whereat every Master ought to be more troubled then at those which tend only to his own loss, or inconvenience." Patriarchs had a particular obligation to deter fornication, a "very brutish" practice that caused "many foul and filthy, besides *painful* diseases" and amounted to "a kind of *sacriledge,* a polluting those bodies, which God hath chosen for his *Temples.*"[34]

Kendall's duty to combat fornication was greater than most patriarchs' because he held the post of churchwarden. Canon 109 of the Church of England required churchwardens to prosecute all people who "offend their brethren, either by Adulterie, Whoredome, Incest, or Drunkennesse, or by Swearing, Ribaldrie, Usurie, or any other uncleannesse and wickednesse of life."[35] A Virginia statute directed churchwardens to present to the county court all persons suspected of "those foule and abominable sins of drunkennesse fornication and adultery,"[36] a task that Kendall performed with the pious rigor his godly neighbors demanded. In June 1664, for example, he prosecuted John Wills and Mary Reddy for fornication. Both confessed and received fines of 500 pounds of tobacco apiece. In addition, Wills had to post bond to hold the parish harmless from the cost of maintaining Reddy's bastard. In a curious twist, he was allowed to work off his fine by continuing to serve as the county whipper, the man who administered corporal punishment to other transgressors of community mores.[37]

Colonel Kendall's role as a member of both the county court and the Assembly compounded people's expectation that he would provide moral leadership. One of the major responsibilities of the county court was to enforce the laws against fornication and bastard-bearing, some of which Kendall helped enact in his capacity as a member of the House of Burgesses. At the 1658 Assembly session, he and his colleagues reenacted legislation mandating that all fornicators and adulterers "of what degree or qualitie soever be seveerly punished" and deemed "incapable of being a wittnes between partie and partie, and of bearing any publique office in the government of this collony."[38] In other words, Kendall and his fellow burgesses proclaimed a policy of zero tolerance toward sexual immorality. Local magistrates had to apply the fornication laws to everyone, regardless of rank and connections, and violators forfeited important civil and political rights. Plainly, the members of the Assembly meant their moral concerns to be taken seriously.

Colonel Kendall's involvement in the campaign against illicit sex placed him in a difficult position. He did not pursue suspected fornicators with any greater zeal than other churchwardens, magistrates, or burgesses, but his humble background left him especially vulnerable to charges of hypocrisy. As the historian Norma Landau has pointed out, a parvenu had to engage in a "constant display of public and private morality" to earn "the veneration of his neighbours — an end most necessary to the new justice who had, aside from office, meager claim to honour."[39] If he failed to maintain proper moral standards in his own household, people might challenge his right to pass judgment on their morality. The desire to avoid such a challenge probably underlay Kendall's decision to remove Anne Orthwood from his household within a few months of her arrival. Kendall parted with Anne after growing increasingly concerned over her budding romance with his kinsman John, a relationship the colonel considered altogether unsuitable. Anne hoped John would marry her and set her free, but Colonel Kendall had different plans. He wanted John to marry a rich woman, as he had, and continue the family's climb up the social ladder. The last person he wished to see John marry was a penniless servant. If a marriage to Anne was unacceptable, so too was a nonmarital relationship, for that path led to illicit sex and bastardy, shameful conduct that a man in Colonel Kendall's position could ill afford to countenance. Kendall therefore resolved to take preventive measures. In the summer or fall of 1663, he brought about a separation of the couple by selling Anne's indenture to another planter and sending her to live at his plantation.

Anne's new master, Jacob Bishopp, was a tenant farmer who had recently settled in Northampton County.[40] His work force consisted of a male servant, a male ward, and one or two female servants, which was about average for a head of household on the Eastern Shore.[41] Bishopp's will, probated in 1675, reinforces the impression that he was more or less of middling status. To his teenage son, Jacob Bishopp Jr., he bequeathed a bed, bolster, pillow, rug, blanket, pair of sheets, pillow case, bedstead, curtains, valance, chest, table, three pewter dishes, a pewter flagon, three pewter porringers, a pewter candlestick, an iron pot, a frying pan, gun, cutlass, two iron wedges, a mare, a cow, two heifers, and his own clothing.[42] These possessions imply a modest level of comfort, but they hardly suggest affluence. Colonel Kendall, by contrast, bequeathed slaves and thousands of acres to various family members, and his heir, William Kendall II, died owning numerous luxury items, such as 20 Russia leather chairs, 27 silver spoons, silver salt cellars, cups, plates, and dishes, two silver-headed canes and a silver-hilted sword, 32 books, several looking glasses, dozens of pieces of furniture, seven pictures, and "one old mapp of the world."[43] Though not part of the emerging elite, Bishopp must have been a respected member of the community, for the county court saw fit to appoint him to several minor posts such as surveyor of highways and constable, a position traditionally given to men of middling status. He also sat occasionally on trial juries and grand juries.[44]

Bishopp's civic responsibilities and business affairs brought him to court from time to time. One of those occasions was the Northampton County Court session on Monday, November 30, 1663, which Bishopp attended because his servant, William Savage, was scheduled to be tried in a civil suit.[45] Anne accompanied Bishopp and Savage, lodging with them in John Webb's tavern-cum-courthouse during the weekend preceding the court session. There she encountered John Kendall, and they rekindled their romance. Even though the inn was crowded with litigants, witnesses, and potential jurors, John and Anne managed to find a private spot, perhaps a storeroom or loft, where they could be intimate. On Saturday night, while the rest of the lodgers were drinking and carousing in the taproom, they slipped away to their trysting place and had sex for the first time. They went there again the next day and repeated the act: "Three tymes She thought hee had to doe with her," Anne later confessed to the midwife who delivered her, "but twice She was Certaine."[46]

A short time later, before Anne's pregnancy started to show, Bishopp decided to sell her indenture. One possible explanation is economic. Tobacco prices dropped in 1663 and 1664, squeezing small farmers like Bishopp. Feeling overextended, he may have chosen to reduce his work force and exchange his least essential employee for cash. A more sinister explanation is that he sold Anne because he knew she was pregnant. Childbearing diminished a female servant's capacity for physical labor, lessening her value. Rather than take the financial hit himself, Bishopp may have tried to shift the loss to an unsuspecting buyer. If that was his aim, he could not have chosen a worse target for deception. The man to whom he sold Anne's indenture, Lieutenant Colonel William Waters, was one of the most influential and legally sophisticated men on the Eastern Shore.

THREE

WILLIAM WATERS,
GENTLEMAN

William Waters, Anne Orthwood's fourth master, was one of Virginia's earliest native-born gentlemen. Although his claim to gentility was tenuous by traditional English standards, he held a secure place in the embryonic colonial elite. His social status enabled him to wield power as a natural right, much to the envy of arrivistes like William Kendall, who had to claw their way to the top. Waters inherited his rank from his father and stepfather, self-made men whose financial and political success paved the way for their descendants to play prominent roles in public affairs well into the eighteenth century.

That William's father, Edward Waters, survived long enough to sire a son was something of a miracle. His journey to the colony was an exciting adventure story, full of hardships, narrow escapes, and derring-do. The 20-year-old Edward left England in 1609 aboard the *Sea Venture,* flagship of a Virginia-bound expedition headed by Sir George Somers. A hurricane struck the fleet, forcing the *Sea Venture* onto rocks off the coast of Bermuda. Edward Waters and the other passengers managed to clamber ashore before wind and waves demolished the ship, an incident that probably inspired parts of Shakespeare's *The Tempest.*[1] After spending a couple of years as a virtual castaway, Waters became one of the leading citizens of the fledgling colony of Bermuda. Later he almost drowned when his ship foundered in the West Indies, and he had to be rescued from a desolate island by pirates. He finally settled in Virginia in 1617 and established a plantation on the north side of the James River, close to the site of the modern-day city of Newport News. He and his wife, Grace O'Neill Waters, whom he married in 1620, nearly lost their lives in the Indian uprising of 1622. Taken prisoner by Nansemond Indians, they were about to be executed when an abandoned boat washed ashore, delighting their captors and distracting them long enough to allow Edward and Grace to slip into a canoe and escape. Amazed by Edward's seemingly endless series of lucky breaks, Captain John Smith could not resist commenting on the capriciousness of fortune: "Thus you may see how many desperate dangers some men escape, when others die that have all things at their pleasure."[2]

The year after they survived the Indian attack, Edward and Grace Waters had their first child, William, followed a year later by a daughter, Margaret. The family enjoyed a steady rise in wealth and prestige during the 1620s. Edward expanded his landholdings on the James-York Peninsula and built one of the largest work forces in the area. The 1625 muster of Virginia's inhabitants called him "Mr Edward Waters," the title reflecting his status as the head of a 15-person plantation community, employer of six servants, and owner of four houses, a boat, and a "pallizado" (small fort). He acquired every office a local grandee could hold: churchwarden, magistrate, burgess, militia commander.[3] Had he lived longer, he might have continued his ascent and eventually won a seat on the colony's preeminent governing body, the Council. In 1630, however, Edward's fabled luck finally ran out; he died on a business trip to England at the age of 41. In his will, written a few days before his death, he styled himself according to the social rank he had attained in the New World: "Edward Waters of Elizabeth Cittie in Virginia Gentleman."[4] He left his land in Virginia and a third of his personal property to his seven-year-old son, William, who was sent to Yorkshire to be educated under the supervision of his uncle.

Edward Waters's stature in Virginia entitled his children to membership in the colonial gentry, and their social position grew even stronger when their mother married Obedience Robins in 1634. The son of a Northamptonshire yeoman, Robins had worked as an apothecary's apprentice in London before emigrating to the colony in the early 1620s and establishing himself as a surgeon on the Eastern Shore. Over the next three decades, he steadily ascended the political hierarchy, serving as county magistrate, sheriff, burgess, militia commander, and, ultimately, as a member of the Council.[5] Power led inexorably to the acquisition of vast tracts of land, and by the early 1640s Robins had amassed over 3,000 acres in the southern part of the Eastern Shore, making him one of the largest landowners in the county. He raised tobacco and livestock and established a wide-ranging transatlantic commercial network. An ardent free trader, Robins opposed the imposition of an English tobacco monopoly, advocated trading with both sides during the English Civil War, and pursued new markets by forming close ties with the Dutch.[6]

Robins was assisted in many of his commercial endeavors by his stepson, William Waters. William joined his family on the Eastern Shore in the autumn of 1641, shortly after he turned 18.[7] He seems to have received deferential treatment from the moment he arrived.[8] The fact that his stepfather was the third-highest-ranking member of the county court contributed to the ease with which he assumed his place among the Eastern Shore gentry. Robins, pleased to have a protege, gave the young man a thorough grounding in business. He assigned William relatively minor tasks at first, such as the sale of a cow, enabling him to learn the rudiments of bargaining firsthand. Then he taught him how to handle more complex transactions by letting him observe the execution of important legal documents. In 1643, for instance, William served as a witness when the Amsterdam merchant Aries Topp signed a power of attorney authorizing Robins to collect Topp's debts in Virginia. As Robins grew more confident in his stepson's skill and judgment, he entrusted him with greater responsibility. In 1644, Robins and his partners sent him as their agent on a 16-month voyage to Holland, Hamburg, and the West Indies. Traveling on a Dutch vessel,

Waters sold consignments of tobacco for his employers, collected their debts, and procured a return cargo. The trip acquainted him with the mechanics of international trade and broadened his knowledge of the legal norms that governed sales contracts. By the time he returned to the Eastern Shore, Waters had become an experienced businessman, well equipped to parlay his inheritance into substantial wealth.[9] He married his first wife, Katherine, in about 1646 and devoted himself to making money through overseas commerce, land speculation, and a large farming operation. Around 1660, he purchased a choice tract near the mouth of King's Creek, where the town of Cape Charles is now located, and built a house for his family's use. This estate, King's Creek Plantation, remained the seat of the Waterses for the next century.[10]

Waters's business dealings frequently brought him into contact with the legal system. He litigated his rights as a creditor and debtor, served on juries, arbitrated disputes, audited controverted accounts, appraised decedents' and orphans' estates, oversaw the performance of wills, and viewed property to ascertain ownership or assist the court in determining damages.[11] He also acted as the attorney for a diverse group of principals, ranging from an Elizabeth City yeoman and a Northampton widow to a New England trader, a Somerset mariner, and a London merchant.[12] Waters's expertise widened in 1650 as a result of his marriage to his second wife, Margaret, the widow and executrix of Dr. George Clarke. He spent much of the next few years litigating on behalf of the Clarke estate, a process that earned him fees and bolstered his legal knowledge. He gained additional fees and experience as the guardian of several orphans and as the trustee for an absent colonist's children.[13] Waters's most significant exposure to the law, however, came from holding public office. Starting with his appointment as a militia lieutenant in 1651, he held governmental posts continuously until his death in 1689.[14]

Waters acquired his first important office — sheriff of Northampton County — in 1652 as a result of Parliament's victory in the English Civil War. The Eastern Shore, like the rest of Virginia, had officially sided with the Stuarts, while maintaining commercial links with their adversaries. In December 1649, the Northampton County Court had proclaimed Charles II king of England and Virginia and pledged the Eastern Shore's unwavering fidelity to the new monarch. Colonial royalists lost their will to fight, however, after Charles suffered a crushing defeat at the battle of Worcester in September 1651 and Parliament dispatched a fleet to reduce Virginia to obedience. Bowing to the inevitable, the governor, Sir William Berkeley, and the Assembly negotiated generous terms and surrendered to Parliament's commissioners on March 12, 1652. The commissioners consolidated control by asking colonists to subscribe to an oath, the Engagement, promising "to bee true and faithfull to the Common-Wealth of England as it is nowe Established without Kinge or howse of Lords." Robins and Waters were among the first Shoremen to sign.[15]

Robins welcomed the change of government, both because his sympathies lay with Puritanism and Parliament and because he had close ties to one of the commissioners, the Puritan leader Richard Bennett, and thus could expect to thrive politically under the new regime.[16] An opportunity to advance his stepson's interests soon presented itself when the Eastern Shore held an election for sheriff. Previous holders of this important office had been appointed by the royal governor on the recommendation of county magistrates. The parliamentarians, though, decided to pick sheriffs by popular election, a novelty designed to ingratiate the new government with the people of the conquered province. With Robins lining up votes behind the scenes, the inhabitants of the county, "By pluralitye of voyces," named Waters as their choice. Following the procedure prescribed by the parliamentary commissioners, the magistrates approved the nomination and, "conferringe with the People," formally elected him. Waters then took his oath of office "In the Name of the Keepers of the Libertys of England by Authority of Parliament" and served as sheriff for the next two years.[17] At the same gathering of the county's electors, Robins engineered his own election as one of the six burgesses who would represent the Eastern Shore in the Assembly at Jamestown.[18]

If the upheaval of the Interregnum created opportunities for well-connected men such as Robins and Waters, it also provided an occasion for ordinary people to vent their frustrations toward government. The "Inhabitants and freemen" who elected Robins and his fellow burgesses passed a resolution instructing them to present the county's grievances to the next session of the Assembly. This resolution, which has come to be known as the Northampton Protest of 1652,[19] sought annual elections of magistrates, better access to justice, and lower taxes. Northampton residents should not have to pay the provincial poll tax, they argued, because the county was not represented in the Assembly when the tax was enacted, rendering the exaction "Arbitrarye and illegall." The county court, responding to the strong antitax sentiments expressed by the voters, ordered Sheriff Waters to refrain from delivering revenues to the provincial government until the Assembly addressed the county's objections.[20] The Assembly disregarded the resolution's call for annual elections of magistrates and more convenient courts but did reduce the tax rate, effectively mooting the main point of the Protest. The incident was significant nonetheless because it demonstrated Shoremen's unwillingness to acquiesce in the imposition of taxes they considered unjustified. The Protest put political leaders on notice that they could expect an angry reaction if they failed to pay sufficient attention to taxpayers' interests.

Shoremen felt "disjoynted and sequestered from the rest of Virginia,"[21] yet they knew full well that their political fortunes would be shaped by the provincial government at Jamestown. The drafters of the Protest prudently ended the resolution with a ringing endorsement of the gubernatorial candidacy of Richard Bennett, who won by unanimous vote of the Assembly in late April 1652.[22] Bennett's victory ensured that Robins and Waters would dominate politics on the Eastern Shore for the next several years. During Bennett's administration, which lasted until March 1655, Waters continued his ascent, first by obtaining a gubernatorial appointment to the county court and then by winning election to the House of Burgesses. Waters's experience on the court, where he served from 1654 to 1685, deepened his understanding of the fields of law that were most important to people's everyday lives. His service in the Assembly in 1654–55, 1660–62, and 1680 exposed him both to the complexities of transatlantic politics and to the delicate interplay of English and colonial law. The Assembly functioned not only as a legislature but also as Virginia's supreme court, deciding an array of criminal and civil causes covering everything from homicide to contracts.[23]

The greatest challenge the Assembly faced during Waters's tenure as a burgess occurred during his second term, when he and his fellow lawmakers, who had faithfully served the Commonwealth and Protectorate, had to apologize to the Crown for their disloyalty and rebuild the legal structures of monarchical rule. The sequence of events that led to the restoration of royal authority in Virginia began in September 1658 with the death of Oliver Cromwell. He was succeeded as lord protector by his son Richard, whose government collapsed in May 1659, plunging England into a year-long state of political confusion. Virginia fared better, thanks to the cooperative spirit displayed by the Assembly and Sir William Berkeley. The Assembly invited Berkeley to resume the governorship in March 1660, and he agreed to serve on a stopgap basis until the burgesses and councillors received instructions from an English regime they deemed legitimate. King Charles II entered London triumphantly at the end of May and immediately set about the task of reasserting his control throughout the empire. One of his earliest acts was to approve the preparation of a new commission for Berkeley. The governor received the king's commission in mid-September, prompting him to summon the Assembly into session for the purpose of giving Virginia's laws a royalist cast.[24]

When Waters, Robins, and the other members of the Assembly gathered in Jamestown in October 1660, their first step was to ask

Berkeley to beg Charles's forgiveness on their behalf. The governor was the perfect intermediary, the Assembly observed, because of his steadfast loyalty to the Crown. The legislators acknowledged that "all the Inhabitants of this Countrey have (though by a forced submission to the parlyment) rendered themselves guilty of . . . rebellion . . . and by that means are legally lyable to the forfeiture of lives and estates." They were "sorrowfully Conscious" of their "Apostacy" and hoped Berkeley could secure their readmission to Charles's favor. Berkeley agreed to intercede and to present the Assembly's request for confirmation of colonists' rights and privileges. In return, the burgesses repealed their declaration of legislative supremacy and amended the colony's statutes to reflect that all legal authority emanated from the Crown.[25] Perhaps Waters, Robins, and the rest of the Assembly felt genuinely contrite over their disloyalty to Charles II during the Interregnum. One suspects, however, that pragmatism motivated them more than guilt. Virginia officials sought Charles's forgiveness for the same reason that they had signed the Engagement and sworn allegiance to Parliament: the king now controlled the machinery of government and the legal system that validated their land titles, protected their markets, and legitimized their right to rule. Although Virginia leaders desired a high degree of political autonomy, they understood that dependence was the paramount colonial reality.[26]

The Assembly spent much of the next two years striving to win the confidence of the Crown. At its 1661 session, the legislature continued its conspicuous display of repentance by creating two royalist holidays. January 30, the date Charles I was beheaded, became an annual day of mourning, to be "solemnized with fasting and prayers that our sorrowes may expiate our crime and our teares wash away our guilt." May 29, the date Charles II entered London and regained the throne, became a day of celebration, when Virginians were to commemorate the restoration of the monarchy.[27] The 1662 session concentrated on a comprehensive overhaul of Virginia's statutes, the first attempt to systematize colonial legislation since the Assembly's creation in 1619. The results appeared in a one-volume work, *The Lawes of Virginia Now in Force*, published in London in 1662. Known simply as "the Printed Lawes," the book was regarded as authoritative for the rest of the century.[28]

The aims of the 1662 revision were as much political as jurisprudential, a reflection of the crucial role that law played in forging the bonds of empire. The dominant theme was penitent colonists' desire to hew closer to the metropolitan model. By Anglicizing their laws and institutions, Virginians hoped to persuade Charles that they had abandoned their independent ways and were now obedient subjects of the Crown. The preamble assured the king that the Assembly had excised all laws that "might keep in memory our forced Deviation from his Majesties Obedience."[29] Conformity, not innovation, was the legislators' ostensible goal. They had "endeavoured in all things, as near as the capacity and constitution of this Countrey would admit, to adhere to those Excellent, and often refined Laws of *England,* to which we profess and acknowledge all Reverence and Obedience." Instead of behaving like a freewheeling mini-Parliament that could pass any law it pleased, the Assembly claimed to have confined itself largely to "brief Memorials" of English law, supplied for the convenience of colonial judges who were "utterly unable" to consult the "vast Volumns" of English statutes and judicial decisions. The revision may have "var[ied] in small things" from rules laid down in England, but any discrepancies resulted from "the difference of our and their Condition" rather than from a desire to contradict English authority.[30]

Evidence of the Assembly's efforts to emulate English law can be found throughout the 1662 revisal. For example, the Assembly eliminated a conflict between Virginian and English jury procedures so trials would "come as near as may be to the laws of England (by which wee are to be governed) as our present capacities will admit."[31] The legislature adopted a statute of Henry VII on weights and measures and directed tavern owners to post bonds as required by English law.[32] Quakers who absented themselves from church were subject to punishment under an Elizabethan antirecusant statute.[33] Church legislation occupied a prominent place in the 1662 revisal, the Assembly explained, "because it is impossible to honour the King as we should, unless we serve and fear God as we ought."[34] Marriages were to be performed "according to the laws of England"; servants were to be bound for "the time lymitted by the laws of England"; accounts against decedents' estates were to be proved in the English manner; and corporal punishment was to be inflicted for offenses "punishable by the laws of England."[35] From a legal perspective, at least, Virginia was to be as English as Devonshire.

The Assembly's reliance on English law was not without precedent, of course. From the earliest days of the colony, metropolitan authorities had enjoined Virginians to pattern their laws on England's,[36] and occasionally the Assembly had complied.[37] In the 1662 revision, though, one senses the strongest commitment yet to achieving the goal of a fully Anglicized colonial law. The 1662 Assembly's self-conscious attempts to conform, like their contrition toward Charles II, resulted from practical political considerations and not from any lack of confidence in their own ability to devise innovative solutions to local legal problems. Virginians felt isolated and vulnerable in the early 1660s. Separated from the mother country by over 3,000 miles of ocean, surrounded by restive and potentially murderous Indians, threatened with invasion by England's continental rivals, and guilty of having turned their coats twice within a decade, colonists craved the imperial government's goodwill and protection. Statutory declarations of Virginians' essential Englishness must have seemed a promising path to that goal.

Waters's participation in the 1662 revision strengthened his grasp of English law, augmenting the knowledge he had acquired earlier through business and government service. He understood both the structure of English justice and the language Englishmen used to frame legal concepts. He had performed every significant role in the colonial legal system: litigant, juror, sheriff, county magistrate, provincial judge, legislator. Although he never studied law in a formal way — few seventeenth-century Virginians did — his experience equipped him with a de facto legal education that was

[handwritten annotation: denoting someone that is in such fact]

vastly superior to that of most Englishmen on either side of the Atlantic. Waters's legal skills, together with his wealth, commercial background, social status, and political power, made him more than a match for Jacob Bishopp.

Bishopp and Waters met in Waters's house at King's Creek Plantation in late 1663 or early 1664 to discuss the sale of Anne Orthwood's indenture. The conversation was witnessed by James Bonwell, who heard Bishopp ask Waters "if hee would buy his Maid." Waters inquired whether Anne "ailed any thing or noe, and whether she were a Maid or noe." Bishopp answered, "she is a Maid, and aileth nothing to the best of my knowledge."[38] Waters was justifiably worried about Anne's maidenhood because he did not wish to get stuck with a servant who was carrying an illegitimate child. Though a Virginia master was not legally obliged to maintain his servant's bastard (that duty fell on the parents or the parish),[39] the possibility of an illicit pregnancy still created reasonable grounds for concern. Even under the best of circumstances, childbearing impaired a woman's ability to work, and occasionally the experience had fatal consequences. It was only prudent for Waters to try to gauge the scope of his risk before making a sizable capital investment in an asset as potentially fragile as an unmarried woman in her early twenties. Satisfied that Bishopp had told the truth, Waters accepted the offer. The records do not say how much he paid for the approximately two and one-half years of service remaining under Orthwood's indenture, only that he made an unspecified down payment and owed Bishopp the rest.[40] Based on inventories and similar sales, Anne probably changed hands for about 1,000 pounds of tobacco, the equivalent of roughly six pounds sterling.[41]

Did Bishopp deliberately set out to cheat Waters? The evidence is ambiguous. The phrase "to the best of my knowledge" sounds suspiciously like an escape clause designed to provide a defense if Bishopp got sued, implying some degree of fraudulent intent. On the other hand, Bishopp simply may have wished to indicate that he was giving honest answers based on limited information, in which case he was guilty of nothing more than an abundance of caution. Assuming that Bishopp behaved rationally, the latter interpretation probably makes more sense. If he had meant to gull someone, Waters is the last person in Northampton County he would have chosen as his victim. The circumstances suggest, therefore, that Bishopp probably was as ignorant of Anne's pregnancy as Waters. Bishopp spoke inaccurately, but he did not lie.

Sometime between April and June 1664, Waters discovered the truth about Anne's condition. The news disturbed him, of course. He had contracted for a healthy maidservant and had gotten instead a woman whose medical condition and child-rearing responsibilities would render her unproductive during a significant portion of her term. He tried to cancel the sale and recover his down payment, but Bishopp refused to take Anne back, contending that the contract was valid and therefore Waters had a legal obligation to support her. Waters, however, considered the contract voidable because Bishopp had misdescribed the servant's fundamental characteristics. Since she must have been pregnant when he bought her indenture, Waters believed he was justified in severing their employment relationship. Under English law, a master's right to discharge a female servant because of pregnancy depended on the date when conception occurred. "If she be with child before the master hire her, and he know it not," the master had a right to fire her, provided he secured the approval of the local justices of the peace, who policed dismissals to prevent unnecessary additions to the poor relief rolls. "But if she be begot with childe during her service, then it seems the Justices cannot discharge her," and the master still had to provide maintenance.[42] Waters thought he could persuade his fellow Northampton justices that the law entitled him to nullify the transaction, so in June he filed suit against Bishopp in the county court. The case came before a five-judge panel headed by Presiding Justice John Stringer, a redoubtable physician-turned-entrepreneur whose career provides yet another example of the success to be had by those with the talent and tenacity to seize the opportunities early Virginia afforded.

*arrives
Pre-Civilwar*

JOHN STRINGER,
PRESIDING JUSTICE

John Stringer and the other four justices who adjudicated *Waters v. Bishopp* came from relatively humble backgrounds. Like William Kendall, they were largely self-made men who achieved economic preeminence by establishing extensive commercial networks, arranging advantageous marriages, and accumulating land and servants. Their wealth, in turn, helped them attain political power and social rank. Obedience by the community did not come easily, however. The justices worried constantly about maintaining their newly minted status, feeling insecure in ways unknown to well-born local leaders in England. Insecurity made them acutely sensitive to perceived slights, but it also spurred them to work harder to win popular approval. The magistrates took their responsibilities seriously, enforcing English and colonial law as well as they could, given the limits of their knowledge. They recognized the importance of maintaining the appearance of fairness and usually dispensed justice impartially, though they missed few chances to nudge the law in directions that coincided with their own economic interests. Their jurisprudence may have looked rustic by contemporary English standards, but the Eastern Shore owed much of its social stability to the justices' resolute, if testy, administration of the local legal system.

Stringer, the presiding justice, was born in England in 1611 and emigrated to the Eastern Shore in the 1630s. The roots of his prosperity lay in the profits from his highly dubious medical practice. The Northampton records contain numerous references to his fees for administering "Phisick,"[1] some of which appear extortionate. In 1639, for instance, Roger and Anne Moy had to bind themselves into servitude to pay Stringer's 1,200-pound bill "For a Cure that hee hath done upon Both [their] Bodyes."[2] (The patients survived the cure but came to a bad end anyway: in 1653, Anne was sentenced to death for murdering Roger.)[3] In 1641, Stringer charged Daniel Cugley's estate over eight pounds sterling, a sum worth more than the cost of a transatlantic passage, for treating Cugley and his wife.[4] For his "Attendance upon Richard Newport gentleman deceased being then sicke and visitted with a Contagious disease call'd the Plague," in 1643, Stringer earned a fee of 500 pounds of tobacco plus the right to "enjoye" the dead man's "weareing apparrell."[5] While remunerative, Stringer's medical practice was less than salubrious. On the same day that the court awarded Stringer the plague victim's clothing, the magistrates had to postpone all litigation involving the physician because he was "now sicke."[6] Unlike many of his patients, Stringer recovered, eventually reaching the age of 78, a remarkable feat in the disease-ridden Chesapeake.[7]

Stringer augmented his medical income with the proceeds from a variety of other economic activities, including land speculation, farming, ship provisioning, money lending, and international trade in wine and tobacco.[8] He must have acquired a reputation for fairness and financial acumen, for he was frequently asked to value property and help the judiciary resolve economic disputes.[9] His success at making money positioned him for political preferment. After serving a year as sheriff, he received an appointment to the county court from Governor Berkeley in 1650. When Virginia surrendered to Parliament two years later, Stringer promptly swore allegiance to the new regime and secured reappointment from Governor Bennett. He switched sides again at the Restoration, and his old friend Berkeley let him keep his seat. He became the senior Northampton justice after the Assembly subdivided the Eastern Shore in 1663, and except for three more stints as sheriff, remained an active magistrate until 1686.[10] He also represented the Eastern Shore in the House of Burgesses from 1659 to 1662 and held various offices in the militia, rising to the rank of colonel in 1663.[11]

Serving alongside Stringer on the Northampton bench was Justice William Spencer, who arrived on the Eastern Shore around 1660 and was appointed to the county court in 1661.[12] Spencer and William Kendall evidently had a close business relationship. In 1663, for instance, Spencer served as Kendall's surety in a lawsuit, and they were later partners in a land deal.[13] Besides his magisterial duties, Spencer served as a captain in the militia, raised livestock and tobacco, and speculated in land.[14] His conduct did not always conform to the patriarchal ideal. Magistrates were supposed to be models for the community, yet on three occasions Spencer subjected himself to fines for dereliction of duty or misbehavior. In June 1663, his fellow justices chided him for habitual tardiness and fined him 300 pounds of tobacco for leaving court before the conclusion of business.[15] They fined him again in December 1674 because he was "for the most part remisse in Attendinge the Publique busines as to the Administracon of Justice very much retardinge his Majesties leige people in their affaires."[16] His worst offense, however, occurred in January 1679, when he confessed judgment for a 1,000-pound fine assessed against him and his second wife, Frances Cowdrey Spencer, for having a child before marriage.[17] If this breach of social and religious norms embarrassed him, Spencer did not let on; he seated himself on the bench immediately after pleading guilty. The following year he tried to rehabilitate his tarnished reputation by donating an acre for the Hungars Parish Churchyard "in reference to [his] Zeale and Devotion to the furtherance of gods worship."[18] Whether this display of late-blooming piety succeeded in changing his neighbors' opinions is anyone's guess. Spencer continued serving as a justice, off and on, until 1683.[19]

If Spencer's behavior made him a rather unconventional JP, Justice John Michael's Dutch origins marked him as another aberration from the magisterial norm. Michael began his career as a merchant in Graft, Holland.[20] He visited the Eastern Shore as early as 1646 and moved there around 1650 to establish a trading base. He shipped tobacco to Amsterdam, served as the resident agent for numerous Dutch merchants, and acted as a middleman for Kendall and other tobacco exporters to the Netherlands.[21] Michael and his fellow Dutch Virginians faced threats of violence during the war between England and the Netherlands in the early 1650s and had to be protected by colonial authorities, whose solicitude toward foreign traders enraged their English competitors. The surgeon on a Bristol ship told Stringer, Obedience Robins, and another local leader "that they had English faces, but Dutch harts." Mocking arriviste Virginians' fondness for titles, the first mate added that he had been afraid to bring his horse to the Chesapeake because the colonists "would have made him either a Collonel, a Major, or a Justice of peace."[22] Ridicule did not deter the Eastern Shore magistrates from trying to safeguard their foreign neighbors. They issued an order prohibiting harassment of the Dutch, and Governor Bennett lent his support by certifying Michael's loyalty to the Commonwealth and granting him equal rights with all other foreigners. Life became easier for Michael and other resident Dutchmen after the war ended in 1654. Two years later, the Assembly made Michael a denizen of Virginia, a legal status entitling him to own land and enjoy all legal privileges except office holding.[23] Taking advantage of these rights, Michael acquired extensive tracts of land and began farming on a major scale, becoming one of the largest employers in Northampton County.[24]

Michael benefited from having influential friends, including Kendall and Waters. When he needed to assert a claim against an estate, for example, Kendall acted as his surety, guaranteeing that the claim was proper. His links to Waters dated back to 1648, when Waters served as Michael's attorney and helped him collect his debts on the Eastern Shore.[25] These ties may have played a role in Michael's appointment to the bench, an action complicated by his foreign birth. Governor Berkeley tried to appoint Michael to the county court in September 1663 but had to revoke the commission when doubts were raised about Michael's eligibility to serve. Under English law, a foreign-born person could not hold public office merely by becoming a denizen; he had to be naturalized by legislative act. Michael produced proof that he had, in fact, been naturalized, so in March 1664 the governor and Council reinstated him as a JP. He took his seat in April, just in time to adjudicate *Waters v. Bishopp,* and continued serving until his death in 1679.[26]

The Northampton bench had another justice with Dutch roots, John Custis II, who was born in Holland in 1628 or 1629. He was one of the 13 children of Henry Custis, an Englishman who operated an inn in Rotterdam. John emigrated to the Eastern Shore in 1649 after his sister Ann married a prominent colonist, Argoll Yardley. With his brother-in-law's help, John grew wealthy in Virginia through trade, land speculation, agriculture, and marriage to two affluent widows.[27] His commercial activities centered on New Amsterdam, a logical trading destination for a man with his background. He assembled cargoes of tobacco for shipment to the Dutch colony and acted as the attorney for merchants from New Netherland and Rotterdam, as well as New England.[28] Custis's facility in the Dutch language enhanced his value as an intermediary in international commerce. When the New Netherland governor, Peter Stuyvesant, corresponded with the governor and Council of Virginia on an important admiralty matter in 1663, for example, the Virginia officials called on Custis to translate the documents.[29] Through headrights and purchases, he accumulated over 1,000 acres by 1664, to which he gradually added another 10,000 over the next quarter century.[30] During the early 1670s, he built a great house—Arlington—which was one of the two finest mansions erected in the seventeenth-century Chesapeake.[31] His affluence and imperious manner earned him the sobriquet "King Custis,"[32] quite a title for the son of an innkeeper.

As Custis's wealth grew, so did his political power. He held several minor posts in the 1650s, such as surveyor and estate appraiser,[33] and was nominated for sheriff in 1655 but did not receive the appointment because of his foreign citizenship. That obstacle to political advancement was removed in 1658 when the Assembly passed a law naturalizing him and his brother.[34] The following year, the county court again nominated Custis for sheriff, and this time he got the post and served until he became a magistrate in 1660. Except for another term as sheriff, Custis remained a justice until 1677, when he was elevated to the Council, where he served until 1692.[35]

William Andrews II, the fifth member of the bench that decided *Waters v. Bishopp*, was the only one born in Virginia. His father, William Andrews I, emigrated to the colony in 1617 and settled on the Eastern Shore in the early 1620s. The senior Andrews became a large landowner and important officeholder, serving on the county court from 1633 through 1655 and eventually becoming the presiding justice.[36] Much as Edward Waters's achievements as a first-generation leader facilitated his son's rise to power, William Andrews I's wealth and position enabled his son to attain public office at an early age. In 1655, when William II was just 23, the governor and Council appointed him sheriff on the recommendation of his father and the other magistrates.[37] William I died the following year, leaving his son 1,800 acres in addition to 500 acres he had given him earlier.[38] Bolstered by his inheritance, William II continued his rapid ascent through the political ranks. He became a member of the county court as soon as his term as sheriff ended in 1656 and, except for a second term in that office, remained an active magistrate until shortly before his death in 1673.[39] In addition, he held the rank of major in the militia and sat as a burgess in the Assembly in 1663–64.[40] Andrews had numerous business and kinship ties to his fellow county leaders. He was related by marriage to Stringer, Custis, and Waters, and the link to Waters was especially close. Andrews's wife, Dorothy, was Waters's beloved half-sister,[41] a connection that can hardly have comforted Jacob Bishopp as he contemplated the prospect of litigating against Waters with Andrews as one of the judges.

The court on which these five men served had grown significantly in importance over the last four decades.[42] From 1607 to

1619, the governor and Council in Jamestown had provided the only source of judicial power. Their jurisdiction extended throughout the colony, embraced both civil and criminal cases, and included petty as well as serious matters. As areas of settlement grew ever more distant from the capital during the 1620s and 1630s, the provincial government delegated increasing amounts of responsibility to county magistrates, who were called commissioners until 1662 and justices of the peace thereafter. The title of justice of the peace is somewhat misleading, for Virginia magistrates possessed judicial powers far beyond those of English JPs. In addition to handling the same kinds of criminal and administrative matters that English JPs adjudicated in their petty and quarter sessions, Virginia magistrates functioned as the colonial equivalents of the central courts at Westminster and the church courts. "The Courts of Justice are not distinct as in England," a late seventeenth-century report noted, "but Causes belonging to Chancery, King's Bench, Common Pleas, Exchequer, Admiralty, and Spirituality, are decided altogether in one and the same Court."[43] At the provincial level, this all-purpose tribunal was the General Court, made up of the governor and councillors, and at the local level, the county court, staffed by JPs.

The jurisdictions of the General Court and the county courts overlapped to some degree, though each had an exclusive domain as well. Under a 1662 law, only the General Court could try "criminall causes that concerne either life or member."[44] County magistrates performed important screening and evidence-gathering functions in capital cases, however. Justices of the peace examined witnesses and suspected felons and, if the evidence warranted, bound over defendants for trial by the General Court.[45] Most noncapital criminal cases began and ended in the county courts, as did the overwhelming majority of civil lawsuits. The General Court's original jurisdiction in civil cases was limited to relatively large matters, namely cases involving at least 1,600 pounds of tobacco or 16 pounds sterling.[46] County courts had much broader civil jurisdiction, encompassing all controversies where at least 200 pounds of tobacco or 20 shillings were at stake.[47] County court judgments were subject to appellate review in the General Court, but because of the Eastern Shore's "remotenesse and [the] dangerousnes of passage" to Jamestown, no appeal could be taken from North-ampton and Accomack Counties unless the litigation concerned at least 3,000 pounds of tobacco or 30 pounds sterling.[48]

The courts of the Eastern Shore generally held about 10 sessions a year. A host of factors — weather, road conditions, crop cycles, the number of case filings, the availability of magistrates — deter-mined when and how often the courts met, although the Assembly did its best to standardize meeting dates.[49] The size of the court de-pended on the governor's wishes and local needs. In theory the governor's power of appointment was unrestricted, but in practice he usually selected men whose names were forwarded to him by in-cumbent magistrates, thereby facilitating county courts' evolution into self-perpetuating oligarchies.[50] Until the Restoration, Virginia law did not limit the number of men whom the governor could elevate to the county bench. So many were appointed during the Interregnum — 20 Eastern Shoremen were commissioned in 1657, for example[51] — that the Assembly intervened to restore the pres-tige of the office. The legislature enacted statutes in 1661 and 1662 limiting the number of appointees to eight per county, at least four of whom had to be present to conduct judicial business.[52] During the 1660s, an average of around six JPs attended each meeting of the court, and those who sat regularly became highly experienced in the administration of justice. The typical Northampton magis-trate who served during 1664, for instance, began the year with 60 court meetings under his belt.[53]

Virginia justices derived their legal knowledge from the acts of Assembly, English treatises, and their own collective experience as working magistrates. The Assembly tried to promote conformity with English law by passing a statute in 1666 ordering all county and provincial courts to acquire Michael Dalton's handbooks for JPs and sheriffs and Henry Swinburne's treatise on wills.[54] The

Eastern Shore records occasionally cite English legal texts, and a few legal works appear on estate inventories, but colonial magistrates were not a bookish lot.[55] The Virginia justice George Webb explained in the preface to his 1736 JP manual that he had "avoided all References to Laws and Law Books" because the "far greatest Part of our Inhabitants are unfurnish'd with those Books, or are diverted from Reading them, by the necessary Affairs of their Plantations, and the innocent Pleasures of a Country Life."[56] Instead of poring over books, Virginia JPs probably learned most of their law by observing their more experienced colleagues.

Critics charged that the lack of formal legal training left county magistrates ill equipped to perform their duties. "[I]t was no Wonder," wrote the authors of a 1697 report to the Board of Trade, "if both the Sense of the Law was mistaken, and the Form and Method of Proceedings was often very irregular."[57] Ignorance was not the only reason why Virginia procedure deviated from the English model, however. Colonists consciously rejected much of the dilatory formalism that characterized English practice, preferring swifter and simpler methods of litigating disputes. Though their procedures were informal, Virginia JPs still expected to be treated with the same deference that was accorded metropolitan magistrates. This was not always a realistic view, particularly in the middle decades of the seventeenth century. Lacking the attributes traditionally associated with gentleman justices, the Eastern Shore magistrates of that period found themselves mired in a ceaseless struggle to coerce lesser men's respect.

Stringer and his colleagues suffered numerous verbal assaults, some of which reflected disdain for the parvenu justices' social pretensions. In May 1660, Stringer and his colleagues fined Samuel Jones 250 pounds of tobacco "for his Scandelous abuse of the Court in calling them Mekannicks."[58] The court also fined John Baddam, John Cole, and Richard Dibbons 50 pounds each "for Righting Contriveing and delivering an Insolent Libell to the Court."[59] Phillip Mongom, a free black accused of hog-stealing, received a fine of 100 pounds for throwing hogs' ears on the court table.[60] Robert Warren was fined 300 pounds for coming "into the face of the Court and then rudely intruding and speaking in unconserned causes, interupting and upbraiding the Court in their pronounceing of Judgments." Warren compounded the offense by approaching Obedience Robins in the yard outside the courthouse and publicly declaring that "hee cared not for him, nor the Court with other words of defiance."[61] At the same tumultuous session, Richard Whitmarsh was fined 300 pounds for swearing "which hee did presumptiously and arrogantly in the presence of severall Magestrates in the Court house,"[62] and Henry Boston was fined 2,000 pounds (later reduced to 400 pounds) for calling the acts of Assembly "Simple foolish things."[63]

Fewer displays of insolence occurred after this crackdown, but contempt of authority remained a problem for Eastern Shore magistrates throughout the early 1660s. Often contempt amounted to little more than rudeness or drunken noisemaking and elicited a fairly lenient response.[64] When misbehavior challenged the foundations of magisterial power, however, JPs came down harder. Disrespect for law seemed tantamount to disrespect for them, and vice versa, so they swiftly punished any criticism of the established legal order. In November 1660, for example, the magistrates fined John Dolby 200 pounds "for misdemeaner to the Court and opprobrious Words Spoke against the Lawes of the Countrey."[65] Since the justices' right to hold office now depended on the Crown, they felt equally obliged to chastise anyone who spoke ill of Charles II. In April 1662, they ordered Alexander Mill to be whipped at a horse's tail for speaking "Irreverent and undecent words . . . concerning his Majestie."[66] Ironically, all five of the magistrates who issued this order had held office under the Commonwealth and Protectorate.

Critics of governmental authority sometimes directed their ire at particular justices, and Stringer seems to have been a favorite target. John Little, a disappointed litigant, called him "a base fellowe" and "a Rascall" for denying him equal justice, "sayeing my flesh trembleth att thee thou dogge thou hellhound." For his verbal assault on Stringer's dignity, Little was fined 1,500 pounds of tobacco.[67] Another critic was ordered whipped for using abusive language toward Stringer.[68] In July 1664, Abraham van Soldt "presented a Scandellous Paper to the Court, wherein hee hath much abused and defamed" Stringer. The court demanded that van Soldt "make good the said Charge or elce Suffer Such punishment as the Court Should thinke fitt to inflict upon him." Van Soldt admitted his charges were false and begged the court and Stringer to be merciful. The court ordered van Soldt to stand at the courthouse door during the next three sittings of the justices "with his fault on his breast in Capitall Letters" and to ask Stringer's forgiveness on his knees in open court on all three days.[69]

Besides punishing people who behaved insolently or challenged their authority, Stringer and his colleagues attempted to win respect by projecting a more genteel image. They found it undignified as well as inconvenient to hold their sessions at hostelries such as John Webb's inn, so in April 1664 they asked Waters to undertake the construction of a proper courthouse, "twenty five foot long, and twenty foot Wide," with a "Nine foot Pitch."[70] To complement their new surroundings, the JPs adopted a code of conduct. Interestingly, two-thirds of the code dealt with the unseemly use of the plant on which Virginia had built her fortune:

It is ordered that if any of the Magistrates Smoake tobacco at the Court table when his Majesties Justice is administered [he] Shall be fined fifty pounds of tobacco to bee disposed of as the Major part of the Court Shall thinke fitt.

It is ordered that if any Officer of the Court Inhabitant or any other person Shall Smoake tobacco in the Court house, when the Court is sitting [he] Shall bee fined thirty pounds of tobacco.

It is ordered that if any Person not Thereby quallified Shall presume to come into the Court with his hatt on his head The Sherriffe or his Deputy Shall take of[f] his or their Hatt and keepe it tell they make payment of thirty pounds of tobacco, And if they Shall offend a Second tyme then to bee fined fifty pounds of tobacco, and for the third Offence, According to the pleasure of the Court.[71]

This earnest campaign of image-building, like the crackdown on insolence, betrayed the Northampton justices' deep sense of anxiety about their status as an elite. For all their pretensions, most knew they lacked the kind of background that naturally commanded deference in early modern English society. Stringer and his colleagues might be wealthy, but they were only gentlemen *manqués,* transparently ambitious men who knew what gentility was and sought it ardently.[72] Until they managed to persuade the community that they deserved places of social superiority, they would continue to worry about being accepted as legitimate rulers.

Magistrates' insecurity made them highly sensitive to public opinion. They worked hard to maintain popular support, especially among free males, the group whose taxes financed government and whose votes determined the outcome of burgess elections. Sometimes the justices appealed directly to the community, urging Shoremen to trust them to govern fairly and in the taxpayers' best interests. In 1661, for example, a rabble-rouser named John Millby accused the sheriff and magistrates of financial misconduct. Millby claimed the governor had empowered him to "call a party of honest godly Men together who were to Question the Commissioners for the wrong they had done the County" and said he would "informe the People" of the magistrates' abuses. The court ordered him incarcerated on the ground that he "would be most dangerous to the peace of the County If hee should be permitted at Large the Ignorant people being all ready possest with many Lyes and falce Relations from the said Millby." But the magistrates did not stop there. Realizing they had "to undeceive those naturally Inocent [people]" who had been corrupted by Millby's charges, they issued a proclamation aimed at "Sattisfying the Expectation of all men in <u>poynt</u> of Justice." This statement reflected the magistrates' awareness that they had to please not only their superiors in Jamestown but also their constituents at home. The proclamation announced the court's intent to examine the sheriff's accounts and to render justice "to the Sattisfaction of all honnest Injenious and good Men" in Northampton County as well as the magistrates' "Superiors to whome wee are to give an Accompt thereof."[73] The authorities in Jamestown upheld Millby's imprisonment and ordered him to apologize for slandering the JPs. He refused and eventually spent over 500 days in jail for his impertinence.[74]

These contempt cases reveal both the vitality of the county court as an institution and the vulnerability of the men who staffed it during the formative years. Waters had a stronger claim to gentility than all the other justices, save perhaps Andrews, yet he too had felt the scorn of his disorderly neighbors. He ran a risk by asking his fellow justices to adjudicate his dispute with Bishopp, for there were those who, like Millby, perceived corruption at every turn. If he won the lawsuit, critics might attribute his victory to cronyism and cite the case as another example of the magistrates' willingness to use the legal system for selfish ends. Consequently, he had to do more than just prevail; he also had to satisfy "all good and moderate Men" that justice was dispensed equitably.[75] The key was to persuade them that his interests coincided with theirs, so a judgment in his favor would benefit not just him but the community at large. This required artful advocacy on Waters's part, both in the court of public opinion and in the judicial tribunal itself. He doubtless had politics as well as law in mind when he prepared his case for trial.

FIVE

ROBERT HUTCHINSON,
CLERK OF COURT

Waters's point of entry into the Northampton judicial system was the office of the county clerk, the
heart of local administration. Virtually every document of legal
consequence passed through the clerk's hands. He kept the records
of court proceedings, issued warrants, enrolled deeds and wills,
compiled tax lists, and memorialized everything county officials
thought worth preserving. His work acquainted him with legal
formalities and enabled him to function as an intermediary between the legal system and the community. Although prohibited
from pleading in court on behalf of a client, the clerk provided a
variety of public services outside the courtroom, such as writing
petitions, wills, and other legal papers, for which he charged a
statutorily prescribed fee.[1] The holder of the lucrative clerkship
in 1664 was Robert Hutchinson, a 34-year-old farmer-bureaucrat
who appears to have had some legal training. He may have been a
Quaker, an unusual affiliation for a Virginia officeholder, given the
provincial government's hostility toward members of that faith.[2]
The governor appointed him to the Northampton post in 1659
following his nomination by the magistrates.[3] When the Assembly split the Eastern Shore into two separate counties in 1663,
Hutchinson became clerk of both. He relinquished the Northampton clerkship to William Mellinge in early 1665 but continued

serving Accomack until being forced out of office in 1670, when the counties were temporarily reunited.[4]

Waters's lawsuit commenced when Hutchinson entered the suit in the court record and collected his fee of eight pounds of tobacco.[5] The purpose of the entry was to reserve a place on the county court's docket and to identify the "form of action" through which the plaintiff proposed to litigate his claim. The forms of action were the various types of civil litigation that courts were willing to recognize, such as trespass and debt.[6] A plaintiff had to fit his grievance into an established category or forgo redress. The choice of form determined how the case would be tried, what the plaintiff had to plead and prove, and what type of remedy he would receive if he won.[7] The entry in *Waters v. Bishopp* has not survived, so we cannot be certain about the precise label Waters affixed to his claim. He probably just called it an action of "trespass on the case," a generic form of action encompassing a wide range of breaches of contract and other nonforcible wrongs.[8]

After entering the action, Hutchinson issued a warrant directing the sheriff or undersheriff to arrest Bishopp and require him to post a bond guaranteeing that he would appear in court on a specified day to answer Waters's accusations and abide by whatever order the justices issued.[9] The warrant, sometimes referred to as the "writ," served an important informational function. Although it did not provide a detailed description of the claim — the plaintiff's initial pleading was supposed to do that — the warrant disclosed the basic nature of the lawsuit. For a warrant to be valid, it had to "express the Cause for which the Party is to be arrested, or summoned, and therefore a General Warrant to cause any Person to appear and answer such Matters as shall be objected against him, without mentioning any particular Matter, is not good."[10] If the officer charged with serving the warrant failed to locate the defendant, he marked "non est inventus" on the paper and returned it to the clerk. That allowed the plaintiff to ask the court for a writ of attachment authorizing the sheriff to seize the defendant's property to satisfy the claim. If the defendant was found and arrested but failed to appear and answer (*nihil dicit*), the court awarded judgment against his surety (the person who provided the bond guaranteeing his appearance) or against the sheriff if he did not obtain adequate bail.[11] In this case, the undersheriff, John Ferebee, had no difficulty locating Bishopp and serving the warrant. Bishopp posted bond, and the suit moved to the next stage, the pleadings.

Waters's initial pleading was a written petition setting forth his cause of action, that is, the facts entitling him to judicial relief. Together with the defendant's response, the petition defined the issues the judges and jurors would be called on to resolve.[12] Virginia law required the plaintiff to file his pleading with the county clerk at least one day before trial. The clerk kept the original, and the defendant received a copy if he wished. For entering the pleading in the court's records, the clerk received a fee of three pounds of tobacco. He earned an additional 10 pounds if he wrote the pleading on the plaintiff's behalf. If the plaintiff entered his suit and had the defendant arrested but failed to file his pleading in a timely manner, the court would order a nonsuit, dismissing the action.[13]

Colonial pleadings were much less formal than those used in the English courts of King's Bench and Common Pleas.[14] Virginians abhorred the notion that technical errors could prevent someone from obtaining justice. At its March 1658 session, the Assembly complained that "there is and daily doth arise excessive charges and greate delaies and hinderances of justice betwixt the subjects of this collony by reason of small mistakes in writts and formes of pleading." To remedy that evil, the legislature instructed courts to "proceed and give judgement according as the right of the cause and the matter in lawe shall appeare unto them, without regard of any imperfection, default or want of forme in any writt, returne plaint or process or any other cause whatsoever."[15] This enlightened measure was repealed in March 1662 as part of the Assembly's effort to conform Virginia's laws with England's.[16] Nevertheless, the secretary of the colony, Thomas Ludwell, could still claim, in a 1666 report to officials in London, that even in Virginia's highest court no advantage was allowed to either party based on procedural error.[17] Colonial judges addressed the merits of a case as soon as they could, "never admitting such impertinences of Form and Nicety, as were not absolutely necessary," and by that method, reported the lawyer and politician Robert Beverley, "all fair Actions were prosecuted with little Attendance, all just Debts were recover'd with the least expense of Money and Time; and all the tricking, and foppery of the Law happily avoided."[18]

If informality prevailed in the General Court, an even more casual approach to procedure characterized adjudication in the county courts, especially in the period before lawyers started practicing regularly at the local level in the late 1660s.[19] Litigants did not enjoy complete freedom in drafting their pleadings, however. At a minimum, a petition had to agree with the warrant that initiated the lawsuit. For instance, the county court would dismiss an action if the plaintiff had a warrant issued for defamation and then filed a pleading alleging that the defendant had committed a different tort, such as battery.[20] Moreover, even if the pleading corresponded to the warrant, the court would dismiss the action if it appeared unduly novel. The Eastern Shore justices' tolerance of informality did not signify an eagerness to invent new grounds for granting judicial remedies. They insisted that litigants use traditional English forms of action, partly because they seemed familiar and therefore somewhat comprehensible, and partly because of the restrictions placed on JPs' authority. The magistrates' commission from the governor authorized them "to Heare and determine all Suits and Causes betweene party and party According to the Knowne Lawes of England, or the Acts of Assembly that are for the tyme being or shall be in force in Virginia."[21] Justices did not have a license to innovate—overtly, anyway—so they refused to hear a claim for monetary relief unless it bore at least a passing resemblance to a traditional action they recognized. A claim for slander would be dismissed, for example, if "the words mentioned in the petition are not Actionable by the Common Law of England" because they were unaccompanied by allegations of falsity, malice, and damage.[22] When a creditor brought an action of "debt upon account" to collect some tobacco he was owed, the court sustained a plea in abatement and dismissed the suit on the ground that "by the Common Law of England there is no Such accon as debt upon account."[23] There was an action called "debt on an account stated," which lay to collect a sum agreed to be outstanding,[24] but the Accomack justices either considered it inapplicable (perhaps because the parties disputed the amount owed) or unavailable because the plaintiff had failed to label his action in the proper English fashion.

To English lawyers, the term "common law" referred to a set of unwritten legal rules, applicable throughout England, based on "the Law of Nature or Reason, the revealed Law of God, the General Customs of the Kingdom, and the Principles and Maxims of the Law."[25] Those rules were developed by the judges and practitioners of the king's courts, who used "common law" to distinguish their handiwork from the other two main categories of secular law, namely, acts of Parliament and the customs of particular localities.[26] Virginians did not always know what they were talking about when they used the phrase "Common Law of England."[27] Nevertheless, the Eastern Shore justices' insistence that lawsuits at least sound reassuringly English reflected their conservative conception of the judicial function. They were aware that the Assembly claimed the right to deviate from English law that did not fit colonial conditions, subject to the Crown's power to veto any deviation it deemed unjustified.[28] Indeed, in their role as burgesses, many magistrates had participated in the enactment of statutes that conflicted with traditional English rules. But colonial legislators did not take such steps lightly. English law was the ultimate source of their authority, and they knew that if they strayed too far from the metropolitan model, they might undercut their own legitimacy. As Governor Berkeley put it, Virginians were determined to "administer Justice according to the lawes of England as farre as [they were] able to comprehend them,"[29] a stance that militated against blatant legal experimentation. When innovation occurred at the county court level, it resulted either from JPs' ignorance of

English doctrine or from their pragmatic and perhaps reluctant decision to modify the mother country's rules to make them better suited to the circumstances of colonial life.

Once the plaintiff had filed his pleading, the defendant had to present a written answer. He could challenge the legal sufficiency of the plaintiff's pleading through a "demurrer," a motion asserting that even if the plaintiff's accusations were true, they did not justify holding the defendant liable. Alternatively, he could plead a special defense such as expiration of the filing period prescribed by the statute of limitations. Or, like most defendants in contested suits, he could plead the general issue ("not guilty") and put the plaintiff to his proof, creating factual issues for the jury or magistrates to decide. Pleading grew more elaborate toward the end of the century as lawyers began augmenting their petitions and answers with replications and rejoinders, a sign that technical English procedural lore was trickling down to the county courts.[30] But in the 1660s, pleading usually concluded with the filing of the answer, which is what happened in *Waters v. Bishopp*. Bishopp's answer simply pled the general issue, putting every aspect of Waters's claim into issue. Waters therefore had to prove that he and Bishopp entered into a valid contract, that Bishopp breached it, and that Waters sustained harm for which he was entitled to redress.

Waters requested two remedies for the alleged breach of contract: termination of his employment relationship with Anne and recovery of his down payment. The petition itself has not survived, but Hutchinson's summary reveals its essence:

> Whereas Lieutenant Colonel William Waters hath petitioned this Court that Jacob Bishopp hath Sould him a maide Servant named Anne Orthwood pretending Shee ayled nothing to his knowledge, Notwithstanding She declareth herselfe with Child and therefore [Waters] Craveth order to bee discharged of the said Servant, and that the said Bishopp may returne payment againe for her with costs of Suit. . . .[31]

Waters's request "to bee discharged" of Anne was perfectly conventional. English law clearly allowed JPs to permit the dismissal of a female servant before the end of her term if her master had hired her without realizing she was pregnant. Waters's request for an order compelling Bishopp to "returne payment againe for her" was more problematic. He was seeking what amounted to rescission and restitution—an order canceling the transaction and requiring the parties to give back whatever they had received from the other so that neither would be unjustly enriched by the aborted sale. A royal court in England would have been unlikely to grant rescission and restitution to a disappointed buyer in Waters's position. To help understand why, a brief examination of buyers' remedies under English common law is needed.

In the seventeenth century, the principal way for a buyer to recover a payment was by suing the seller in an action of "indebtitatus assumpsit for money had and received," a subcategory of trespass on the case. The plaintiff alleged that the defendant had received a sum of money rightfully belonging to the plaintiff and had breached his subsequent promise to pay it. The promise to pay was wholly fictitious, and the real purpose of the action was to enforce the courts' view that under certain circumstances fairness obligated a defendant to hand over money to the plaintiff.[32] The King's Bench held in *Lady Cavendish v. Middleton* (1628)[33] that a buyer could sue in indebtitatus assumpsit if the seller had deceived her into mistakenly paying more than the agreed price. Courts later extended the action by allowing buyers to recover money paid under a contract of sale where the seller, although innocent of fraud, failed to deliver anything.[34] A sharp distinction was drawn, however, between nondelivery and defective delivery. A buyer could bring an indebtitatus action if he never received the thing contracted for but not if it arrived in a damaged condition.[35] Thus, a buyer who paid 50 pounds for a horse that was never delivered could recover the 50 pounds in an action for money had and received, but a buyer who took delivery of a horse that was too lame to ride could not return the animal and get his money back.

The difference in outcomes stemmed from the doctrine of *caveat emptor*—let the buyer beware. Once a sale had been executed and the goods delivered, ownership passed from the seller to the buyer, and the transfer could not be undone by a court.[36] Generally this meant that a seller did not have to stand behind the accuracy of his statements or the quality of his merchandise; instead, the onus of verification fell on the purchaser. If a buyer got less than he bargained for, he had only himself to blame for neglecting to take adequate precautions. *Caveat emptor* encouraged sellers to puff their wares with abandon, secure in the knowledge that so long as they did not overcharge or give warranties, they could not be held accountable for their exaggerations. The rule exacerbated the amorality of the marketplace, but it produced benefits as well. To the extent that gullible buyers believed the extravagant sales pitches and purchased goods they otherwise would have done without, *caveat emptor* stimulated the flow of commerce and fostered economic growth.

The best way for a buyer to protect himself in the world of *caveat emptor* was to obtain an express warranty from the seller guaranteeing that the quality of the goods was as high as he claimed. If a seller warranted his goods and they turned out to be defective, the buyer could seek compensation from the seller in an action of "deceit on a false warranty," another subcategory of trespass on the case. The gist of the action of deceit was not that the seller had intended to defraud the buyer but that the false warranty itself had induced the buyer to make a contract he would have shunned if he had received accurate information. The warranty had to relate to the present condition of the goods, and the falsehood must not have been evident to the buyer. In an action of deceit on a false warranty, the buyer had to keep the defective goods, and he did not get his money back. His remedy was damages, not rescission and restitution. The measure of damages was the difference between the goods' actual value and what they would have been worth had they conformed to the warranty.[37] The leading case on a buyer's right to recover damages for defective goods was *Chandelor v. Lopus* (1604).[38] The buyer, a merchant, exchanged a diamond ring worth 100 pounds for a lump that the seller, a goldsmith, affirmed to be a bezoar stone, a hard gastric or intestinal mass found chiefly in ruminants and considered an antidote to poison. When the buyer learned that his purchase was not a bezoar, he sought damages through an action of deceit. The judges held the declaration insufficient, "for the bare affirmation that it was a bezar-stone, without warranting it to be so, is no cause of action."[39] The seller could say whatever he wished without fear of damages liability provided he did not formally warrant the product.

English court decisions continued in this proseller vein for the rest of the seventeenth century. William Sheppard, writing in the early 1650s, emphasized the central role that warranties had come to play in sales law. "If a man sell me any living or dead thing, as Cattel, Cloth, or the like, and at the time of the sale he doth warrant it to me good and right, and it be otherwise," the buyer could sue the seller in deceit. That principle applied, Sheppard noted, even though "the fault is such as the seller did not know of it." In other words, the buyer did not have to prove that the seller knew his warranty was false. But if the fault was so "apparent that the buyer may discern it by one of his five senses," no action would lie because the false warranty was not what induced the sale. A special rule governed sales of "corrupt victual or wine"; there the buyer who had purchased without knowledge of the contamination could bring an action of deceit even in the absence of an express warranty. "But if one sell corrupt, or false and sophisticated wares" of another type, Sheppard added, "it seems no Action of the Case will lie upon this sale without a warranty be made."[40]

Waters's claim for rescission and restitution fit neither indebtitatus assumpsit nor deceit on a false warranty. Indebtitatus was not an appropriate action because Waters did not accuse Bishopp of inducing him to pay money by mistake or of failing to deliver. Deceit on a false warranty was unavailable because Waters lacked the crucial ingredient of a warranty. Bishopp's statement that Anne was "a Maid and aileth nothing to the best of my knowledge"[41] amounted to a bare affirmation of quality rather than an explicit guarantee. Until late in the seventeenth century, when the distinction between affirmations and warranties started to blur, the word "warrant" or something close to it was necessary for a warranty.[42] Waters's petition, in essence, urged the court to disregard the technicalities of indebtitatus assumpsit and deceit and to make *caveat venditor* — let the seller beware — instead of *caveat emptor* the central principle of Eastern Shore sales law. That would enable a buyer to rescind a contract if the goods did not conform to the seller's description regardless of whether the seller knew the truth about them or warranted the accuracy of his description. Waters's request for restitution rather than damages implied that deficient performance of a contract should be regarded as the legal equivalent of total nonperformance. If this view prevailed, a misled buyer of defective goods (or, in Waters's case, a pregnant servant) could return the items and get his money back, just as he could recover his payment if the seller delivered nothing at all.

The legal theory best suited to implementing *caveat venditor* was the concept of the conditional sale. Courts in England had long allowed a disappointed buyer to recover his payment if he and the seller had expressly agreed that the validity of their transaction depended on the fulfillment of a condition pertaining to the quality of the goods.[43] They also had permitted a buyer to invoke an implied condition of quality in defense to a seller's suit to collect the price of a defective item.[44] Waters wanted the county court to go a step further and hold that nonfulfillment of an implied condition of quality enabled the buyer to recoup his down payment as well as cancel any remaining debt. Had he made that argument in England, he might well have encountered resistance from judges influenced by *caveat emptor,* but in Virginia precedent was on his side. Eastern Shore contract law already pointed in a probuyer direction.

Three Eastern Shore cases decided a few years before *Waters v. Bishopp* illuminate some of the similarities and differences between the colonial and metropolitan versions of the common law of sales contracts. The first, *Jones v. Selby* (1658),[45] illustrates the overlap between the two approaches. In *Jones,* the Eastern Shore justices applied conventional *Chandelor* principles to a deceit action involving the delivery of a defective mare. The seller, Thomas Selby, said "hee was Sure [the mare] was with foale and therefore hee Could warrant her without danger." The mare turned out to be barren, prompting the buyer, Samuel Jones, to sue Selby. The jury found that Selby had warranted the mare to be pregnant and returned a verdict for the plaintiff, whereupon the court ordered Selby to "forthwith make Satisfaction to the Said Samuel Jones for a foale." The "Satisfaction" took the form of 1,000 pounds of tobacco in damages rather than rescission of the transaction and restitution of any money that had changed hands.[46] The buyer kept the mare, and the seller retained the full purchase price. The outcome was consistent with the English rule that an executed sale transferred property in spite of a breach of warranty, leaving the disappointed buyer with a damages award as his sole remedy.

Stringer v. Selby (1662),[47] the second important pre-*Waters* contract case, also involved the delivery of goods that did not conform to the seller's description, but this time the seller (again the exaggerator Selby) affirmed rather than warranted the quality of the items sold. The litigation arose from an exchange of livestock between Selby and the wife of Justice John Stringer.[48] Selby offered to take Mrs. Stringer's milk cow and calf in exchange for "A very gentle heifer . . . of the Dutch breed and a Lusty Calfe of six weekes old." Mrs. Stringer was reluctant to make the swap, but Selby assured her that the heifer was so gentle anyone could handle her. Finally Mrs. Stringer agreed to the exchange, "provided the heifer and Calfe are so good as he [Selby] declared them to be." When Selby delivered them three or four days later, however, the supposedly "Lusty" calf was "almost dead with poverty." The poor animal moaned so pitifully that Mrs. Stringer ordered its throat cut to end its misery. As for the "gentle" heifer, she was "so wilde that their was noe dealing with her, neither by faire means, nor beating, neither would she suffer any one to come neare her." That night the heifer ran off, headed for Selby's field. Mrs. Stringer realized she had made a bad bargain and asked Selby to undo the sale. He refused, so she brought suit through her husband to cancel the contract and recover her former property. Ignoring the *Chandelor* rule and *caveat emptor,* the justices concluded that the sale had been subject to an unfulfilled condition of quality and was therefore void. They ordered Selby to return Mrs. Stringer's cow and calf and required her to pay for his butchered calf,[49] putting the parties back into the position they occupied prior to the transaction, precisely the same relief that Waters sought. *Stringer v. Selby* provided an important precedent for Waters's lawsuit, and since he was one of the justices who decided the case, Waters was fully aware of its significance. So too, of course, was the victorious plaintiff's husband, Justice Stringer, and that gave Waters a major advantage in his litigation against Bishopp.

The third pre-*Waters* case meriting discussion, *Waggaman v. Wingfield* (1662),[50] holds particular interest for us because it involved the sale of a pregnant servant. James Wingfield, the defendant, sold Henrik Waggaman, the plaintiff, a woman servant for around 2,800 pounds of tobacco. Unfortunately, Hutchinson's brief account of the case does not say whether the seller made any warranties or affirmations of quality at the time of the sale. The clerk merely noted that the servant proved to be with child. Waggaman did not react to the pregnancy in the same fashion as Waters. Instead of canceling the transaction, Waggaman explicitly affirmed the sale and formally acknowledged his indebtedness for the purchase price. Then he successfully sought a court order requiring Wingfield to compensate him for any damages he might sustain as a result of the servant's medical condition.[51] The decision is important doctrinally because it indicates that Eastern Shore judges regarded rescission and restitution as an optional rather than mandatory remedy. A disappointed buyer was not obliged to seek restoration of the status quo ante, as Mrs. Stringer did. If the buyer wished, he or she could affirm the sale, keep the defective property or servant, and sue for damages.

These three cases suggest that Waters's contract claim had a solid basis in prior Virginia law. Eastern Shore precedents were more protective of buyers' interests than were *Chandelor* and other English decisions, while also affording plaintiffs a wider range of remedial choices. The magistrates of the Eastern Shore rejected *caveat emptor* for the same reasons that some antebellum Southern courts declined to apply the doctrine to slave sales.[52] They recognized that sellers usually have an informational advantage over buyers, especially in transactions involving people and livestock. Latent defects, such as diseases or pregnancy, may be known to the seller but be difficult for the buyer to detect in the brief time allowed for inspection before the sale. Magistrates identified closely with the interests of buyers because, as major plantation owners, they viewed themselves primarily as consumers of labor. They acquired servants as fast as visiting ships could unload them and, like other planters, found *caveat venditor* appealing because it gave them a measure of protection from the sometimes unscrupulous merchants and mariners who sold workers at dockside. The doctrine's attractiveness increased as JPs sank more and more capital into slaves, who cost two to three times as much as white servants with long terms.[53] By 1664, slaves constituted over a third of the work force belonging to Justices John Custis, John Michael, and William Spencer, Northampton County's three biggest employers. The percentage in Michael's household approached two-thirds.[54] The enslaved portion of Northampton's dependent work force grew from roughly 16 percent in the 1660s to over 50 percent by the 1720s. For slaveowners — around 12 percent of households in the 1660s and 1670s and twice that in the 1720s[55] — the demise of *caveat emptor* was one of the most important developments in early American law.

Caveat venditor did not spring entirely from judicial self-interest.

The notion that fairness required sellers to tell the truth had religious origins as well. In *The Whole Duty of Man,* theologian Richard Allestree excoriated sellers who misrepresented the quality of their wares, either by denying or concealing faults, or by taking advantage of the buyer's ignorance. "[H]e that will do justly," Allestree wrote,

> must let [the buyer] know what he buyes; and if [the buyer's] own skill enable him not to judge, (nay, if he do not actually find out the fault) thou art bound to tell it him, otherwise thou makest him pay for somewhat, which is not there, he presuming there is that good qualitie in it, which thou knowest is not, and therefore thou mayest as honestly take his money for some goods of another mans, which thou knowest thou canst never put into his possession, which I suppose no man will deny to be an arrant cheat.[56]

Making a buyer "pay for what he hath not" is "an abomination to the Lord," Allestree warned, and those who practiced overreaching could expect to burn in Hell.[57] He also condemned buyers who took unfair advantage of a seller who was ignorant of an item's worth. He observed, however, that "On the Buyers part there are not ordinarily so many opportunities of fraud" as sellers have,[58] which is why *caveat venditor* promotes fair dealing more effectively than does *caveat emptor.* Eastern Shore magistrates were not naive enough to think they could mandate perfect equality in bargaining. Nevertheless, their decisions endorsed behavioral norms closer to Allestree's biblically based ideal than to the amoral marketplace envisioned in *Chandelor.* Tough and acquisitive though they were, Virginia JPs believed people should be able to rely on each other's word even as they pursued their fortunes.

Waters, then, had religious as well as legal precedent on his side. He also enjoyed overwhelming political advantages. He was rich, powerful, well-connected, and highly experienced in legal matters. His adversary, Bishopp, knew the odds were against him, yet he could not bring himself to concede victory to Waters, for that might be taken as a confession that he had perpetrated a fraud. Small planters valued their reputations no less than magistrates did, and Bishopp was determined to defend his if he could. For the moment, the best strategy appeared to be delay, for the longer Anne's pregnancy lasted, the greater the likelihood that the court would eventually conclude that conception probably occurred after the sale of her indenture, in which case Bishopp could not be held liable. When *Waters v. Bishopp* came before the county court on June 28, 1664, Bishopp played for time and asked for a postponement until the following month. The justices, conscious of the need to look evenhanded, granted his request.

There remained the question of what to do about Anne Orthwood. Waters's lawsuit had alerted the court and community to her pregnancy, and the justices were eager to learn her lover's identity so they could hold him responsible for paying all the ensuing costs. Anne resolutely refused to cooperate, however. JPs usually determined paternity by interrogating the mother under oath,[59] but if that did not work, they resorted to coercion. In 1663, for example, the Accomack JPs questioned a pregnant servant, Ruth Colledge, who "being examined would not confess the father of the said Child, but obstinately and audaciously behaved herselfe towards the Court." The justices responded by sending her to the house of correction for a month.[60] They took even stronger action against Jaccominta Bottella in 1667, ordering her whipped when she refused to name her bastard's father. She escaped corporal punishment when Nicholas Laylor (possibly the child's father) stepped forward and agreed to pay her fine and support the child.[61] In 1703, Mary Case, who bore several bastards, was brought before the Accomack court by her mistress, and when asked to identify the children's father, "most audaciously and impudently said . . . that She did not Know who was the father." For her "great contempt," the court sentenced her to receive 25 lashes forthwith and another 25 at the next court session.[62] Anne probably would have suffered a similar fate had she behaved insolently, but she managed to hold her tongue. Instead of ordering her incarcerated or whipped, the Northampton justices decided to subject her to a form of psychological abuse. They remanded her to the custody of a midwife, Eleanor Gething, with instructions to extract the father's name by interrogating her during labor.[63]

SIX

ELEANOR GETHING,
MIDWIFE

Eleanor Gething, the matron assigned to "performe the office of a Midwife"[1] at Anne Orthwood's delivery, was 50 years old in 1664, and a longtime resident of the Eastern Shore. Her husband, Matthew, was an illiterate small planter and the neighborhood constable.[2] Like most midwives of the period, Gething was a respected figure in the local community, admired for her technical skills and knowledge of the mysteries of childbirth. She advised on the management of pregnancy, supervised preparations for delivery, took charge of labor, and ensured that mother and child received proper care. A woman of exceptional authority, she crossed social boundaries and received deference wherever she went.[3] The Northampton magistrates signaled their confidence in Gething by, in effect, deputizing her as a law enforcement officer. They entered an order on June 28, 1664, directing her to "forthwith Repaire to the next Magistrate and their take her Oath" to question Anne during delivery as to "who is the true Father of the Child."[4]

Gething's appointment as an official inquisitor followed a longstanding English practice of enlisting midwives' help in policing sexuality. The Church of England licensed midwives and required them to take an oath promising to "straightly charge" every unwed mother to declare the name of the father and the circumstances of conception. Midwives had a duty to report the information to the ecclesiastical authorities, who used it to determine paternity and to discipline the parents for their sinful behavior.[5] Secular judges relied on midwives as well, although they generally preferred to question pregnant women directly.[6] The most effective way for a midwife to obtain information was to threaten that she would withhold assistance unless the mother revealed her secrets. Fearing death from an unaided delivery if she said nothing and God's wrath if she lied, the woman usually spoke truthfully, or so people claimed.[7] A woman's statement to a midwife was not considered as reliable as her testimony in court, however. If she identified one man as the father while in labor and a different man when questioned under oath by the justices, the latter version prevailed, for the law deemed sworn testimony in court "the most strong assurance of the truth."[8]

Midwives' interrogations were as common in Virginia as in England. Since Virginia did not have a separate system of church courts, colonial midwives took their oaths of office from JPs, but in all other respects they followed the English pattern, demanding fathers' names and dates of conception from women in the throes of labor and reporting their findings to the justices. Alice Wilson, an Eastern Shore widow, testified, for instance, that "she urginge Ollive Eaton in the instant tyme of her payne in travell, to declare who was the true father of the child she was then to be delivered of, she answered William Fisher."[9] Merle Hewett and Katherine Gray told the Accomack County Court that, at the request of a JP, they had examined the justice's servant, Eleanor Tanner, and "the said Eleanor did declare in the extremity of her Labour and about the tyme of her delivery that the Childe she went with and was then to be delivered of was begoten by James Davis late servant to Mrs Tabitha Browne."[10] Socially prominent women such as Mrs. Grace Robins, William Waters's mother, sometimes attended births and helped midwives with their inquiries. Mrs. Robins was present during the delivery of Frances Smyth, a servant, and demanded to know the father's identity and "what tyme it was that she had done such an Accon."[11] Interrogations almost always yielded the name of a man whom the authorities could pursue for child support, but for mothers the process added to the trauma of an experience that was already terrifying enough.

For centuries, the church had tried to compel parents to maintain their illicit offspring, and if they failed to perform their duty, the child's parish had to step in and supply food, clothing, and shelter. Parish taxpayers were understandably reluctant to assume parents' financial obligations and sometimes went to extreme lengths to protect themselves.[12] Parliament shared taxpayers' concern over the rising cost of supporting illegitimate children, a responsibility that burdened respectable folk, consumed charitable resources that should have gone to "the Releife of the impotente and aged true Poore," and furnished an "evell Example and Encouradgement of lewde Lyef." To deter out-of-wedlock births and relieve the pressure on parish treasuries, Parliament included a tough antibastardy provision in the Poor Law of 1576. The act provided an effective secular means of enforcing the child-support obligation long mandated by the church. The statute allowed any two justices of the peace who lived in or next to the parish in which an illegitimate child was born to punish the parents, require them to reimburse the parish for any costs it had incurred, and order them to make payments to maintain the child. If the mother or father disobeyed any of the JPs' commands, the magistrates could send the recalcitrant parent to jail until he or she posted bond to guarantee performance.[13]

The 1576 statute and subsequent parliamentary legislation regulating the poor laid the foundation for Virginia's bastardy laws. In the colony, as in England, parishes had to support bastards whose parents could not or would not fulfill their responsibility.[14] Parishes obtained their funds through the collection of compulsory tithes, a form of taxation based on the number of workers a head of household employed. During the latter part of the seventeenth century, the overall annual tax rate in most counties was about 100 pounds of tobacco for every taxable servant and male family member over 16. Half went to the parish to finance poor relief and church operations and the other half to the provincial and county governments.[15] To put parish taxation in perspective, a Chesapeake field hand could produce about 1,500 pounds per year in the 1660s;[16] at 50 pounds per person, parish taxes consumed 3.3 percent of a worker's productive capacity. Magistrates felt the impact of parish taxation more than most planters because of their relatively large work forces. In the 1660's, the average Eastern Shore JP had roughly three times as many taxable household members as the typical planter and therefore paid triple the taxes. Collectively, the justices accounted for between a sixth and a tenth of total parish levies,[17] a tax burden that gave them a significant stake in efforts to contain parish costs. We do not know the exact amount spent by the three Eastern Shore parishes[18] on poor relief, but data from other parts of Virginia suggest that the figure probably approached 40 percent of parish budgets.[19] Much of that was devoted to bastards, who were expensive to maintain. The standard fee for nursing or caring for an illegitimate child was 1,000 to 1,200 pounds of tobacco per year,[20] an expenditure that all taxpayers, especially JPs, bitterly resented.

The members of the Assembly attempted to mollify taxpayers — and protect their own pocketbooks — by targeting bastard-producing servants for special punishment. Ever sensitive to the financial interests of masters, lawmakers increased the compensation that employers could claim when a servant gave birth outside of marriage. Until the late 1650s, the burden of compensating masters had fallen only on males. A man who impregnated a servant not only had to pay a fine for fornication and support the child but also had to pay the woman's employer for the loss of her labor, either by serving him for a year or by giving him 1,500 pounds of tobacco.[21] In 1660, the Assembly made female servants "lible to equall punishment" with males[22] and then went to the other extreme two years later by making females solely responsible for compensating their masters, raising the amount to 2,000 pounds of tobacco or two years of labor.[23] As further punishment, a servant who bore an illegitimate child had to pay her parish a fornication fine of 500 pounds of tobacco. If her master paid the fine, he was entitled to another half year of service; if he refused to pay, the servant would be whipped.[24]

Some "dissolute masters" took unfair advantage of this legislation by deliberately impregnating their servants so they could demand extra work. Decency demanded that the legislators stamp out this outrageous practice, yet they also realized that if they adopted a rule whereby "a woman gott with child by her master should be freed from that service it might probably induce such loose persons to lay all their bastards to their masters," a prospect the Assembly, composed entirely of masters, found unappealing. So the legislators crafted a compromise. If a master impregnated his servant, she had to serve two extra years, but not for him; the churchwardens were to sell her services to a third party and put the proceeds in the parish treasury.[25] The statute had an important loophole, however. If the master's son, rather than the master himself, got the servant pregnant, the master still was entitled to two more years of labor.[26]

By imposing a disproportionate financial burden on females, Virginia law left pregnant women heavily dependent on the protective mercy of men. A woman risked the magistrates' displeasure if she remained silent in the face of their questioning, but she hazarded a far worse fate if she alienated her lover. Since it was practically impossible for a serving woman to accumulate 2,500 pounds of tobacco on her own, the only way she could avoid extra service and corporal punishment was to persuade her lover or some other person to make the payment on her behalf. That probably explains why Anne concealed John's identity as long as she did. She could have spared herself the rigors of interrogation during labor by simply divulging his name in a private conversation with the midwife. She had plenty of opportunities to do so during the month she spent as a lodger in the Gethings' home, waiting to give birth. Nevertheless, she remained stoically silent, hoping John's conscience would compel him to step forward and marry her or at least satisfy her financial obligations so she would not have to serve longer. Anne found herself in a position similar to that of another pregnant Northampton servant, Jane Clark, who was ordered to remain with her master unless her lover chose to "Redeeme the said Jane Clark from servitude, by gieving good satisfaccon."[27] John was Anne's only realistic prospect for redemption, and the desire to stay in his good graces led her to keep her vow of silence right to the bitter end.

While Anne waited anxiously for John to come to her rescue, he pondered his options. Should he admit responsibility, pay Anne's fine, and compensate her master (Waters or Bishopp, depending on the outcome of their lawsuit) or deny paternity and hope to get away with it? An admission would have shamed both him and his uncle, and to compound his embarrassment, he probably would have needed to borrow money from Colonel Kendall to pay the 2,500 pounds that Anne owed. A denial, on the other hand, would have required him to deceive his neighbors and probably would not have worked anyhow. If Anne broke down during interrogation and named John as the father, as she was almost certain to do, John would face moral opprobrium and legal liability. Unable to see a way out of his dilemma, he turned to his uncle, William Kendall, for help. John evidently made a full confession, and one can imagine Colonel Kendall's reaction when he learned of the mess his young kinsman had created, both for himself and for his extended family. Besides breaching the community's moral code, John's behavior reflected poorly on Kendall's performance of his patriarchal duties, and therefore the problem of Anne Orthwood's bastard was now his problem too.

Hoping to save his family's honor, Colonel Kendall took charge and began developing a strategy of damage control. He also moved to disqualify himself from further participation in all litigation involving Anne's pregnancy.[28] Disqualification, or "recusal," was the standard practice in seventeenth-century Northampton County whenever judicial business affected a magistrate or close family member. Justices considered themselves legally bound to refrain from participating in such cases because of the common-law rule that a man cannot be a judge in his own cause.[29] Kendall's recusal extended to *Waters v. Bishopp,* as well, so when the county court took up the breach-of-contract suit at its next meeting, on July 28, Colonel Kendall exited the courtroom along with Waters. While they were outside, the other justices decided to suspend the litigation "untill the production of the Child or Miscarriage of the same." Then a "Jury of able women" would determine the duration of Anne's pregnancy, information that would help the justices figure out whether her condition arose before or after the sale of her indenture.[30]

The next day, July 29, Anne went into labor at the midwife's house. Gething handled the delivery, assisted by Hannah Harmer, age 37, and Elizabeth Harper, age 26. All three later testified that while Anne was giving birth, Gething "desired her as she should answer at that dreadfull Day of Judgment where all harts shall be opened and all secretts made knowne, To Speake who was the father of the Child she went with." Frightened and exhausted, Anne yielded at last, naming John as the father and identifying John Webb's inn as the place where the conception occurred "the Court before Christmas one Satterday neight, the Monday following being the Court." That night — November 28, 1663 — was "the first tyme John Kendall ever knew her." When Gething asked Anne "if John Kendall had any thing to doe with her any where but at John Webbs," she answered that he had not. The two or three encounters they had at the inn that late November weekend were the only times they had ever engaged in intercourse, she insisted.[31]

Gething thought Anne's story sounded implausible because it conflicted with the midwife's understanding of reproductive timing. By Anne's account, conception occurred eight months before delivery, yet Gething had witnessed enough pregnancies to know that nine months was the normal gestation period. Like many early modern people, she probably believed an eight-month child could not survive.[32] If Anne gave birth to a live, full-term child, Gething reasoned, she must be lying and someone other than John Kendall had to be the real father. The skeptical midwife pressed on with her interrogation. "[A]ccording to Computation of the tyme of your Reckninge,"[33] Gething told Anne, "if you goe your full tyme you wronge the young Man." When Anne protested "That God did know she did not wronge him," Gething answered, "certainly you wronge the young Man, but I cannot certainly tell untill I see you delivered."[34]

The midwife finally saw Anne delivered after a long and difficult labor. She screamed John's name as she struggled to give birth, denouncing with "bitter Execrations" the man who had gotten her pregnant. She had twins, one of whom was stillborn or died soon after birth, and the other of whom survived. After seeing the babies, Gething declared that they had "come their full tyme"; in other words, they looked fully developed and their gestation seemed to have taken the usual period of nine months.[35] Appearances were deceiving, however. The newborns may have been as big as some full-term babies, but since one-quarter to one-half of twins are born early, there is a good chance they were premature.[36] Gething was unaware of that possibility because multiple births are exceedingly rare, only 1 percent of all pregnancies,[37] and this may have been the first twin birth the midwife had ever seen.

For Anne herself, childbirth was an unmitigated catastrophe. She had come to America full of hope but had not been able to realize any of her ambitions. Husband, freedom, economic security, a stable family — all eluded her. Even the joy of motherhood, her sole consolation for all the shame and suffering she endured, proved fleeting. Her brief, sad life ended shortly after she gave birth. The records do not say whether she perished during or following delivery, only that she "died in Child bed of two Children."[38] The odds are that she did not die during delivery. Most women who died in childbed in the early modern period did so not as a result of complicated births but because of puerperal fever, a postpartum infection caused by bacterial invasion of the uterine cavity.[39] Anne probably succumbed a few days after delivery, living long enough to name her surviving child Jasper. If she selected that unusual name in memory of her original master, Jasper Cross, the man who brought her to America, the choice seems ironic indeed.

Whatever the actual cause of Anne's death, rumors circulated that the midwife was to blame. The court observed that "Sum Reports hath past that Ellinor Gething appointed Midwife at the Labour of Ann Orthwood late Servant to Lieutenant Colonel William Waters used harsh Useage to her the said Ann by neglecting her in the tyme of her Labour." The implication of the charge was that Gething treated Anne badly to punish her for immoral behavior, a practice not unknown among midwives.[40] If the accusation had been true, Gething's conduct would have violated the community's ethical norms. Shoremen sometimes subjected bastard-bearers to corporal punishment, to be sure, but they did not condone deliberate medical malpractice. The justices recognized the seriousness of the slur on Gething's reputation and felt obliged to come to her defense. For the sake of her "future Vindication from the said Aspertion," they placed a statement in the record noting that the two assistant midwives, Harmer and Harper, had exonerated her of abusing her office.[41]

Anne's death mooted her master's claim for extra service, but the contract and child-support issues arising from her pregnancy remained very much alive. *Waters v. Bishopp* was still on the county court docket, set for trial on August 29. The justices also had to decide who bore responsibility for feeding, clothing, and housing Jasper and for finding him a master to teach him some vocational skills. Since parishes had a major stake in child-support enforcement, suits against putative fathers typically were initiated by churchwardens,[42] many of whom were also JPs, providing a strong link between the governing structures of church and state.[43] In 1664, the churchwardens for the lower parish of Northampton County, where Jasper was born, were William Kendall and John Custis.[44] Colonel Kendall had disqualified himself, so the burden of suing John Kendall to force him to support Jasper rested entirely on Custis. This put Custis in an embarrassing position, for it required him to impugn both John's morality and Colonel Kendall's competence to supervise his own household. Custis was quickly extricated, however, when John took the unusual step of initiating the litigation himself. He launched what amounted to a preemptive strike, filing a petition asking the court to declare his innocence. This clever move not only spared Custis's feelings but also allowed him to sit in judgment of John's case. Since Custis would not have to litigate before the court in his capacity as a churchwarden, he did not have to disqualify himself from considering the petition in his capacity as a magistrate.[45] As Colonel Kendall's friend and colleague, Custis could be counted on to lend a sympathetic ear to John's side of the story.

One senses the colonel's guiding hand behind John's petition, along with a hint of the strategy that Kendall had devised to clear his nephew's name. He would try to dispel the notion that John was a sexual predator and depict him, instead, as the innocent victim of a woman's lie, the kind of man who was confident enough of his rectitude to invite — no, demand — judicial scrutiny of his most intimate behavior. It was a gamble, but John had an important factor in his favor: the principal witness against him was dead.

SEVEN

JOHN WATERSON,
TRIAL JURY FOREMAN

The litigation over the legal consequences of Anne Orthwood's pregnancy came to a head on the morning of August 29, 1664, when the magistrates of the Northampton County Court convened at John Webb's inn to adjudicate Waters's lawsuit, John Kendall's petition, and a half-dozen other matters. Justices John Custis II, William Andrews II, and John Michael sat behind the court table, along with Waters and William Kendall. The crier (bailiff), Charles Holden, called the proceedings to order, proclaiming:

> O Yes O Yes O Yes silence is comanded in the court while his Majesties Justices are sitting, upon paine of imprisonment. All manner of persons that have any thing to doe at this court draw neer and give your attendance and if any one have any plaint to enter or suite to prosecute lett them come forth and they shall be heard.[1]

The first item of business was the punishment of a man who had defamed Justice John Stringer at the previous court session.[2] Waters temporarily took the chair while the court exacted an appropriately groveling apology from the miscreant. Then Stringer, who had absented himself from the courtroom while his colleagues vindicated his reputation, entered and assumed his customary place as presiding magistrate. The second case on the docket was *Waters v. Bishopp,* and now it was Waters's turn to recuse. He rose from his place at the court table and stepped outside, signaling that he was temporarily abandoning his judicial post and assuming the role of a litigant. Kendall also disqualified himself because he knew that some of the testimony would implicate his nephew John. That left Stringer, Custis, Andrews, and Michael to hear the case. At some point during the trial, William Spencer joined them on the bench, and all five participated in the judgment.

The trial began when Waters returned to the courtroom and Holden called on him to "come forth, and prosecute thy Action against Jacob Bishopp or else thou wilt be nonsuite[d]."[3] Waters already had filed his petition accusing Bishopp of failing to perform his bargain, and now he formally asked the court to consider his claim. Having verified that the plaintiff was present and ready for trial, Holden called on Bishopp "to come forth and save thee and thy Bail, or else thou wilt forfeit thy Recognizance."[4] Bishopp responded that he was ready to answer Waters's complaint and wished to try the case before a jury. His reason for demanding a jury was largely tactical. Even though his adversary had relinquished his judicial role, Bishopp still worried about possible bias because of Waters's various family, business, and political ties to the other justices. Bishopp believed he might fare better if the facts were determined by jurors drawn from the community at large rather than by Waters's colleagues. Consequently, he requested "that a Jury bee impannelled to examine the ... Difference" between him and Waters "and give Report thereof to the Court."[5]

Although civil jury trials were readily available in theory, they were rarely utilized in the 1660s. Magistrates usually ascertained the facts themselves and applied the relevant legal standard to their findings. Trial by jury remained every Englishman's birthright, however, and colonists occasionally availed themselves of the privilege. Civil juries were employed by the General Court in the 1630s and on the Eastern Shore by the early 1640s.[6] Under legislation enacted in the early 1640s, either party had the right to request a jury provided he or she filed a written motion in advance of trial and the justices concluded that the lawsuit was proper for jury consideration.[7] The jurors were to be "chosen of the most able men of the county" and impaneled by the sheriff. During their deliberations, the jurors were "to be kept from food and releife till they have agreed upon their verdict according to the custome practised in England."[8] Jury trials proved too costly to furnish as a public service, so the legislature passed a statute in 1646 requiring the party who requested the jury to pay a fee of 72 pounds of tobacco per cause, regardless of the outcome of the litigation. This requirement marked a departure from the usual English rule that the loser paid all the costs and discouraged suitors from opting for juries over magistrates. At the same time, though, the Assembly took steps to safeguard the integrity of jury trials by prohibiting litigants from discussing the case with jurors after they received their instructions from the court.[9]

In 1662, the Assembly reviewed the legislation on jury trials as part of its comprehensive overhaul of Virginia statutes and found some of the restrictions to be "quite contrary to the law of England." The legislature rewrote the colonial provision as part of its Anglicization effort and made jury trials more accessible to people of modest means. Litigants no longer had to give advance notice of their desire for a jury trial and did not have to pay a fee merely for requesting one. Sheriffs impaneled juries as a matter of course, and the jurors had to wait in or near the courtroom, ready to serve if called on. The sheriff's fee for summoning and impaneling the jury was paid by the loser as part of the costs.[10] If neither party asked for a jury, as happened most of the time, the taxpayers had to bear the expense of the unnecessary impanelment. This became a major source of annoyance. When Northampton County submitted its grievances to the royal commissioners dispatched to Virginia in 1676, following Bacon's Rebellion, county residents complained about the "summonsing of Juries before need, when often times in 3 or 4 courts not one cause is put to a Jury."[11] Although impanelment of juries was automatic, the county court still had the power to decide whether a particular cause was suitable for them. For those cases where jury trials were appropriate, the 1662 act codified the traditional division of responsibility between the bench and the jury. Jurors resolved factual disputes and reported their findings to the court. Magistrates decided questions of law and determined the appropriate judgment.

Given the 1662 act's liberal approach to the availability of jury trials, the outcome of Bishopp's request was never in doubt. Waters's breach-of-contract claim clearly fit within the category of matters that Virginians considered jurors competent to decide. The claim more or less resembled indebitatus assumpsit for money had and received, a common-law action traditionally regarded as suitable for fact-finding by a jury. Moreover, the politics of the situation favored granting Bishopp's motion. The Northampton magistrates wanted the community to see them as disinterested patriarchs rather than as self-serving parvenus. If they had denied Bishopp's request and then ruled for Waters on the merits, critics might have accused them of unfair favoritism toward one of their own. By submitting the case to a jury, the magistrates shifted the community's gaze away from themselves, thus giving their own eventual decision an aura of objectivity.

Sheriff William Jones had assembled a jury panel earlier in the day, and it took only a few moments to gather them in the courtroom for the purpose of hearing evidence. The jury had a dozen members, but the order book names only the foreman, John Waterson, a 35-year-old tailor.[12] His pre-*Waters* experience as a juror consisted of three cases, only one of which involved a civil action. In February 1662, he sat on a grand jury that charged several people with selling liquor illegally; in June 1663, he served on a coroner's jury that investigated the death of a female servant who hanged herself; and in December 1663, he was a trial (*nisi prius*) juror in *Scott v. Cowdery*, a damages action arising from the destruction of a cornfield by trespassing cattle.[13] Following his service in *Waters v. Bishopp,* however, Waterson became virtually a professional juror. He served on at least 72 civil jury panels between 1663 and 1678 and was the foreman of 13 of them.[14] He also sat on the grand jury, a coroner's jury, and the petit jury in a larceny case.[15] The fact that sheriffs kept selecting Waterson for jury service in case after case, year after year, implies a high level of confidence in his reliability. Since the office of sheriff rotated among the magistrates on an annual basis, we may assume that the court as a whole held Waterson in high regard. To some extent, this probably stemmed from his personal qualities, including perhaps intelligence and integrity, but ideological compatibility certainly played a role as well. Waterson's votes as a juror must have coincided with the magistrates' views, in the main, or sheriffs would have stopped choosing him. Jurors and JPs may have performed distinct functions, but to consider them independent actors would be naive. The 15-year collaboration between Waterson and the Northampton magistrates suggests that they were partners who complemented each other in pursuit of common goals.

Waterson occupied a middle rung in Northampton society. He held minor offices, such as highway surveyor and churchwarden, and often served as an appraiser of decedents' estates.[16] Like the magistrates, Waterson was a landowner and an employer. He owned 355 acres, which he had purchased from Waters's stepfather, Obedience Robins, in 1660.[17] He had more servants than the average head of household but fewer than most magistrates. In 1664, for example, Waterson employed three servants compared to an average of two for all heads of household and eight for JPs.[18] Though of lower economic status than the magistrates, Waterson could identify with their interests. He was a farmer as well as a tailor, and he too had invested much of his resources in his work force. He shared the justices' distrust of the men who purveyed servants and slaves and felt no less vulnerable to the pressures imposed by Virginia's tight labor market. To Waterson, the case for jettisoning *caveat emptor* in favor of a rule requiring greater candor from sellers would have seemed self-evident. We do not know the identities of his 11 fellow jurors, but judging from the composition of other jury panels, Waterson's middling background was typical. The jury as a whole therefore provided a receptive audience for an argument in support of *caveat venditor.*

Besides the intrinsic appeal of Waters's legal theory, personal ties may also have predisposed Waterson to take his side. When William Mellinge, with whom Waterson had a longstanding relationship, died in 1671, he named his "Deare and lovinge freinds" Waterson and Waters as overseers of his estate.[19] If a friendship existed between Waterson and Waters seven years earlier, when the lawsuit was tried, Waters may have enjoyed yet another advantage in his quest to undo his bad bargain.

The court gave Waterson and his fellow jurors little in the way of instructions. Stringer simply directed them "to inquire whether the plaintiff hath cause of action" against the defendant and to report their findings.[20] Since neither side was represented by counsel, Waters and Bishopp handled the presentation of evidence themselves. They did not get a chance to tell their stories directly to the jurors because as litigants they were incompetent to testify. English law forbade the parties from serving as witnesses because their inherent bias was thought to render them incapable of providing reliable information.[21] Waters and Bishopp had to make their respective points through the testimony of bystanders and others with no obvious axe to grind.

The first witness was James Bonwell, who was present at the sale of Anne's indenture and heard what Bishopp and Waters said to each other. Bonwell did not testify in person at the August 29 trial because he had already given his testimony, under oath, in a deposition taken in court on June 28. Waters introduced Bonwell's deposition to prove that Bishopp's description of Anne's condition formed part of the basis of the bargain. If the description was inaccurate, Waters argued, the transaction rested on a false premise and ought to be set aside. Waters's theory was complicated by the ambiguity of Bishopp's statement, however. Bishopp did not state unequivocally that Anne was a healthy virgin, much less warrant her to be one. He merely affirmed that she had nothing wrong with her *so far as he knew*. The qualifying phrase "to the best of my knowledge" should have warned Waters not to give much weight to Bishopp's speculative assurance that Anne was "a Maid" who "aileth nothing." Therefore, Bishopp maintained, Waters had only himself to blame if he felt misled.

Next the jury heard live testimony from the midwife Eleanor Gething and her two assistants, Hannah Harmer and Elizabeth Harper, concerning the circumstances of Anne's delivery and death. They recounted Anne's claim that conception occurred in late November 1663 and characterized the newborns as fully developed.[22] The purpose of this evidence was to establish that Anne was pregnant when sold and thus not in the chaste and healthy condition that Bishopp described. Waters did not try to prove that Bishopp was aware of Anne's true condition when they made their contract because scienter (guilty knowledge) was not essential to his claim. Waters based his lawsuit on the principle of *caveat venditor*, under which a seller bore responsibility for all misrepresentations of quality regardless of whether he actually knew the truth at the time of sale. Bishopp, on the other hand, grounded his defense on the traditional English rule that a buyer had a duty to look out for himself. Since Waters did not impugn Bishopp's integrity by suggesting that he had committed fraud, Bishopp did not feel obligated to introduce any evidence justifying his conduct. He simply relied on *caveat emptor* and hoped the jury would conclude that Waters was foolish to put so much faith in sales talk.

After the reading of Bonwell's deposition and the testimony by the three midwives, the jury went out and deliberated. Upon their return, their names were called and answered to, and Stringer asked whether they all had agreed on a verdict. They responded affirmatively, and then Stringer inquired, "Whoe shall speake for you?" "Oure foreman," they replied.[23] The verdict was a complete triumph for Waters:

> The Jury finde that Jacob Bishopp sold the said Lieutenant Colonel William Waters A Maid that ayled nothing, but she proved to bee with Child, Therefore they finde Jacob Bishopp hath not performed his Bargaine therefore hee ought to Repay the said Lieutenant Colonel the Tobacco back hee hath received and discharge him of the Residue behinde, and pay costs of suit.
>
> [signed] John Waterson[24]

The verdict contained five elements: two explicit findings of fact, one implicit finding, a conclusion, and a suggested remedy. The express findings were, first, that Bishopp described Anne as a healthy virgin; and second, that she was pregnant when sold and thus did not correspond to the description. The implied finding was that the parties intended the sale to be conditional rather than absolute, the condition being Anne's conformity to Bishopp's description. Based on the three findings, the jurors concluded that "Bishopp hath not performed his Bargaine." They recommended restitution of Waters's down payment and cancellation of his debt as the appropriate means of redress.

The linchpin of the verdict was the jurors' understanding that the parties meant their contractual obligations to be mutually dependent. If Anne's true condition matched Bishopp's description of her, Waters had to pay for her; if they did not match, he owed nothing. Waters had neglected to hedge his acceptance with overtly conditional language of the type used by the buyer in *Stringer v. Selby*, who said she was willing to purchase a heifer and calf "provided [they] are so good as [the seller] had declared them to be,"[25] but such provisos were not essential, in the jurors' view. By asking about Anne's health and virginity, Waters plainly signaled their importance to him, and the jury reasonably inferred that the sale hinged on the accuracy of Bishopp's answers. Bishopp was not found guilty of intentionally misrepresenting Anne's physical and moral characteristics or of breaching a warranty of quality. He forfeited his right to keep the purchase price not because he lied or gulled Waters with a false warranty but because one of the contract's preconditions was not satisfied, rendering Bishopp incapable of performing his side of the bargain.

The JPs probably were not surprised to receive a probuyer verdict, coming as it did from a panel whose foreman bought servants and thus had economic interests similar to the magistrates' own. The court accepted the jury's findings and entered judgment accordingly:

> The Difference depending between Lieutenant Colonel William Waters plaintiff and Jacob Bishopp defendant concerning a woman servant sould by the said Bishopp to the said Lieutenant Colonel Waters, being at the Request of the said Bishopp referred to a Jury, Whose Verdict is That they finde Jacob Bishopp hath not performed his Bargaine, therefore hee ought to Repay the said Lieutenant Colonel Waters the tobacco hee hath received, and discharge him of the Residue behinde and pay cost of suit, The Court therefore Order that the said Lieutenant Colonel William Waters according to the Verdict of the said Jury be discharged from the said servant and the said Bishopp to pay cost of suit Els Execution.[26]

Discharging Anne from Waters's service was a bit gratuitous. After all, she had been dead for almost a month. Nevertheless, the judgment got across the magistrates' two main points: jurors, rather than Waters's colleagues on the bench, were responsible for his victory in court; and sellers, particularly of servants, should beware of how they described their wares, lest inaccuracy invalidate their bargain.

The outcome of *Waters v. Bishopp* illustrated colonists' ability to use old devices to push the law in new directions. English juries long had been able to mitigate the harshness of *caveat emptor* by finding implied dependent conditions of sale, and in a narrow sense that is all Waterson and his fellow jurors did when they decided in Waters's favor. Viewed from a broader perspective, though, their verdict signified more than just an ad hoc decision to deviate from *caveat emptor. Waters v. Bishopp* formed part of a pattern of decisions in which Eastern Shoremen rejected the *Chandelor v. Lopus* legacy and embraced *caveat venditor* as a principle more in keeping with Virginia values and the realities of the colonial economy. If the nature of the transaction was such that the seller probably had better access to information than the buyer, the seller had to bear any loss caused by the buyer's justifiable reliance on a material misrepresentation of quality.[27] Liability attached even though the seller acted unwittingly and merely described, rather than expressly warranted, the object sold. Decades before English warranty law emerged from the formalism that retarded its expansion,[28] the jurors and magistrates of the Eastern Shore fashioned sales doctrines that placed greater emphasis on the parties' expectations than on the terms they used while bargaining.[29] Unencumbered by the technical knowledge possessed by English judges, they devised remedies to fit the circumstances and their own sense of fairness.

This protective attitude toward buyers had limits, however. *Caveat emptor* no longer held sway to the same extent as in England, yet Shoremen still expected buyers to look out for themselves to some degree. *Caveat venditor* prohibited sellers from misleading buyers through exaggeration or unfounded assurances of quality, but it did not permit buyers to plunge blindly into transactions and expect sellers to make them whole if things turned out badly. In cases where the buyer and seller had equal access to information, and the seller said nothing that deceived the buyer but merely took advantage of his negligently caused ignorance, judges and juries refused to redress the buyer's loss.[30]

Eastern Shore sales cases adjudicated before and after *Waters v. Bishopp* show that the decision was neither anomalous nor the cynical product of wealth and influence. Waters's power in the community greatly exceeded Bishopp's, to be sure, but that factor did not dictate the result. Waters prevailed primarily because his position coincided with the probuyer direction of Eastern Shore contract law, a development deeply rooted in the economic system of Virginia. This trend continued into the eighteenth century at the provincial as well as the local level. In a 1735 decision, *Waddill v. Chamberlayne,* for example, the General Court rejected *caveat emptor* and held the seller of a slave liable for failing to disclose a defect even though he did not expressly warrant the slave's soundness.[31] Colonial Virginians expected to get what they paid for, and if they were misled through no fault of their own, the judiciary stood ready to alleviate their disappointment. The judges' willingness to police the marketplace reduced the risk of investing in human capital, livestock, and other components of plantation agriculture, contributing significantly to the economic and demographic expansion that characterized the Chesapeake for much of the century between 1660 and 1760.[32]

EIGHT

JOHN KENDALL,
PUTATIVE FATHER

John Kendall's petition seeking exoneration from Anne Orthwood's paternity charge came before the Northampton County Court on August 29, 1664, right after the justices disposed of the contract claim in *Waters v. Bishopp.* The magistrates construed the petition as presenting two distinct issues. One was the legal question of whether Anne's accusation provided a sufficient basis for holding John liable for Jasper's support. The other was the moral question of whether John actually engaged in the sinful conduct attributed to him. The court's bifurcated approach was highly unusual. Eastern Shore magistrates did not ordinarily distinguish between legal and moral culpability even when dealing with subjects having strong religious overtones, such as illicit sexuality. Sometimes they ignored a law if they considered its application unjust, but they seldom spoke openly about the propriety of holding someone legally accountable for something he did not do. In this instance, though, the JPs perceived an irreconcilable clash between law and truth and took pains to note the conflict for the record.

The justices ruled against John on the legal question, holding that even though the timing of Anne's pregnancy indicated that he was not Jasper's biological father, the law still required him to provide for the child until he could be bound into servitude. The ruling presupposed that JPs had to take a woman's accusation of paternity at face value regardless of proof to the contrary. In legal terms, they accorded her words an "irrebuttable presumption" of truthfulness, conclusively assuming that if she made her allegations under oath or during labor, they must be worthy of belief. Instead of weighing competing evidence, as in other types of lawsuits, the magistrates felt constrained in bastardy cases to consider only the woman's side of the story. Liability followed automatically once a charge was made, no matter how innocent the man otherwise appeared to be. No exceptions were allowed, the JPs said, because "the Law peremptorily declareth that person, who shall at the delivery of such Child or Children be charged with gitting of the same, shall keepe the Child or Children unavoydably." Since Anne "did positively declare that she the said Anne was gotten with Child by John Kendall affirmatively declaring the tyme and tymes of his lying with her, and never before," they had no choice but to assign him responsibility for Jasper's maintenance.[1]

When the magistrates decided the moral question, on the other hand, they felt free to consider all of the relevant evidence, including proof pointing to John's innocence, and they found Anne's account "not to bee Just." According to Anne, John impregnated her on November 28 or 29, 1663, eight months before the birth of her twins on July 29, 1664. Her version of events was contradicted by Eleanor Gething, the midwife, who testified that the babies had "come their full tyme." The justices took this to mean that the babies were conceived around October 29, nine months before they were delivered. The medical basis of their premise was wrong, but the magistrates had no way of knowing that. They thought the discrepancy undermined Anne's credibility, the "Court finding by Just calculacon that the said Children, were not gott within that Computacon of tyme as she the said Anne so positively charged him, but wanted about a Month of the tyme of produccon according to the Rules of Phisick, It being not above eight Months tyme." If she misrepresented the time of conception, they reasoned, she probably lied about her lover's identity as well. The law required them to hold John legally responsible, but for the sake of his "future Reputacon,"[2] they recorded their finding that he did not, in fact, have extramarital sex with Anne and therefore was innocent of violating moral norms.

The judgment in *Ex Parte Kendall,* holding John morally innocent yet legally guilty, raises several interesting issues. Did English law require this seemingly bizarre result, or was it the product of colonial innovation? What social and economic factors underlay the irrebuttable presumption of paternity? Given the rule's obvious unfairness to men who were falsely accused, why did colonists accept it? Why did the Northampton justices depart from their usual practice of confining themselves to legal questions and attempt to clear John of the stigma associated with breaking the moral code?

The imposition of "unavoydable" liability based solely on a woman's allegation cannot be ascribed to traditional English legal doctrine. The rule in England was that a mother's accusation of paternity, made under oath or during labor, should be given great weight but not be regarded as conclusive.[3] Although legal scholars such as Michael Dalton emphasized that putative paternity "dependeth chiefly" on the mother's word,[4] metropolitan JPs remained open to persuasion that a particular charge was false. The English rebuttable presumption allowed men to avoid liability by producing clear and convincing evidence of their innocence, a standard few could actually meet. Even if the accused managed to cast doubt on a woman's veracity, he stood virtually no chance of escaping responsibility unless he proved another man's guilt.[5] If the defendant fell short of rebutting the presumption but still managed to impeach the woman's credibility, JPs sometimes compromised and entered judgment for a reduced amount.[6]

English justices permitted men to offer exculpatory evidence because they realized that the method they used to determine the size of child-support payments essentially created a bounty for perjury.[7] One of the primary factors JPs considered was the putative father's wealth. "[I]f he be of ability," Dalton wrote, magistrates should "charge him the more deeply," and if he refused to pay, they should jail him. "And if the reputed Father be of small ability, and shall not find friends to yield some reasonable allowance," he continued, the man should "undergo the more punishment."[8] An unscrupulous mother could increase her income substantially by blaming her illicit pregnancy on an affluent man instead of the real father. Many yielded to temptation, and the English quarter sessions records contain numerous cases in which women were caught lying about paternity.[9]

False testimony had the potential to inflict significant financial damage because English child-support obligations usually lasted a long time. A father typically had to make weekly payments to the churchwardens "towards the Relief of [the] Bastard Child"[10] until the child reached the age of seven and became eligible to be bound out as an apprentice or servant.[11] Males had to serve until 24 and females until 21 or the time of their marriage, whichever came first.[12] Masters often demanded a premium for taking on a servant, so bastardy orders generally included a provision requiring the father to make a lump-sum payment of around three to five pounds for this purpose.[13] George Meriton, the author of a 1669 handbook for parish officials, suggested that bastards and other poor children be indentured as soon as the law allowed, before they developed bad habits. "[P]ut them out timely, and while they are young and tractable," Meriton counseled, "otherwise by reason of their idle and base Educations they will hardly keep their Service, or imploy themselves to work."[14] This did not apply to "nurse children" (those under seven), however, and the expense of maintaining them at home with their mothers became part of the price men had to pay for extramarital procreation.[15] When one adds up the various costs an Englishman incurred if found guilty of fathering a bastard — including the midwife's fee, a minimum of seven years of child-support payments, and a hefty indenture premium — it is easy to see why English JPs afforded accused fathers at least a modicum of procedural protection.

The Northampton justices, by contrast, did not think such protection was necessary even though they knew that women sometimes lied about paternity. Masters made an especially inviting target for pregnant servants who wished to conceal the identity of the real father — often a fellow servant — and pin the blame on a man with deeper pockets.[16] Yet colonial magistrates still refused to give men a chance to rebut the charges against them. Instead of spending time delving into the facts of particular sexual encounters, they streamlined paternity adjudication by transforming it into what amounted to an ex parte proceeding. In place of the traditional English rule, which weighted the scales in favor of the woman but permitted rebuttal evidence on behalf of the man, Eastern Shore magistrates adopted a policy of nearly always taking a woman at her word. If the mother of a bastard identified the father during labor or while giving testimony under oath, the court simply assumed the charge was true, dispensed with a trial on the merits, and swiftly entered judgment against the accused. Proceeding in this summary fashion enabled magistrates to assign responsibility for child support with ruthless efficiency, though at considerable cost in terms of fairness. To understand why the Eastern Shore justices adopted this procedure, one must understand the similarities and differences between the colonial and metropolitan systems of bastard maintenance.

Fathers' basic support obligations were the same in Virginia as in England. Eastern Shore bastardy orders typically required men to provide for their illegitimate children and to post bonds guaranteeing that they would hold the county or parish harmless from the cost of rearing them.[17] Colonial magistrates also required fathers to pay women's lying-in expenses, maintain them while disabled by pregnancy, and compensate third parties who helped care for their children.[18] A variety of people faced secondary liability if a father failed to provide support. The guarantors of the father's bond could be required to assume his obligations, and so could people who helped him flee the county. If the sheriff neglected to take adequate security, or if the father escaped from the sheriff's custody before posting bond, the sheriff became liable for nursing fees and other child-care expenses.[19] Parishes functioned as custodians of last resort, taking care of bastards whose fathers died, disappeared, or lacked the means to maintain them. Whenever possible, churchwardens arranged for those children to be nursed by their mothers at parish expense.[20] Parishes also advanced the funds necessary to support illegitimate children fathered by servants and were entitled to recoupment after the fathers gained their freedom.[21]

In Virginia, as in England, the support obligation ceased when the child entered indentured servitude. Many bastards were bound to their mother's employer, a practice that enabled servants to raise their own children.[22] Once a master agreed to assume responsibility for an illegitimate child, he had to provide "sufficient meat Drink washing Lodgeing and apparrell and keep [the child] in sikeness and in health."[23] The right to choose the master belonged to whoever underwrote the child's initial maintenance. If the father fulfilled his duty, he obtained "good and Lawfull title in the Law to dispose" of the child without the mother's consent.[24] He lost that right if the parish provided support or if the mother released him from liability by arranging for another person to assume his obligation.[25]

The triracial composition of the Eastern Shore produced additional exceptions to the rule that fathers ordinarily controlled the selection of masters. If the father was a slave, the power to dispose of the child belonged to the mother, though if she was a servant she had to secure her master's consent before binding out the child.[26] The mother's rights were less clearly defined if the father was an Indian. In an Accomack case, for example, Elizabeth Long, a servant of William Custis, had a bastard by Oni Kitt, an Indian rug weaver. Kitt had a duty to maintain the child, and normally that would have given him the right to determine his future. Long objected, however, and petitioned the justices to rule that a "Pagan may not have my Child." She implored the court to bind the child to her master until he reached 24 so the boy could remain with her. To bolster her argument, she promised to serve Custis an additional three years if the justices would terminate the Indian's paternal rights. Concerned by the religious and cultural implications of allowing an Indian to raise a half-English child, the magistrates granted Long's request, thereby giving a handsome windfall to Custis, a fellow JP.[27]

Although the Eastern Shore's system of bastard maintenance resembled England's in many respects, it deviated from the metropolitan model in two important ways that had a major impact on the size of fathers' financial obligations. First, whereas England's population surplus allowed employers to command large fees for taking bastards as servants, Virginia's labor shortage caused colonial masters to dispense with premiums for the most part.[28] The near-abolition of premiums meant that Shoremen avoided one of the most costly consequences of being adjudged the father of an illegitimate child. Second, colonial masters were so eager to obtain additional workers that they accepted bastards as servants long before they were old enough to earn their keep, cutting off fathers' liability at an early stage. Bastards on the Eastern Shore were indentured at astoundingly young ages, ranging from two months to around two years. One child was bound for 24 years just nine days after he was born.[29] Planters viewed indentured children as an incipient worker corps, a home-grown group of eventual tobacco cultivators whose presence reduced their masters' dependence on the vagaries of the transatlantic labor market. Agreeing to support a bastard from infancy to adulthood was risky, since many children died before their masters could recover the cost of raising them. Investing in imported servants also involved a gamble against death, however, yet that never stopped planters from sinking money into them. Virginians probably viewed infant and immigrant mortality in much the same light: both were hazards an investor had to endure to make his fortune on the tobacco coast.

Besides helping the labor supply, the practice of binding out infants became popular on the Eastern Shore because it alleviated the tax burden. Early indenturing reduced the likelihood that the parish would have to provide support if a bastard's father failed to fulfill his obligations. Many of the men who sired bastards were servants or young freemen with meager estates. As long as they bore primary responsibility for child support, taxpayers stood a good chance of having to make up a shortfall. Once the child was indentured, however, his master — generally a man of substance — stepped into the father's shoes, and the taxpayers' secondary liability became less worrisome. The taxpayers' exposure was largely limited to the first few months of a child's life, a result especially pleasing to the Shoremen with the biggest tax bills, the magistrates.

Fathers profited most of all from the indenturing of infants because it significantly lowered the price of illicit sex. Being adjudged the father of an illegitimate child had serious financial ramifications in England, but fathers on the Eastern Shore usually got off lightly, paying only the mother's lying-in costs and a fee for nursing the child during the brief period between its birth and indenturing. That does not mean Shoremen regarded accusations of paternity as trivial. Begetting a bastard injured a Virginian's "Reputacon and Creditt,"[30] particularly if the child resulted from the "hainous" offense of miscegenation.[31] Nevertheless, from a fiscal standpoint, a colonial child-support order caused a putative father far less harm than did a maintenance order issued by English JPs. This difference in economic impact explains why the Eastern Shore magistrates thought they could afford to take shortcuts when they determined paternity. The justices' refusal to listen to the man's side of the story did not signify a sudden rise in the credibility or status of women. Rather, their use of the irrebuttable presumption reflected the fact that bastardy litigation on the Eastern Shore involved much smaller stakes than in England. Even if a woman's lie went unexposed, the man she falsely accused probably would not suffer substantial financial loss from an unjust imposition of liability.

The contrast between England's rebuttable presumption and the Eastern Shore's irrebuttable presumption provides a good illustration of the dichotomy between individualized and categorical decisionmaking.[32] When a court or other governmental body uses an individualized approach to allocate benefits or burdens, it judges people on the basis of their own conduct or characteristics.

Categorical decisionmaking, by contrast, classifies people into groups and presumes that all members of a group behave the same way or share certain traits and thus deserve identical treatment. Both modes have strengths and weaknesses. Categorical decisionmaking is the more efficient of the two because it does not entail costly, time-consuming factual inquiries. Individualized decisionmaking is the more accurate because of its attention to detail. It is also fairer because, unlike the categorical approach, it bases legal consequences on actual rather than imputed conduct. One can learn much about a society's values by examining its ratio of individualized and categorical decisionmaking. If a society places greater reliance on the former, it prizes accuracy and fairness more than efficiency. If it emphasizes the latter, it prefers efficiency to equity, and its legal system has a comparatively high tolerance for error. Most societies try to strike some sort of balance between the two modes of decisionmaking; hence public law consists largely of rules designed to maximize governmental efficiency without generating any more unfairness than the society is willing to accept. Eastern Shore society accepted a high level of unfairness in the enforcement of the bastardy laws because the consequences to wrongly accused individuals were relatively slight, at least in economic terms, and the benefits to the population as a whole were considerable. The irrebuttable presumption kept costly bastards off the welfare rolls while freeing magistrates to concentrate their energies on matters more pressing than resolving swearing matches about sex.

Like most deviations from the English legal model, the irrebuttable presumption did not develop instantly as part of a conscious decision to innovate. The rule emerged gradually as the practice of early indenturing became increasingly common. As late as 1650, Eastern Shore judges still followed the traditional English approach and allowed rebuttal. When Frances Smyth asserted during labor that Claus Johnson fathered her child, for instance, the court invited Johnson to "produce his Evidence and testimony for cleareinge of the question which hath relacon unto the child laid to his charge."[33] At midcentury, a man became liable for child support only if he failed to deny paternity or if extrinsic evidence corroborated the woman's charge.[34] Within about a decade, his right of rebuttal had vanished. The change is perceptible in a 1663 case in which Elizabeth Shepway accused William Onoughton of fathering her illegitimate child. Onoughton denied the charge, yet the court held him liable anyway "forasmuch as the said Shepway made oath in open Court that the said William Onoughton was father of her said Child."[35] In a 1667 Northampton case, Richard Ridge was ordered to support Margaret Morgan's bastard even though the justices had received "noe posietive proofe" of his paternity "but onely the womans affirmation."[36] Magistrates ignored even the most vehement denials by the accused. So powerful did the presumption become that men occasionally agreed to assume financial responsibility if a woman merely *offered* to identify the father under oath.[37] Accomack magistrates augmented the general presumption with a special, and equally conclusive, presumption that applied when a woman had multiple illegitimate children. A 1668 county bylaw provided that if a man admitted fathering a woman's first bastard, the court would assume, "without further inquest," that he also sired her second "unless Some other doe voluntarily owne the Second bastard."[38]

The efficiency of the irrebuttable presumption lost its allure, however, when the rule clashed with white supremacy. Such a conflict occurred in Northampton County in 1695, when a free black servant, Frances Driggus, accused her white master, John Brewer, of fathering her second bastard.[39] Driggus "not only declared but profered to sweare that her said master John Brewer was the only man that knew her." Brewer insisted that he was innocent, creating a dilemma for the justices. They knew they were supposed to give conclusive weight to a woman's oath, yet they also realized that they might upset the racial order if they accepted the word of a black woman over that of a white landowner. Eventually they decided the case was "soe tender" that they "would not presume to take her Oath." Instead, they referred the matter to the governor and Council "for their direction therein." Brewer, the magistrates noted, was "A free borne Subject of the Kingdome of England and A freeholder of this County" who was willing to swear that "hee was Nigh A hundred miles from home (by computacon of time) when his said servants childe was gott: And hee never knew her or was Concerned with her in any Such way." If he could be adjudged the father of a mulatto bastard on the strength of Driggus's testimony, who knew "what evill consequence such Presidents may futurely be If unduely grounded."[40] The county court's reaction to Driggus's charge is interesting because it shows there were limits to the colonial legal system's tolerance for unfairness. Eastern Shoremen would accept a certain amount of injustice to individuals in order to dispose of bastards quickly and cheaply, but this case crossed the line. Applying the irrebuttable presumption to Brewer would have burdened him not only with a possibly undeserved child-support obligation but also with the stigma of having committed miscegenation. The magistrates' decision to send the case to Jamestown reflects their suspicion that this combination of adverse consequences exceeded the price Shoremen were willing to pay for efficiency.[41]

John Kendall's case was not complicated by miscegenation or other extraordinary circumstances, so the Northampton justices lacked a plausible justification for exempting him from the irrebuttable presumption. Had they tried to spare him, they would have risked antagonizing the tithe-paying heads of household who formed the backbone of the political community. Taxpayers would have resented having to pay the costs associated with Jasper's birth and might have expressed their anger through further defiance of the court's authority. Moreover, an acquittal would have offended the community's sense of justice. Shoremen believed that the law applied equally to all people, regardless of their family and social connections. Excusing John from liability would have exposed magistrates to the charge that they had bent the rules to help a JP's kinsman, further weakening their already fragile claim to legitimacy as a ruling elite. Political self-interest therefore compelled the magistrates to treat John as arbitrarily as they had treated other putative fathers, despite their ostensible belief in his innocence.

If the justices felt bound by the irrebuttable presumption, and if the purpose of the rule was to avoid time-consuming inquiries into the truth, why did the court delve so deeply into what actually happened between John and Anne? Again the explanation was rooted in politics. The procedural novelty of John's petition gave the magistrates an excuse to say far more about the defendant's side of the story than was customary, and they took advantage of the opportunity to help the Kendalls save face. Probably after having a quiet word with the colonel, the justices handed down a decision that was designed to assuage public opinion while simultaneously salvaging the Kendalls' honor. They held John liable, shielding the parish and its taxpayers, and in the same breath proclaimed his moral innocence, enabling him to depict himself to the community as the hapless victim of a legal technicality rather than as the wilful transgressor of religious and social norms.

John had little reason to complain about the judgment. Although he lost on the issue of liability, he reclaimed his reputation, a significant victory for him and his politically ambitious uncle. He promptly obeyed the court's order, compensating the midwife for her services and arranging to reimburse the parish for the cost of a wet nurse whom the churchwardens had hired to suckle Jasper after his mother died.[42] Then he turned to the task of finding a master to take the baby off his hands. Fathers on the Eastern Shore took an active role in the recruitment of masters for their illegitimate offspring. Their principal motivation was probably a desire to cut their losses, but some fathers also took their child's welfare into account when they looked for a potential master. Thomas Barnes, for instance, arranged for his bastard son to be placed with his friend Peter Morgan "in regard that he and his Wife being so Carefull of it now and so loveing to it."[43] John likewise may have been thinking of Jasper's best interests when he indentured the infant to his friend Richard Patrick, a 41-year-old farmer and community leader.[44] Patrick, a resident of the Shore since about 1640, was of middling rank and generally employed one or two servants a year.[45] He held 1,200 acres on the north side of Indiantown Creek, abutting the tidal flats of Ramshorn Bay on the eastern side of the peninsula.[46] Near the mouth of the creek, he and his wife, Eleanor, had built a three-room home and "side house" (where he stored a large quantity of pins and dry goods, probably for resale), planted orchards, erected fences, and stocked their farm with horses, cattle, and hogs.[47] The Patrick's plantation—Homesett—would become Jasper's home for the next 22 years.

At this point, John undoubtedly thought he had put the Orthwood scandal behind him. He had fulfilled his financial responsibilities, found Jasper a master, and done everything he could to clear his name. He did not reckon, however, on the maverick natures of the 12 men who made up the Northampton County grand jury. On February 23, 1665, the jurors embarrassed the Kendalls anew by charging John with the crime of fornication. The justices, who just six months earlier had declared John blameless, found themselves in the awkward position of having to direct the sheriff to summons him for trial.[48]

NINE

JOHN STOCKLEY,
GRAND JURY FOREMAN

Powerful

The foreman of the grand jury that prosecuted John Kendall for fornication was John Stockley, a 44-year-old farmer who had lived on the Eastern Shore since the 1640s.[1] Like John Waterson, Stockley belonged to the modestly prosperous middle stratum of Northampton society. He raised hogs, cattle, and tobacco, owned a few hundred acres, and employed a handful of servants, giving him a personal stake in preserving order and stability.[2] He and others of his ilk formed the respectable core around which local government was organized. Magistrates depended on them to police the community and provide the political support necessary for effective rule. Self-interest encouraged them to take an active role in law enforcement, for they had more to lose from disorder than did those farther down the economic scale. As taxpayers, masters, and property owners, middling planters such as Stockley felt threatened by bastard-bearing and other types of undisciplined behavior and stood ready to help the JPs combat it. The "jury of inquest," or grand jury, provided a convenient mechanism for converting their impulse to control their neighbors into a powerful instrument of state.

Grand juries had operated in Virginia since at least 1645.[3] They were abolished in 1659 on the ground that they had "not produced such success as was expected for detection of offences" but were restored three years later because the penal laws had "become wholly uselesse and ineffectuall" without them.[4] Impaneled by the sheriff for a one-year term, grand jurors took an oath to "make diligent inquiry after Drunkes, Adulterers, and Bastard Bearers, Extortioners, . . . Lenders of Gunns, powder and shott to the Indians," and other miscreants and to present their names to the county court.[5] Grand jurors shared their law enforcement responsibilities with churchwardens, who made semiannual presentments to the county court of all persons suspected of "foule and abominable sins" such as fornication.[6]

Fornication cases fell under the county court's general jurisdiction to punish wrongdoers in conformity with English law, taking "speciall care that the Acts of this Country" — meaning Virginia — "are not broken nor infringed."[7] Rape and sodomy lay beyond JP's purview because both were capital crimes within the exclusive jurisdiction of the General Court at Jamestown. Eastern Shore JPs ordinarily tried noncapital sex cases without juries, although they occasionally impaneled one if the offense involved conduct more serious than garden-variety fornication. In 1681, for example, Dorothy Arew was presented to the Accomack County Court on a charge of copulating with a dog, and the magistrates "left the matter of fact to a Jury," which acquitted the poor deranged woman.[8] Incest was regarded as too serious for the county court to handle, with or without a jury. When a man was accused of fornicating with a mother and daughter, the Accomack justices deemed the offense "a crime of so high a nature that it merrited the Censure of a superiour Court and therefore thought it necessary to be preferred to the Honorable Governor and Councell," sitting as the General Court.[9] For the most part, Accomack and Northampton justices confined themselves to cases of extramarital heterosexual misconduct involving consenting unrelated adults. Although they sometimes disciplined married couples who conceived a child before their wedding, the overwhelming majority of fornication prosecutions resulted from illegitimate births.

Virginians patterned their fornication statutes, in part, on the punitive sections of the parliamentary poor laws. English magistrates sometimes incarcerated or fined fathers[10] and occasionally sentenced one to be whipped, particularly if he conceived several illegitimate children or impregnated a woman under offensive circumstances. In 1617, for instance, the Somerset justices ordered Nicholas Ruddock and his paramour, Katherine Canker, whipped through the high street of Glastonbury while two fiddlers played before them "to make known their lewdness in begetting the base child upon the Sabbath day coming from dancing."[11] From the reign of Charles I onward, magistrates tended to confine whippings to men who could not afford to pay child support.[12] For a man of means, having to make weekly maintenance payments over a period of several years was considered punishment enough.[13] English JPs often took a more explicitly punitive stance toward women, ordering them whipped in the middle of town on market day, a shaming ritual intended to deter others from indulging in risky and immoral behavior. JPs could inflict a lesser form of humiliation by requiring fornicators to make a public confession in church, a sanction borrowed from the ecclesiastical courts.[14] Under a 1610 statute, the justices also had the authority to send a woman to the house of correction for a year if she had a bastard who might become a burden to taxpayers.[15]

English JPs seldom encountered problems of proof when meting out punishment to women because most female defendants were visibly pregnant, but they often had a hard time deciding whether to punish men beyond ordering them to fulfill their support obligations. Metropolitan magistrates were reluctant to chastise men who professed to be innocent if the only evidence against them was a woman's allegation. They realized that many bastardy cases were little more than a credibility contest between two people with incentives to lie, yet they lacked an effective way to probe the parties' consciences and determine who was telling the truth. Making a possibly innocent man support someone else's child was bad enough; subjecting him to painful and humiliating punishment was intolerable. Consequently, if a male defendant refused to confess and the woman's accusation was uncorroborated, English

JPs merely entered a maintenance order and left disciplinary sanctions to the church courts, which had a larger arsenal of truth-discovering devices at their disposal.[16]

Ecclesiastical judges in England conducted twice-yearly visitations of parishes to accept churchwardens' presentments of fornicators, adulterers, and other violators of canon law.[17] If a defendant denied engaging in extramarital sex, the judge would order him to purge himself of suspicion by declaring his innocence under oath, supported by a specified number of compurgators who were willing to swear that they believed him. If the defendant confessed or failed purgation, the judge either admonished him to improve his conduct or imposed some sort of penance.[18] Public penance punished the breach of religious norms, extracted an expression of remorse and a promise of reformation, and served as a warning to others. It was especially embarrassing for people of high social standing. Rather than risk their honor and reputation, high-status defendants often asked church courts to commute their sentences to a monetary payment for the benefit of the poor.[19]

Ecclesiastical justice drew vigorous criticism, particularly from those who questioned the fairness of compelling people to swear to their own guilt or innocence.[20] In 1641, Parliament eliminated church courts' power to inflict punishment, barred ecclesiastical judges from accepting churchwardens' presentments, and prohibited church officials from administering any oath that required a person to accuse himself of misconduct. Five years later, Parliament stripped ecclesiastical courts of the rest of their powers.[21] They regained much of their authority in 1661, but opposition to compulsory self-incrimination remained so strong that Parliament reenacted the 1641 prohibition against forcing people to swear to their guilt or innocence.[22] Although the 1661 act barred mandatory oathtaking, ecclesiastical judges still allowed men accused of sexual misconduct to clear themselves by offering a voluntary oath or unsworn declaration of innocence.[23]

Colonists' memories of English ecclesiastical practices had a strong influence on early fornication prosecutions in Virginia. The

Assembly, at its first session, in 1619, ordered ministers and church-wardens to present fornicators to the governor and Council, sitting as the Quarter Court (the forerunner of the General Court). In 1627, the Court sentenced a male defendant, John Ewins, to 80 lashes, a penalty rooted in the 1576 Poor Law, and his sex partner, Jane Hill, was ordered to do penance by standing in church during divine service clad in a white sheet, a typical ecclesiastical punishment.[24] Mixed secular and ecclesiastical sanctions also appeared in a 1630 order directing that Hugh Davis "be soundly whipt before an assembly of negroes and others for abusing himself to the dishonor of God and shame of Christianity by defiling his body in lying with a negro, which fault he is to acknowledge next sabbath day."[25] The Quarter Court even had the power to excommunicate people who failed to perform a prescribed punishment for an ecclesiastical offense.[26]

As the colony grew, primary responsibility for disciplining sex offenders devolved to county magistrates.[27] Churchwardens started presenting fornicators to the Accomack-Northampton court in 1638. Like the Quarter Court, Eastern Shore magistrates imposed a combination of secular and ecclesiastical punishments, ordering some fornicators whipped and others subjected to humiliating penance.[28] The Assembly underscored magistrates' role as surrogate ecclesiastical judges in 1643 by requiring the ministers and church-wardens in each county to hold an annual meeting with the justices "in [the] nature of a visitation according to the orders and constitutions of the church of England"[29] so church officials could report any misconduct that had come to their attention. The legislature continued tinkering with the laws against sexual immorality in an attempt to make them more effective and in 1658 passed a statute providing that "every person," male or female, who committed fornication had to pay a fine of 500 pounds of tobacco to the parish where the act occurred or be whipped.[30] The Assembly kept the fine at that level when it overhauled Virginia's laws in 1662 and adopted a statute "for restraint of the filthy sin of fornication."[31] As a special deterrent to miscegenation, the legislators set the fine for interracial sex at 1,000 pounds of tobacco,[32] a sign of the escalating racism that accompanied the growth of slavery.

Stockley and his fellow grand jurors brought charges against John Kendall under the 1662 act as part of a general crackdown on misbehavior. They presented him at the February 23, 1665, court session along with 10 other defendants, including three couples charged with premarital fornication, a man accused of swearing, a man who had neglected to attend church regularly, and a couple of local officials who were derelict in performing their duties.[33] The prosecutions came at a time when the pursuit of fornicators on the Eastern Shore was reaching its zenith. A larger portion of the population (about 1 percent a year) was hauled before the magistrates for sexual misconduct in the 1660s than in any other decade of the seventeenth century.[34] The rise of prosecutorial activity in the 1660s had several causes, the most important of which was demographic. The Eastern Shore's population increased substantially in the early part of the decade with the arrival of several hundred immigrants, many of whom were young, unmarried servants. The zealous prosecution of fornicators was designed to deter these indentured newcomers from having sex before they had fulfilled their service obligations. Local government's ability to carry out this function improved in 1663 when the Assembly divided the Shore into two counties, doubling the number of grand jurors who were available to ferret out wrongdoers. The surge of prosecutions also stemmed from insecure magistrates' desire to curry favor with taxpayers and the Crown. In 1661, the Council for Foreign Plantations in London had admonished Virginians "that above all things they doe prosecute in their severall places and qualities the Reformation of the Debaucheries and licentious Conversation of Planters and servants whose ill example doth bring scandal upon Christianitie."[35] Tightening control over colonists' sexual conduct provided a way for local officials to demonstrate both a commitment to holding down welfare costs and their adherence to the policies of Charles II.

Even so, the grand jury's decision to include John in the crackdown seems remarkable, given the county court's opinion exonerating him of moral responsibility for Anne's pregnancy. One possible interpretation is that it was a symbolic action designed to register the jurors' disagreement with the justices' transparent attempt to help the Kendalls save face. John Stockley had an iconoclastic streak and was certainly capable of such a gesture. Less than two years earlier, the justices had ordered him arrested for having "disturbed and abused" the Hungars Parish vestry by accusing them of injustice and questioning the legality of their selection.[36] Stockley subsequently apologized and regained enough of the court's confidence to be named grand jury foreman, however, so we cannot assume that the presentment was just another expression of contempt for the justices. A more likely explanation is that Stockley and his fellow jurors decided to prosecute John because they did not differentiate between civil and criminal standards of proof. They appear to have assumed that since a woman's accusation created an irrebuttable presumption of guilt in a civil child-support case, her charge should receive the same weight in a criminal prosecution. In other words, if Anne's allegation provided a sufficient basis for ordering John to support Jasper, her statement furnished adequate grounds to fine him for fornication.

The magistrates, by contrast, perceived that the community was unwilling to go that far. No matter how committed they were to curbing illegitimacy, the justices could not countenance fining or whipping possibly innocent men on the strength of uncorroborated accusations. Like English JPs and ecclesiastical judges, Eastern Shore magistrates thought men deserved the right to present rebuttal evidence in criminal cases and adhered to that traditional practice even as they developed the irrebuttable presumption for civil cases. In 1663, for example, an Accomack man, Japhet Cooke, managed to overcome a woman's accusation and avoid a fornication fine by swearing to his innocence under oath and producing a prominent colonist as his compurgator.[37] A Northampton defendant, Richard Ridge, was acquitted of fornication in 1667 because there was no proof of his guilt besides the woman's affirmation (but, thanks to the irrebuttable presumption, he still had to support her child).[38] In fornication prosecutions, Eastern Shore justices applied what amounted to a two-witness rule. Unless a male defendant confessed, he could not be convicted solely on the word of his sex partner; another person had to corroborate the truthfulness of her charge.

The county court's willingness to throw out presentments based on uncorroborated accusations should have led John to file a motion to dismiss the prosecution as soon as he received his summons. The grand jury statute provided that the justices could convict on the strength of a presentment only "if made upon the certaine knowledge" of a juror or if supported by a witness's sworn testimony before a JP in the presence of the accused.[39] The first condition was not satisfied in John's case because nobody on the grand jury had firsthand evidence of his culpability. All the jurors had to go on were the equivocal paternity judgment and John's "common fame" as Anne's lover, information that fell short of certain knowledge.[40] The second condition was not met either because the only potential witnesses against him were the midwives, who could merely repeat Anne's uncorroborated allegations, which were insufficient to convict. Instead of moving swiftly to dismiss the flawed presentment, however, John displayed his contempt for the grand jury by ignoring the summons. Disobedience to a court order was intolerable, so the justices issued another order on September 4, 1665, demanding that John appear before them to answer the charge. This time he acted sensibly and challenged the presentment, putting Stockley on the defensive. The magistrates issued an order on November 6 directing Stockley to appear at the next court and "make good" the presentment or abandon the prosecution.[41] They also must have indicated the amount of evidence they would require to let the case go forward because Stockley abruptly gave up the fight. Daunted by the difficulty of satisfying the two-witness rule, Stockley dropped the charge, sparing John and his uncle a further round of embarrassing litigation.

John's victory did not end the controversy over the proper standard of proof in fornication cases, however. Two years later, the magistrates of Accomack County had to decide whether to apply the two-witness rule or the irrebuttable presumption in a case against Hugh Yeo, a burgess and former JP whom Ann Morfee accused of fathering her illegitimate child. Yeo denied the charge and contested both civil and criminal liability, contending that the county court could neither order him to pay child support nor fine him "unless hee would confess the fact or . . . [an]other Oath besides the Mother was produced as a witnesse of the act." The magistrates postponed judgment pending instructions from Governor Berkeley, the colony's chief justice. Berkeley informed them that the woman's uncorroborated oath provided all the evidence the court needed to convict Yeo of fornication and hold him liable for child support:

> Upon peruseall of this paper I am of Opinion that it is Consonant and agreeable both to Law justice and the practice of England that the reputed father be convicted by the sole Oath of the Mother of a bastard Child provided the Oath bee taken as the Law requires and that the reputed father convicted as aforesaid shall Suffer such punishment as the Lawes in that case doe provide.[42]

Under Berkeley's view, a woman's oath was not merely sufficient to support a conviction in a case where the man failed to adequately rebut it; the oath constituted conclusive proof of guilt in *all* cases.

Berkeley's opinion eviscerated the two-witness rule that had saved John Kendall and pushed the irrebuttable presumption well beyond its previous boundaries. Far from being "consonant and agreeable" to English practice, Berkeley's extension of the doctrine to criminal cases violated the fundamental principle that an accused person always had the right to reply to the prosecutor's evidence. Indeed, since the presumption of innocence had not yet taken root, a defendant had a positive duty to rebut the prosecutor if he possibly could. English law permitted the accused to cross-examine witnesses, introduce evidence, and speak in his own defense, and if he failed to avail himself of those opportunities, the judge and jury were entitled to assume that he was unable to deny the truth of the prosecutor's evidence.[43] The irrebuttable presumption would not have made sense in the context of seventeenth-century England's criminal justice system, and it did not, in fact, exist there. It was another colonial innovation—one that proved short-lived.

The governor's opinion left county officials with two options. They could continue prosecuting males for fornication, knowing they were now practically defenseless to perjury, or they could obviate the unfairness of the new rule by removing males from the criminal process. After a brief period of confusion and equivocation, Eastern Shore officials settled on the latter course. Starting around 1670, grand jurors, churchwardens, and JPs effectively nullified the criminal part of Berkeley's policy by declining to prosecute males for fornication. They still applied the irrebuttable presumption in child-support cases, thereby protecting taxpayers from the costs of bastardy, but criminal prosecutions for illicit sex became confined largely to females. Whereas males constituted 51 percent of the people who were prosecuted for sex offenses on the Eastern Shore in the period 1633 through 1669, men accounted for only 14 percent of those charged between 1670 and the end of the century.[44] A breakdown by decade makes the change even clearer. In the 1630s, 1640s, and 1650s, males were prosecuted more often than females, and in the 1660s, the percentages were roughly equal. In the 1670s, however, females were charged in three times as many cases as males, and in the 1680s and 1690s, women were prosecuted 10 times as often as men.[45]

The sharp decline in the prosecution of male sex offenders after 1670 reflected Eastern Shoremen's increasing sensitivity to procedural rights. Berkeley's attempt to enlarge the scope of the irrebuttable presumption clashed with the more demanding standards of proof that began to emerge in the 1660s, when lawyers started appearing regularly in the county courts. The notion that a man could be punished on the uncorroborated word of an unchaste woman grew less and less acceptable as Virginians endeavored to bring their legal system into closer conformity with England's. With the rise of men's procedural rights came a concomitant decline in the status of women. As the historian Cornelia Dayton observes in her study of women in the courts of colonial Connecticut, lawyers and the Anglicization of legal process played key roles in diminishing women's effectiveness as witnesses against male sex offenders. Lawyers' push for more stringent corroboration requirements resulted in the devaluation of women's accounts of sexual encounters and induced local officials to curtail their efforts to hold men answerable for breaching the community's moral code. Women ended up bearing almost all of the criminal responsibility for illicit sex while males shouldered only the relatively light financial burden of bastard maintenance.[46]

Broader social and political trends also contributed to the decriminalization of male sexual misconduct. Beginning in the 1660s, the Chesapeake colonies experienced a fundamental shift in their attitude toward the regulation of family life. This process, the historian Mary Beth Norton has explained, entailed the gradual replacement of the traditional patriarchal model of social organization, under which the community aggressively regulated both male and female sexuality, with a new consensus-based model that concentrated more on preserving lives and property than on enforcing moral norms. The change of emphasis helped create a climate in which men could avoid scrutiny of their sexual conduct provided they bore all the resulting costs themselves rather than imposing them on the community.[47] Bacon's Rebellion probably accelerated the trend toward the development of a prosecutorial double standard. The violent upheaval of the mid-1670s taught Virginia's rulers to adopt a more responsive leadership style and to work harder to avoid alienating the white male underclass.[48] By easing up on male sexual transgressions, leaders sought to reduce tensions between respectable society, which they represented, and the volatile mass of poor young men they wished to dominate. By concentrating their prosecutorial energies on wayward females, particularly white servants who bore mixed-race bastards, the Virginia elite gratified white men's desire to control access to white women's bodies. This strategy, the historian Kathleen Brown has powerfully argued, fortified the post-Rebellion alliance that white men of all classes formed around the issues of male privilege and racial solidarity.[49]

Another factor fostering the decriminalization of male fornication was the waning influence of religion on the criminal process. Pre-1670 fornication prosecutions had strong religious overtones. Officials described out-of-wedlock sex as a filthy sin and tried to punish it even if it did not produce an illegitimate child, as in the case of married couples prosecuted for antenuptial fornication. Magistrates further emphasized the religious origins of sex regulation by allowing the church-court defense of compurgation and by inflicting ecclesiastical punishments. Early Virginians' adherence to the traditional religious concept of fornication as an egregious form of sinful behavior that required atonement by men and women alike may explain why Eastern Shore prosecutions in the period 1633–69 formed a pattern resembling that of Puritan New Haven. After 1670, however, the pattern of prosecutions changed, just as it did in Connecticut after about 1690. Despite an Anglican renaissance in the last quarter of the century, Virginia officials became more concerned about the economic effects of bastardy and the need to protect men's procedural rights than about securing contrition from all sinners. With rare exceptions, they stopped prosecuting married couples, abandoned compurgation, and ceased imposing ecclesiastical punishments.[50] The secularization of law enforcement facilitated the reemergence of a double standard of sexual conduct long embedded in English culture. Late seventeenth-century Virginians, like eighteenth-century New Englanders, embraced the view that women were chiefly responsible for upholding society's moral standards and that fornication was basically a crime associated with female lewdness.[51]

Virginians' attitude of "prudent inattention"[52] to the noneconomic aspects of sinful behavior by males did not meet with universal approbation. In 1690, the Reverend James Blair, the bishop of London's colonial representative, advocated the establishment of church courts as a way to counter local officials' failure to enforce morality, but the provincial government blocked implementation of the plan.[53] Blair's proposal collapsed because Virginians had grown comfortable with the double standard, and, as the eighteenth-century clergyman Hugh Jones put it, "The people hate[d] the very name of the bishop's court."[54]

The opponents of Berkeley's policy eventually achieved total victory. After two decades of successful resistance to the criminal version of the irrebuttable presumption, the Assembly officially rejected it and adopted the two-witness rule long favored on the Eastern Shore. Under an act passed in 1691, a person could be fined or whipped for fornication only if "convicted by the oath of two witnesses, or by confession of the party."[55] Confessions by males were difficult to obtain because by the 1670s the privilege against self-incrimination guaranteed that "noe law can compell a man to sweare against himselfe in any matter wherein he is lyable to corporall punishment."[56] Unless a man confessed voluntarily, the only way to convict him of fornication was to elicit incriminating testimony from both his sex partner and a corroborating witness. Given the private nature of most sex acts, corroboration was rarely available. The 1691 statute therefore essentially exempted most males from prosecution, codifying the protection that Northampton County's informal two-witness rule had long given to men such as John Kendall.

TEN

JASPER ORTHWOOD,
FREE MAN

The years following the dismissal of John Kendall's criminal case were eventful for both him and his son, Jasper Orthwood. Jasper spent his youth as a servant at Richard Patrick's seaside farm, Homesett Plantation, learning how to cultivate tobacco and grain and care for livestock. John too immersed himself in agriculture, trying to get rich enough to become a grandee like his uncle. Sometime between the summers of 1665 and 1666, he left Colonel Kendall's household and established his own plantation. A desire for independence was natural for a male Virginian in his midtwenties, but few men John's age could muster the capital necessary for large-scale farming. With his uncle's help, John launched his enterprise employing at least six servants, which was triple the work force of the average head of household.[1] His economic prospects grew even brighter in 1667 when he became engaged to Susannah Savage, the eldest of the three daughters of John and Ann Elkington Savage, a wealthy couple with ties to most of the Eastern Shore's leading families.

The Savages owed their affluence to a pioneering ancestor, Ensign Thomas Savage, who settled on the Eastern Shore in 1619 and ingratiated himself with the Indians by serving as their interpreter. As a token of his affection, Esmy Shichans, chief of the Accomac tribe, gave Ensign Savage a large strip of land stretching across the peninsula from the Chesapeake Bay to Indiantown Creek on the sea side.[2] Ensign Savage died in the early 1630s, and on the strength of the chief's grant, his widow, Hanna, and son, John, obtained patents to 9,000 acres. When Hanna Savage died in 1641, John Savage became the sole owner of one of the largest tracts in Virginia.[3] Wealth brought political influence, and eventually Savage attained almost every kind of office a man could hold, including membership in the House of Burgesses.[4] Forging a marriage alliance with the powerful Savage family marked yet another milestone on the Kendalls' climb to the summit of Eastern Shore society.

The match between John Kendall and Susannah Savage almost did not occur, however, because of a quarrel over the terms of Susannah's dowry. Depositions describing the dispute provide a fascinating vignette of seventeenth-century matrimonial negotiations. William and John Kendall instructed their lawyer, John Tankard,[5] to draw up a contract requiring Savage to give John Kendall 100 acres on Cherrystone Inlet immediately and to bequeath a third of the rest of his land to his prospective son-in-law in his will. On the day of the wedding, June 4, 1667, while the guests were assembled in Savage's house awaiting the ceremony,[6] William Kendall and Tankard took Savage aside "in a private place" and presented the bridegroom's proposal. Savage objected to leaving his property to John, preferring instead to bequeath it to Susannah's future children. That was unacceptable to the Kendalls because it would have denied John the power to sell the land if he chose. "[T]here had like to have been variance betweene them" until Savage finally capitulated and agreed to leave his land to John, Susannah, and her heirs, giving John effective control of the property. Savage balked at the large portion John demanded, protesting that "hee must not undoe the rest of his children for one, besides hee did not know whether hee might have any more children." John could "have equall share with the rest of his children when hee dyed," but no more. After further argument, Savage and the Kendalls reached a compromise: John would get a third unless Savage had additional children, in which case the land would be "devided proportionably."[7] By this stage, the wedding guests were becoming impatient, so the parties gave the marked-up contract to the minister, Thomas Teackle, and went on with the ceremony.

After the wedding, Savage let John and Susannah anticipate their inheritance by taking up residence on Savage's land along the south bank of Indiantown Creek. They built a house there and, over the next decade, had four children: John Jr., Susannah, Thomas, and William.[8] John's other child, Jasper Orthwood, lived just a stone's throw away at Homesett Plantation, on the north side of the creek. John must have seen a great deal of Jasper as he passed through childhood into adolescence and perhaps allowed him to play with his half-brothers and half-sister from time to time. John never acknowledged that Jasper was his son, however, and it is unlikely that he and Susannah treated the boy like a member of their family. William Kendall took an interest in Jasper after he reached adulthood,[9] and John may have cared about him as well, but no trace of paternal concern appears in the surviving records.

Despite the many advantages that John enjoyed, his career ended largely in failure. People may have addressed him as "Mister,"[10] in deference to his family connections, but he did not achieve the stature necessary for appointment or election to a major public office. He sat on trial juries at least 15 times between 1669 and 1678[11] but never attained militia rank, nor did he join his uncle William on the bench or in the Assembly. He fared no better in the economic sphere. The size of his work force shrank, a sure sign of his inability to turn a profit as a planter.[12] Much of his energy was squandered on a long-running boundary dispute with his neighbors, the Gingaskin Indians, whom he "often threatened, Disturbed and affrightned." The conflict became so serious that the provincial government in Jamestown had to intervene. In 1674, the General Court ordered John to post a bond guaranteeing that he would stop harassing the Indians while the Northampton JPs tried to work out a peaceful solution.[13] John's hopes of becoming a land baron on the strength of Susannah's dowry were dashed when

John Savage had five more children, reducing John and Susannah's share of Savage's estate from a third to an eighth.[14] All they got in Savage's will was title to the 800-acre tract they had occupied since their marriage, a far cry from the riches John had once expected.[15] Even that small bequest came too late, for his fecund father-in-law came within two months of outliving him.

Around the beginning of February 1679, John was stricken with a fatal illness. His family summoned a physician, Dr. Richard Fortescue, who left a poignant account of the deathbed scene. Sensing the end was near, John called Susannah to his side, "and takeinge her . . . by the hand declared to her . . . Love[,] All my whole estate I have in this world I leave it wholly to you for you to dispose of it when you shall see cause." Then he asked for his four legitimate children and "blessed them severally and comaunded them to serve god and to keep the Sabbath day holy and to bee dutifull to their mother." Entreating Susannah "to bee a lovinge mother to all his Deare children," he quietly passed away, dead before the age of 40. If John made any reference to Jasper in his final moments, neither Fortescue nor the other witness, Mary James, thought it worth mentioning.[16]

Susannah remained a widow for about a year and a half. Shortly before marrying her second husband, Henry Warren, she conveyed much of the personal property she had inherited from John to the Reverend Mr. Teackle in trust so it would remain at her "owne disposeinge" for the use of her children "without the contradiction or Molestacon of [her] Intended husband."[17] Susannah's conveyance provides a good indication of the modest amount of wealth John possessed at the time of his death. She listed 15 cattle, three mares "branded with my late deceased husbands marke J.K.," two horses, three feather beds and bolsters, two iron pots, one large iron kettle, three large pewter dishes, one great oak chest, one round table, one cupboard, one small trunk, and one small chest.[18] For all his family's pretensions to gentility, John died owning little more than a yeoman.

Jasper remained a presence in the lives of Susannah and her family as the servant of her new brother-in-law, John Warren. Jasper's original master, Richard Patrick, died in 1676,[19] and the 12-year-old boy descended to Patrick's heir like a piece of property. Patrick bequeathed portions of his plantation to each of his four surviving children, giving his son, Richard Jr., Homesett House and Jasper along with it. Richard Jr. was a lifelong invalid whose infirmities rendered him "Alltogether Incapable and unable to worke whereby to mainetaine [him]selfe in Apparrell and Dyett." His disability gave him "greate cause to feare" that he would "want Extreamely" if he tried to look after himself. Consequently, in 1683 he entered into a contract with his sister Elizabeth and her husband, John Warren, under which the Warrens promised to care for Richard Jr. for the rest of his life, and in return he assigned them Homesett House and all the land he inherited from his father.[20] As a result of this assignment, John Warren, the younger brother of Susannah's husband, Henry Warren, became Jasper's master.

John Warren was hardly an ideal employer. He was young — just four years older than Jasper[21] — and unaccustomed to managing other men. His father, Robert Warren, an illiterate small landowner and minor officeholder, did not have any servants,[22] so John grew up without a paternal role model on which to base his conduct as a master. He had a hot temper and tended to employ force when angry. In 1678, for example, Henry Mathews, keeper of the inn next to the courthouse, complained that John and his brother Henry had started a barroom brawl.[23] Five years later, John, Henry, and their brother Argoll got into another fight at the Mathews tavern, and again John was the initiator. He quarreled with Bartholomew Taylor, prompting Andrew Carr to come to Taylor's defense. Henry and Argoll intervened, and in the ensuing struggle Carr seriously wounded Argoll with a sword.[24] In 1686, while John was serving as constable, he and Henry exchanged harsh words with Charles Geldinge, and John violently pushed Geldinge to the ground three or four times, injuring his leg.[25] Given John's volatility, he probably treated Jasper at least as roughly as he treated everyone else who crossed him. That would not be surprising in a society where cruelty to servants was commonplace and the exploitation of labor sometimes became so harsh that the worker responded by murdering his master.[26] Jasper, in turn, may have placed further strains on their relationship by resisting authority and stubbornly insisting on doing as he pleased.

We catch a glimpse of Jasper's headstrong personality in a 1683 incident that led John Warren's neighbor, Joseph Godwin, to sue Warren for trespass. Godwin alleged that horses belonging to Warren and his disabled brother-in-law, Richard Patrick Jr., broke down Godwin's fence and trampled his crops. To establish ownership of the animals that inflicted the damage, Godwin's servant Anne Merrick testified that she saw "Richard Patrick and John Warrens man," Jasper, fetch the horses out of Godwin's wheat patch, and on another occasion she "did see the said John Warrens man in a morninge come and tooke his Masters horse in the Corne field and did pull downe the fence and lett him out a New way." When Merrick asked Jasper why he had knocked a second hole in the fence instead of taking the horse out the same place it had entered, he "went his way and made noe answer."[27] If Jasper displayed a similar attitude around his short-fused master, clashes were inevitable.

In the spring of 1686, Jasper decided that he had worked for Warren long enough. He had turned 21 the previous July and was ready to strike out on his own. He told Warren of his desire to leave and requested a freedom certificate to protect him from being arrested as a runaway. He also asked for the corn and clothes to which emancipated servants were customarily entitled. Warren refused to release him, claiming that he had a right to Jasper's labor until the age of 24. Warren evidently based his refusal on the parliamentary Poor Law of 1601, which required male bastards who were bound out as parish apprentices to serve until the age of 24.[28] In 1672, however, the Virginia Assembly had lowered the age of emancipation to 21.[29] If the English statute applied, Jasper owed

Warren another two years of service; if Virginia law trumped it, Jasper gained his freedom, and Warren owed him almost a year of back wages.

Jasper scarcely could have appreciated the complexity of the conflict of laws his case presented, but he understood enough about his situation to realize that he needed professional legal advice. The attorney he retained, Charles Holden, did not need to be briefed on the background of the case. Holden had been present in the courtroom, in his capacity as crier,[30] when the circumstances of Jasper's conception and birth were litigated in 1664. He had parlayed his courtroom experience into a career as an advocate for hire. He started appearing as a private attorney in 1667 and maintained an active law practice until his death in 1690.[31] He reached the pinnacle of his legal career in 1687, when he was appointed deputy attorney general of Virginia in charge of prosecuting criminals on the Eastern Shore.[32] Holden may have lacked the sophistication of a barrister practicing in England, but he was a skillful litigator nonetheless. He had at least a passable command of common-law writs[33] and knew how to raise technical challenges to opponents' pleadings by "showinge Law."[34] He did not doubt his grasp of the mother country's jurisprudence. When a litigant tried to refer the court to particular pages of an English law book, Holden declared the references "to bee None of the Lawes of England" and therefore not binding.[35] Holden's legal acumen was occasionally flawed,[36] yet he had sufficient respect from the bench to be named foreman of the grand jury, a panel "of the ablest and most Knowinge now present at Court."[37]

Holden's clientele spanned the social spectrum. At various times, he represented a slave accused of assault; a white servant who bore a bastard; a burgess's widow seeking a larger share of her husband's estate; and a member of the governor's Council who was involved in civil litigation.[38] Like all aggressive trial lawyers, Holden expected his clients to keep quiet and let him take charge. He once told a client who was about to be tried for hog killing, "bee damned: hold your tongue[;] will you bee Upon record by your owne confession[?]"[39] Holden sometimes handled cases with such zeal that he strayed across the thin line separating forcefulness from insolence. In 1689, the Northampton bench fined him 50 pounds of tobacco "for his passionate swearinge in Court."[40] Holden and his friendly rival, John Tankard, litigated hundreds of cases, but neither became rich. After spending over 20 years at the bar, Tankard died in 1689 "much incumbred with debt,"[41] and Holden left only a modest 300-acre estate.[42]

Holden filed suit on Jasper's behalf against John Warren in the Northampton County Court by early June 1686, asking the court to declare his client a free man. The lawyer simultaneously filed a motion in Warren's defense in a trespass and battery suit brought against him by his barroom adversary, Charles Geldinge.[43] Modern ethical rules ordinarily prohibit a lawyer from acting as an advocate against a person the lawyer represents in some other matter, even if it is wholly unrelated.[44] This kind of conflict of interest was unavoidable in the seventeenth century, however, because of the shortage of lawyers. Holden and Tankard were the only professional attorneys in Northampton County in the 1680s, and if they had labored under the same strict duty of loyalty that lawyers owe their clients nowadays, a large segment of the population would have been denied legal services. Holden's ability to sue a man in one case and represent him in the next meant that people throughout the county, including those near the bottom of the social scale such as Jasper, had access to experienced counsel.[45]

Warren probably had mixed feelings about being sued. He surely resented Jasper's effrontery, yet he may also have felt relieved that Jasper sought redress through the legal system rather than resorting to violence or running away. He evidently did not take the servant's claim seriously, though, because instead of hiring Tankard to handle his defense, he elected to represent himself. By arrogantly assuming he would win, Warren deprived himself of the professional assistance that might have made victory a real possibility. An experienced advocate would have seen the weaknesses in Holden's case and exploited them. Holden not only had to persuade the justices that the 1672 Virginia statute superseded the 1601 act of Parliament — no mean feat — but also had to convince them that the Assembly intended the colonial act to apply retroactively to servants like Jasper who were indentured before 1672. Holden had lost when he made the same retroactivity argument in *Webb v. Bowman,* an Accomack County case decided just ten weeks earlier.[46] Tankard had witnessed the establishment of that precedent, and had he represented Warren, he could have informed the Northampton justices that their Accomack colleagues already had rejected Holden's contention. The Northampton magistrates would not have been obliged to follow the Accomack decision, but the precedent might have been enough to persuade them to rule against Jasper. Warren's ignorance of *Webb,* coupled with his lack of forensic skills and experience, put him at a significant disadvantage in courtroom combat with Holden.

Orthwood v. Warren appeared on the Northampton JPs' docket on June 4, 1686. They hesitated to proceed to judgment, however, because the case involved much thornier legal issues than they were accustomed to handling and because Jasper was not an ordinary plaintiff. Most aggrieved servants were poor and powerless, and their legal concerns commanded cursory attention at best. Jasper's, on the other hand, had drawn the notice of the county's most influential figure, and that was reason enough to give the magistrates pause.

Colonel William Kendall was now the senior justice of Northampton County and speaker of the House of Burgesses. His elevation to the speakership in 1685 capped a career of nearly a quarter-century as a legislator, during which he had chaired or served on all of the House's principal committees.[47] His most important governmental role was that of peacemaker, constantly striving to conciliate the warring factions that threatened the colony's security and stability. He considered moderation and restraint the most effective tools for keeping resistance at bay and instinctively opposed heavy-handed exercises of power. During Bacon's Rebellion, for instance, he initially sided with Sir William Berkeley and then broke with the governor over the ruthlessness with which he had treated his opponents.[48] Kendall later proved himself to be an artful diplomat while serving as one of Virginia's two envoys at a peace conference with the Iroquois in Albany, New York,[49] and when he became speaker, he tried to use his mediation skills to break a bitter deadlock between the burgesses and the governor, Lord Howard of Effingham.[50] Although his diplomatic efforts ended largely in failure, Kendall never lost faith in his ability to help men resolve their differences through negotiation and compromise.

The dispute between Jasper and John Warren gave Kendall another opportunity to play peacemaking patriarch, and this time he had a personal stake in the outcome. When he learned of Jasper's lawsuit, Kendall informed his colleagues on the bench that he was "Concerned therein" and wished to be present when they decided the case, an acknowledgment that in some sense he felt responsible for the young man he had once gone to great lengths to disown. Kendall's intervention on Jasper's behalf showed that much had changed in the 22 years since John Kendall's paternity trial. William Kendall was no longer an insecure ex-servant struggling for acceptance. He was now a rich, well-respected leader, firmly established at the apex of colonial society. He had just prevailed on the governor to commission his son a JP and thus could look forward to passing along power to his descendants, the ultimate measure of political success in early Virginia.[51] Having solidified his family's position, the 65-year-old colonel could afford to take a more magnanimous view of his moral obligations to Jasper, even if that meant tacitly admitting the existence of a relationship he formerly denied.

Kendall could not attend the June 4 hearing because he was "absent over the Bay"[52] on affairs of state, probably visiting Jamestown in yet another quest to improve relations between the quarreling governor and legislature. In deference to the colonel's wishes, the justices postponed the trial of *Orthwood v. Warren* until the next county court session, scheduled for late July. Kendall returned to the Eastern Shore sometime in early June, but within a few days he was summoned back across the Bay, this time to Rappahannock County. He had made countless trips to the Western Shore during his political career and had always made it home safely, yet he had an uneasy feeling about this particular journey. In 1684, he had married his fourth wife, Sarah Mathews Kendall,[53] who was now expecting their first child, and he worried that if anything happened to him, Sarah might be left without sufficient resources to care for herself, the baby, and her young children from a previous marriage. Placing himself "in the hands of Allmighty God as to [his] Returne," Kendall amended his will and instructed his executor to pay Sarah 30,000 pounds of tobacco, worth a penny per pound, as soon as possible after his death.[54] Unfortunately, the colonel's premonition of imminent mortality proved all too accurate: he was dead within a month.

Kendall had served on the Northampton County Court for three decades, so the July 28 session, the first meeting since his passing, must have been a somber occasion. Its poignance was heightened by the presence of his pregnant widow, Sarah, who presented his will to the magistrates and asked them to begin the process of probating his estate. Her stepson, Justice William Kendall II, who inherited much of his father's property, "conceded to" Sarah's wish that she and her children continue living in the colonel's house "untill the production of the childe shee now goeth withall by him."[55] The will's recitation of Kendall's acreage, slaves, livestock, and other holdings bore witness to the magnitude of his material success, and the long list of relatives who received bequests further evidenced the achievement of his dynastic ambitions.[56] Among the many beneficiaries of the colonel's largesse was his legitimate grandnephew, John Kendall Jr. His illegitimate grandnephew, Jasper Orthwood, got nothing.

Although Kendall did not leave Jasper any property, his death probably helped the young man win his freedom. Jasper's suit against John Warren was brought up shortly after the presentation of Kendall's will. The seven Northampton magistrates who heard *Orthwood v. Warren*[57] knew that one of the colonel's last wishes was to aid Jasper, and the desire to honor his memory may have predisposed them in Jasper's favor. That advantage, coupled with Holden's advocacy skills and Warren's lack of counsel, produced victory for the servant. The court implicitly held not only that the 1672 Virginia statute took precedence over the 1601 act of Parliament but also that the colonial measure applied retroactively to servants indentured before its enactment. The court concluded that Jasper "was not Obliged by Law to serve any longer then till Twenty one yeares of Age to which he Attained the 29th of July 1685: from which time hee was free." Because Warren had detained him a year longer than the law allowed, he had to pay Jasper 600 pounds of tobacco.[58] The amount awarded as compensation for the extra service fell far below the prevailing wage for adult males. A year earlier, a master had been ordered to pay 100 pounds a month—double Jasper's award—for work a male servant performed past the date when he should have been emancipated.[59] The stinginess of Jasper's compensation might have been the result of a compromise by the JPs, at least some of whom may have been troubled by the retroactive application of the 1672 statute.

The conflict between the act of Parliament and the Virginia statute resurfaced in 1694, and again the Northampton bench held that the colonial law controlled. Ironically, the 1694 case, *Gale v. Guilden,* also involved John Kendall, albeit indirectly. In 1673, Kendall's servant, Mary Gale, gave birth to a male bastard, Jephtah, who was bound out to the age of 24. Jephtah turned 21 in 1694 and, like Jasper, requested his freedom. His master, Charles Guilden, refused to release him, so he hired the former JP John Custis III to file a freedom petition. Custis turned out to be a very wise choice. As one of the justices who decided *Orthwood v. Warren,* he knew about the precedent and used it to his client's advantage. The court, citing the 1672 Virginia law, discharged Jephtah from further service.[60]

After *Orthwood* and *Gale,* the people of Northampton County regarded 21 as the age of emancipation for indentured white male bastards and considered the debate closed. The issue remained unresolved in Accomack County, however, until 1698, when the county court there decided *Morgan v. Bally*. In 1677, Bridget Morgan named Edward Jellson as the father of her illegitimate son, Joseph Morgan,[61] and to terminate his child-support obligation, Jellson arranged for Joseph to be bound to Richard Bally until the boy's twenty-fourth birthday. When Joseph became 21, he asked Bally to free him. Bally refused, so Joseph retained Custis (who was now practicing law in Accomack as well as serving as a justice in North-ampton) to petition the Accomack justices for his freedom. Bally offered to prove that "by the Statute Laws of England he could make out that Bastard Children are to be bound out untill they at-taine unto the age of twenty foure yeares,"[62] and his lawyer later produced a copy of the 1601 act of Parliament in support of that contention. Custis responded by arguing that the 1672 Virginia statute required that Joseph be freed at 21.[63] Critics sometimes ac-cused colonial judges of failing to follow clear choice-of-law rules, forcing litigants "to depend upon the Crooked Cord of a Judge's Discretion,"[64] but in this instance the Accomack justices found no room for doubt. Holding that the act of Assembly "was bindeing to us in this Country," they ordered Joseph released from servitude immediately.[65]

The three Eastern Shore emancipation decisions did not signify by any means a wholesale rejection of parliamentary authority. They did, however, underscore magistrates' belief that the colonial legislature had the right to determine the extent to which general English laws applied in Virginia.[66] The Assembly was the best in-stitution to make that judgment, they maintained, not only be-cause it was made up of men like themselves but also because its conclusions were disseminated throughout the colony in the form of written statutes, an efficient means of notifying people of what was and was not the law.[67] Parliament had not specifically man-dated that Virginians enforce the Poor Law of 1601, and colonial legislators had therefore felt free to supplant it with a statute they deemed better suited to their needs. The 1672 Virginia act reflected the Assembly's conclusion that holding males in servitude from infancy until 24 would cause deep resentment and thus become a potential source of social unrest, a concern that deepened in the wake of Bacon's Rebellion. So far as the magistrates were concerned, the Assembly's decision settled the issue, and the act of Parliament no longer bound them.

Freedom had once been the key to opportunity, but by the 1680s it conferred fewer practical benefits than it had earlier, which may partially explain why the Assembly was willing to lower the emancipation age. Release from servitude did not give Jasper any political rights, for instance, because he did not possess land. In 1670, the Assembly had stripped landless ex-servants of the right to vote in burgess elections in reaction to their supposedly tumultuous behavior at polling places. Their suffrage was briefly restored during Bacon's Rebellion and then taken away again in 1677 on orders from the Crown.[68] Until Jasper could scrape together enough capital to set up his own household, he would not have any more say in community governance than he had as a servant. Theoretically, freedom meant he could marry and start a family if he wished,[69] but without land he would be hard pressed to support them. Land was essential to Jasper's future, yet few things were harder for a Northampton freedman to obtain. Real estate, which had been plentiful and affordable in the middle decades of the century, had grown increasingly scarce and expensive after 1660 as magistrates and other speculators had amassed all the property they could get their hands on. Very few ex-servants — perhaps one in ten — ever succeeded in becoming landowners.[70] Most either descended back into servitude or left the Eastern Shore for less settled areas where land was cheap and men could still hope to experience the sort of meteoric rise that William Kendall enjoyed in the 1650s.[71]

Kendall's death took away Jasper's only reason to stay on the Eastern Shore after emancipation. Had the colonel lived, his guilt might have induced him to help Jasper acquire a little land and start a farming operation, but that was not to be. Kendall's widow and son did not share his newly awakened sense of responsibility toward Jasper, nor did the young man's stepmother, Susannah, and her husband, Henry Warren. Jasper was essentially on his own, facing slim odds of attaining even a modest level of prosperity at home. Like his mother and grandmother before him, he decided that the wisest course of action would be to migrate to another part of the world, where opportunities were more abundant and nobody knew his past.

The records do not indicate where Jasper went after he won his lawsuit. Maybe he headed north, through Maryland, Delaware, or Pennsylvania, or crossed the Chesapeake Bay, bound for the unclaimed lands beyond the fall line in western Virginia. Whatever his destination, one would like to think that he finally got a chance to fulfill his potential, unencumbered by the circumstances of his birth. For he was no longer just a bastard—the son of nobody—but a free man.

CONCLUSION

As a tale, the story of Anne Orthwood's bastard is almost operatic in its drama and pathos. A poor, illegitimate young woman binds herself into servitude and braves an Atlantic crossing to find a husband and establish a new life. She falls in love with a cad, becomes pregnant, conceals her lover's identity as long as she can, and dies for her sins. Scorned by society and brutalized by a legal system that cares more about property than about human dignity, she perishes without ever knowing the joys of marriage and parenthood. Her lover's rich and powerful uncle tries to squelch the ensuing scandal by concocting a clever plan to clear his nephew's name. The young man emerges largely unscathed and goes on to marry an heiress, but he gets his just deserts in the end, dying a failure at an early age and leaving his uncle to bear the full weight of the family's guilt. Meanwhile, his bastard son languishes in involuntary servitude, hopeless and unloved, until a smart lawyer helps him cast off the shackles of illegitimacy and win his freedom. A historian can do his best to relate this story, but it would take a Verdi or a Puccini to do it justice.

As legal history, the Orthwood-Kendall cases are interesting because of the light they shed on the way law actually functioned in an early American community. The purpose of law was to maintain order, protect and enhance property, and safeguard reputations.

The men who operated the Eastern Shore's legal system in the seventeenth century displayed considerable skill in manipulating law to their advantage in each of these respects. The malleability of the English doctrines and institutions that colonists brought with them as part of their cultural inheritance made it relatively easy for ambitious leaders to shape the law to conform to their social and economic goals. Within a couple of generations, they had constructed a legal regime far different from England's, a system reflective of the tobacco economy and labor market on which it was based. The rhetoric of law still sounded basically English, both because of its origins and because outward Anglicization furthered colonial officials' political agenda. In a substantive sense, however, a distinctive legal dialect had emerged.

This study has identified four significant examples of self-interested innovation by the magistrates and jurors of the Eastern Shore. They altered English law to allow the assignability of servants without their consent in order to keep down the cost of workers and maintain a free-flowing labor supply. To protect themselves and other buyers of servants, they replaced the English contract principle of *caveat emptor* with *caveat venditor*, using the concept of the implied conditional sale to force sellers to give more accurate descriptions of workers' physical characteristics. They lowered the age at which illegitimate children could be bound into servitude from seven years to just a few weeks, expanding the number of cheap laborers and cutting the price men paid for fathering bastards. They invented an irrebuttable presumption of paternity to shield parish taxpayers from the costs of supporting illegitimate children, making Virginia's system of poor relief less fair than England's but more efficient. In each instance, they acted subtly and incrementally, never acknowledging that they had strayed from the well-worn paths of English law.

Besides revealing Shoremen's creative side, the Orthwood-Kendall litigation shows how early Virginians regarded the hierarchy of authority. Modern Americans are accustomed to thinking of law as a pyramid, with federal law at the top, state law in the middle, and local law at the bottom. When conflicts arise, federal law trumps state law, and state law trumps local law. One might assume that an analogous pyramid existed in the seventeenth century, with metropolitan English law (acts of Parliament) on top, provincial law (acts of Assembly) in the middle, and local law (county or parish bylaws and customary practices) on the bottom. To some extent that was true. Virginians recognized the English government's authority to override colonial statutes, and they deemed local bylaws invalid if they contradicted acts of Assembly.[1] But they sometimes inverted the pyramid when it suited them to do so. They gave their own 1672 emancipation act precedence over Parliament's 1601 Poor Law on the theory that the Assembly knew what was best for the colony and could do as it pleased since the English authorities had not specifically ordered Virginians to apply the metropolitan statute. And the Eastern Shore's local practice of requiring testimony from at least two witnesses in order to convict a man of criminal sexual misconduct effectively nullified the provincial fornication act as far as males were concerned. "[T]he practice is the law," declared a seventeenth-century English chief justice,[2] and Shoremen demonstrated their adherence to that view by occasionally subordinating the written law to their conception of higher values.[3]

This story reminds us that seventeenth-century justice was very much a community affair. One of its most striking aspects is the number of people who were eventually drawn into the four cases stemming from Anne's weekend of sex with John Kendall. The litigation involved 12 justices, 24 jurors, at least five sheriffs and undersheriffs, five litigants, four witnesses, two clerks, a crier, a lawyer, and countless spectators who watched intently as the drama unfolded. The outcome makes sense only if one bears in mind that the actors were keenly aware of their audience. Although political stability had been achieved in Virginia by the 1660s,[4] the parvenu rulers of Northampton County felt profoundly insecure, hence they courted public opinion almost as assiduously as they pursued their economic policy of "looking out for number one."[5] The county court's ruling that John was legally guilty but morally innocent, for example, looks more like an appeal to the crowd than like a judgment grounded in orthodox legal reasoning.

In the end, the story of Anne Orthwood's bastard illustrates the utility of English law as an instrument of empire. It conferred authority on local elites, enabling quack physicians, ex-servants, naturalized aliens, and the sons of tailors and innkeepers, armed with little more than their JP commissions, to keep the peace and exploit the resources around them. It lent legitimacy to their judicial processes, linking them, politically and ideologically, to the English legal system and its long tradition of deference and obedience. Above all, it gave them the flexibility they needed to pick and choose among the rules they inherited[6] and to fabricate new legal doctrines without appearing any less English, thus allowing them to rule in the king's name while governing in their own interest.

NOTES

Acc O, 1717–19	Accomack County Orders, 1717–1719
Acc-Nor Rec, 1632–40	*County Court Records of Accomack-Northampton, Virginia, 1632–1640,* ed. Susie M. Ames. Washington, DC, 1954.
Acc-Nor Rec, 1640–45	*County Court Records of Accomack-Northampton, Virginia, 1640–1645,* ed. Susie M. Ames. Charlottesville, VA, 1973.
BRO	Bristol Record Office (Bristol, England)
GCL	Gloucestershire County Library (Gloucester, England)
Nor DWO, 1645–51	Northampton County Deeds, Wills, [Orders,] etc., 1645–1651
Nor DWO, 1651–54	Northampton County Deeds, Wills, [Orders,] etc., 1651–1654
Nor DWO, 1654–55	Northampton County Deeds, Wills, [Orders,] etc., 1654–1655
Nor O, 1655–56	Northampton County Orders, 1655–1656
Nor DWO, 1655–57	Northampton County Deeds, Wills, [Orders,] etc., 1655–1657
Nor O, 1657–64	Northampton County Order Book, 1657–1664
Nor DW, 1657–66	Northampton County Deeds, Wills, etc., 1657–1666
Nor O, 1664–74	Northampton County Order Book, 1664–1674
Nor DW, 1666–68	Northampton County Deeds & Wills, 1666–68
Nor D, 1668–80	Northampton County Deeds, etc., 1668–1680
Nor OW, 1674–79	Northampton County Order Book, Wills, etc., 1674–1679
Nor O, 1678–83	Northampton County Order Book, 1678–1683
Nor DW, 1680–92	Northampton County Deeds, Wills, etc., 1680–1692
Nor OW, 1683–89	Northampton County Order Book & Wills, 1683–1689

Nor OW, 1689–98	Northampton County Orders & Wills, 1689–1698
Nor DW, 1692–1707	Northampton County Deeds & Wills, 1692–1707
Nor OW, 1698–1710	Northampton County Orders, Wills, etc., 1698–1710
Nor O, 1710–16	Northampton County Order Book, 1710–1716
Nor WD, 1711–18	Northampton County Wills, Deeds, etc., 1711–1718
Nor O, 1716–18	Northampton County Order Book, 1716–1718
Nor W, 1717–25	Northampton County Wills, etc., 1717–1725
Nor DW, 1718–25	Northampton County Deeds, Wills, etc., 1718–1725
Nor O, 1719–22	Northampton County Order Book, 1719–1722
Nor WD, 1725–33	Northampton County Wills, Deeds, etc., 1725–1733
NRO	Norfolk Record Office (Norwich, England)
PRO	Public Record Office (London)
Statutes at Large	*The Statutes at Large; Being a Collection of All the Laws of Virginia, From the First Session of the Legislature, in the Year 1619,* ed. William Waller Hening. 2nd ed. New York and Philadelphia, 1823.
WRO	Worcestershire Record Office (Worcester, England)

Introduction

1. Whitelaw, *Virginia's Eastern Shore,* i. 187; Nor O, 1657–64, p.-f. 196.
2. Acc O, 1666–70, p. 75.
3. Nor O, 1657–64, pp. 187, 191.

4. Isaac, *Transformation*, p. 90.

5. *Portsmouth Record Series Borough Sessions Papers*, p. 4.

6. See Amussen, *Ordered Society*, pp. 110, 116; Godbeer, *Sexual Revolution*, pp. 33–34, 37, 127–28. For other cases involving sex accompanied by promises of marriage, see *Portsmouth Record Series Borough Sessions Papers*, pp. 2, 24; Norton, "Gender, Crime, and Community," pp. 123–24; and *Churchwardens' Presentments in the Oxfordshire Peculiars*, p. 28 (curate promised to marry woman "before and after the childe was begotten . . . but he durst not doe it untill his father was dead").

7. 43 Eliz. I, c. 2, s. 3 (1601).

8. *Statutes at Large*, ii. 298.

9. Friedman, Introduction to *Common Law, Common Values* p. 11.

10. Macfarlane, *Justice and the Mare's Ale*, p. 24. For other outstanding examples of case studies, see Davis, *Return of Martin Guerre;* Simpson, *Cannibalism and the Common Law;* Lewis, *Gideon's Trumpet.*

11. See Ames, "Law-in-Action," p. 177; *Minutes of the Council,* pp. vii–xvi; Friedman and Shaffer, "Conway Robinson Notes," pp. 259–60; Flaherty, "Select Guide," pp. 112–37.

12. The records for Accomack-Northampton (1633–63) and Northampton (1663 to present) are kept in the courthouse in Eastville, and those for Accomack (1663 to present) are at the courthouse in the town of Accomac. Photocopies and microfilms of the Eastern Shore archives are available at the Library of Virginia in Richmond. Historians have put the Eastern Shore records to good use. For especially fine works based largely on the Northampton and Accomack County archives, see Breen and Innes, *"Myne Owne Ground";* Perry, *Formation of a Society;* Ames, *Studies;* Deal, *Race and Class.*

Chapter 1

1. Anne's family spelled its name in a variety of ways, including Harwood, Harewodd, Horwood, Horwodd, Herwod, Herwodd, Herwood, and Herward. See WRO, All Saints, Worcester, Parish Register, i and ii. Her baptismal record spells her surname as "Harwood," ii. 5. The Northampton County clerk misspelled her name because Harwood, Horwood, and Orthwood sounded a lot alike. The "H" in Harwood and Horwood probably was silent. "Whoredom," for example, often was pronounced as "oredom" in the early modern period. Anne probably called herself "Arewood" or "Ore-wood," but the clerk heard the name as "Orth-wood" and spelled it accordingly. See Dobson, *English Pronunciation,* i. 389, ii. 991;

Kökeritz, *Shakespeare's Pronunciation*, pp. 307–9, 320–21; Nor O, 1657–64, p. 194 (first use of "Orthwood" in court records).

2. Styles, "City of Worcester," p. 187.

3. All Saints Parish Register, i (unpaginated), ii. 3–6; Glare, *Oxford Latin Dictionary*, p. 1192. *Notha* referred to a female bastard and *nothus* to a male. Ricketts occasionally used the Latin word *spurius* to indicate that a male child was illegitimate and *spuria* to signify the illegitimacy of a female. See, e.g., All Saints Parish Register, ii. 18, 20, 23. When Ricketts knew the identity of the man who fathered an illegitimate child, he listed his name in the parish register. For example, he placed an asterisk beside the February 4, 1642, baptismal entry for "Robert the son of Robert Rode & Joan Potter," followed by "spurius"; ii. 18.

4. Ingram, *Church Courts*, pp. 3, 53–54.

5. WRO, Worcester Consistory Court Papers, 1626–42, bundle 3, item 917. A chancellor was normally a layman and an experienced lawyer with a doctorate in civil law. Ingram, *Church Courts*, pp. 59–60.

6. McGrath, "Bristol and the Civil War," p. 92; Sacks, *Widening Gate*, p. 251.

7. GCL, St. Mary Le Port, Bristol, Parish Register, 1560–1654, p. 71, in Hockaday, "Abstracts," vol. 442. The original parish register was destroyed during an air raid in World War II.

8. Laslett, "Introduction: Comparing Illegitimacy," pp. 14–17.

9. Macfarlane, "Illegitimacy," p. 71 (quoting Kingsley Davis, "Illegitimacy and the Social Structure" [1939, reprinted 1964], p. 21).

10. Brydall, *Lex Spuriorum*, pp. iii, 15–16, 18.

11. I have averaged three scholars' estimates: Main, *Tobacco Colony*, p. 10 (113,400); Menard, "British Migration," p. 105 (108,400); Gemery, "Emigration," p. 216 (114,000).

12. Galenson, *White Servitude*, p. 217 (34,122); Menard, "British Migration," p. 105 (34,900). In addition, around 3,100 blacks, most of whom were enslaved, went to the Chesapeake from Africa and the Caribbean in the 1650s and 1660s. Galenson, *White Servitude*, p. 217.

13. Horn, *Adapting to a New World*, p. 25.

14. Galenson, *White Servitude*, pp. 220–25; Horn, *Adapting to a New World*, pp. 32–44; Horn, "Servant Emigration," pp. 66–69; Horn, "Tobacco Colonies," pp. 176–78; Souden, "'Rogues, Whores and Vagabonds,'" pp. 29, 31; Fischer, "*Albion* and the Critics," pp. 280–81; Salerno, "Social Background," pp. 35, 41–43. For a spirited debate over emigrants' social origins, see Campbell, "Social Origins," pp. 63–89; Galenson, "'Middling People,'" pp. 499–524; "Mildred Campbell's Response," pp. 525–40;

Galenson, "Rejoinder," pp. 264–77; "Mildred Campbell Replies," pp. 277–86.

15. Bullock, *Virginia Impartially Examined,* p. 54.

16. Acc-Nor Rec, 1640–45, pp. 6, 185–86; Nor DWO, 1645–51, p. 168.

17. See Menard, "Population, Economy, and Society," p. 71; Menard, "British Migration," pp. 102–5; Morgan, *American Slavery,* pp. 181, 404; Walsh, "Servitude and Opportunity," pp. 116, 130; Anderson and Thomas, "Growth of Population," pp. 298–99; Menard, "Growth of Population," p. 403; Carr and Menard, "Immigration and Opportunity," pp. 208–9; Rutman and Rutman, *Place in Time,* p. 258 nn. 15, 16; Menard, "Immigrants and Their Increase," p. 100; Rutman and Rutman, "'Now-Wives and Sons-in-Law,'" p. 178; Walsh and Menard, "Death in the Chesapeake," p. 214; Rutman and Rutman, "Of Agues and Fevers," p. 52.

18. Walsh, "'Till Death Us Do Part,'" pp. 127–28; Carr and Walsh, "Planter's Wife," pp. 552–53; Menard, "Population, Economy, and Society," pp. 72–73; Menard, "Immigrants and Their Increase," pp. 98–102; Main, *Tobacco Colony,* p. 15; Horn, "Tobacco Colonies," pp. 182–83.

19. This practice was especially common among mariners sailing to Virginia. Souden, "'Rogues, Whores, and Vagabonds,'" p. 36.

20. *Bristol Registers, 1654–1686,* pp. 35, 79, 90, 114, 148, 166, 178, 194, 195, 207, 212, 213, 223, 224; Coldham, *Complete Book of Emigrants, 1607–1660,* pp. 334, 409, 439; Coldham, *Complete Book of Emigrants, 1661–1699,* pp. 5, 23, 33, 51, 52, 73, 83, 98.

21. Three-quarters of the registrations for Chesapeake-bound servants occurred in July through October, with August being the peak month. Galenson, *White Servitude,* pp. 87–88.

22. BRO, Register of Servants to Foreign Plantations, p. 508. The Register lists Anne's surname as "Horwood."

23. See Menard, "Tobacco Industry," p. 156; Gladwin, "Tobacco and Sex," pp. 57–72.

24. See Pagan, "Growth of the Tobacco Trade," pp. 248–62.

25. See Pagan, "Dutch Maritime and Commercial Activity," pp. 485–501; Menard, "Tobacco Industry," pp. 123–24, 157–59; Menard, "Farm Prices," pp. 80–85; Menard, "Note on Chesapeake Tobacco Prices," pp. 401–10.

26. *Acts and Ordinances of the Interregnum,* ii. 425–29, 559–62; 12 Car. II, c. 18 (1660); 15 Car. II, c. 7 (1663); see McCusker, "British Mercantilist Policies," pp. 344–55.

27. See McCusker and Menard, *Economy of British America,* pp. 120–26; Clemens, *Atlantic Economy,* pp. 30–35, 52; Menard, "Economic and Social Development," pp. 261–63.

28. The farm price of Chesapeake oronoco tobacco slid from 2.4 pence per pound in 1657 to 1.9 pence in 1658, 1.65 pence in 1659, and 1.5 pence in 1660 and 1661, then rose to 1.6 pence in 1662, followed by a sharp decline from 1.55 pence in 1663 to 1.35 pence in 1664, 1.1 pence in 1665, and 0.9 pence in 1666. Menard, "Tobacco Industry," pp. 158–59.

29. Hammond, *Leah and Rachel,* p. 12.

30. Carr and Walsh, "Planter's Wife," p. 547; Carr and Walsh, "Economic Diversification," pp. 151, 161; Main, *Tobacco Colony,* pp. 108–9.

31. Steele, *English Atlantic,* pp. 10, 41–51; Canny, "Origins of Empire," pp. 27–28.

32. Cressy, *Coming Over,* pp. 146, 162, 168–71.

33. Duffy, "Passage to the Colonies," pp. 22–23.

34. Deal, *Race and Class,* p. 3; Ames, *Studies,* p. 4; Perry, *Formation of a Society,* pp. 15 n. 9, 16, 31–35.

35. For a detailed analysis of the Eastern Shore's population growth in the seventeenth century, see Pagan, "Law and Society," pp. 416–34.

36. *Statutes at Large,* i. 224, 249; Ames, *Calendar,* p. 4. The two Eastern Shore counties were formally reunited in 1670 under the name "Northampton," but they continued to function as separate administrative units. The Assembly divided them again, this time permanently, in 1673. See Ames, "Reunion of Two Virginia Counties," pp. 536–48.

37. Nor DW, 1657–66, p. 156; Nor O, 1657–64, f. 149.

38. Nor O, 1657–64, p. 153; Nugent, *Cavaliers and Pioneers,* ii. 9. Her name is recorded as "Anne Norgood" on the headright certificate.

39. Nor OW, 1674–79, p. 136.

40. Morgan, *American Slavery,* pp. 128–29.

41. Bullock, *Virginia Impartially Examined,* pp. 13–14.

42. The custom of London allowed a master to transfer an apprentice to another master if the guild approved. That practice may have provided a precedent for the assignment of colonial indentured servants. Steinfeld, *Invention of Free Labor,* pp. 46, 220 n. 70. According to Richard B. Morris, however, transfers made under the custom of London usually required the apprentice's consent. Morris, *Government and Labor,* p. 402.

43. Dalton, *Countrey Justice,* pp. 93–94.

44. See Ames, *Lectures,* pp. 212–13; Teeven, *History of the Anglo-American Common Law of Contract,* p. 116; Simpson, *History of the Common Law of Contract,* pp. 459–65.

45. Morris, *Government and Labor,* pp. 402–3, 409–11.

46. Nor DWO, 1645–51, f. 167.

47. Ibid., f. 140.

48. Acc-Nor Rec, 1640–45, p. 260.

49. E.g., ibid., pp. 429, 440; Nor DWO, 1645–51, p. 21, f. 205; Nor DWO, 1655–57, p. 4.

50. Acc-Nor Rec, 1640–45, p. 221.

51. Ibid., p. 235.

52. Nor O, 1657–64, f. 150–p. 152, p. 156.

53. See Galenson, "Settlement and Growth," pp. 153–58.

54. Kussmaul, *Servants in Husbandry,* pp. 32, 148.

Chapter 2

1. NRO, Brinton Parish Register, 1547–1728, f. 3v, baptismal entry for September 2, 1621.

2. William Kendall's great-grandfather Robert Kendall was a Brinton yeoman (a substantial farmer of less than gentry status) as were both of his grandfathers, Richard Kendall Sr. and Robert Pleasance Sr., and his great-uncle William Kendall of Thornage. See Robert Kendall's will (1566), NRO, Norwich Consistory Court Register of Wills, vol. 74, 1566–67, MF 59, pp. 77–78; Richard Kendall Sr.'s burial record (1623), NRO, Brinton Parish Register, 1547–1728, f. 23r; Robert Pleasance Sr.'s burial record (1613), f. 23r; will and burial record of William Kendall of Thornage (1613), NRO, Archdeaconry of Norwich Register of Wills, 1612–13, MF/RO 309, p. 341; but see NRO, Thornage Parish Register, 1561–1743, PD 507/1, f. 34r (calling William of Thornage a husbandman or small farmer). One of William's uncles, William Kendall of Brinton, was a husbandman, as was his eldest son, Richard. See will of William Kendall of Brinton (1638), NRO, Archdeaconry of Norwich Register of Wills, 1638–39, MF/RO 326, p. 8-f. 9; will of Richard Kendall (1696), NRO, Norwich Consistory Court Register of Wills, vol. 143, 1694–98, MF 426, pp. 315–18; but see NRO, Brinton Parish Register, f. 23v (calling William of Brinton a yeoman). For a discussion of the social categories of yeoman and husbandman, see Sharpe, *Early Modern England,* pp. 199–202. William's uncle Christopher Kendall was a blacksmith, and his uncle Nicholas Kendall was a carpenter. William's brother Philip was a blacksmith, and another brother, John, was a laborer. See will of Christopher Kendall (1632), NRO, Archdeaconry of Norwich Register of Wills, 1632–34, MF/RO 318, f. 46- p. 47; NRO, Brinton Parish Register, f. 23v; will of John Kendall (1665), NRO, Archdeaconry of Norwich Register of Wills, 1664–65, MF/RO 330, p. 224; *Norfolk and Norwich Hearth Tax Assessment, Lady Day 1666,* p. 45.

3. Ruth's first husband was Thomas Larrington, who died in 1643. NRO, Great Yarmouth Parish Register, 1558–1653, PD 28/1, burial entry

for April 19, 1643; "Norwich Consistory Administrations, 1588–1646," ch. 1634–46, pp. 16, 19. For the marriage of Ruth and Kendall, see NRO, Bradwell Parish Register of Baptisms 1560–1680, Marriages 1565–1677, and Burials 1556–1680, PD 581/1, marriage entry for February 29,1644. For the death of the Kendalls' child, see Great Yarmouth Parish Register, burial entry for August 16, 1647.

4. See will of William's aunt Marian Kendall (1648), NRO, Archdeaconry of Norwich Register of Wills, 1648–52, MF/RO 301/4, f. 98.

5. Horn, *Adapting to a New World,* p. 36.

6. Nor DWO, 1651–54, f. 15, p. 48, f. 79; Nor DWO, 1645–51, p. 240.

7. Perry, *Formation of a Society,* pp. 93, 116; Whitelaw, *Virginia's Eastern Shore,* i. 188; Nugent, *Cavaliers and Pioneers,* i. 46, 117; Meyer and Dorman, *Adventurers of Purse and Person,* p. 69; Acc-Nor Rec, 1632–40, pp. 27, 130; Acc-Nor Rec, 1640–45, pp. 451, 452; Nor DWO, 1645–51, f. 70, p. 98.

8. Acc-Nor Rec, 1632–40, p. 44.

9. Acc-Nor Rec, 1632–40, pp. 67, 127; Acc-Nor Rec, 1640–45, p. 267; Nor DWO, 1645–51, f. 179.

10. Nor DWO, 1651–54, p. 13, ff. 18–19; Nor DWO, 1654–55, p. 21.

11. Nor DWO, 1645–51, f. 239, p. 240; Nor DWO, 1651–54, f. 93.

12. Perry, *Formation of a Society,* p. 154; Nor DWO, 1651–54, p.-f. 93.

13. Nor DWO, 1651–54, p. 145, ff. 147, 171, 186; Nor DWO, 1654–55, ff. 30, 33, f. 36–p. 37, f. 55, pp. 56, 73, ff. 82, 93; Nor DWO, 1655–57, pp. 2–3, f. 12.

14. Nor DWO, 1654–55, p. 21.

15. Nor DWO, 1651–54, f. 197; Nor DWO, 1654–55, f. 24, f. 36–p. 37.

16. Nor DWO, 1655–57, pp. 2–3, f. 12.

17. Acc-Nor Rec, 1632–40, p. 27; Nor DWO, 1654–55, f. 143.

18. Nor DWO, 1654–55, f. 129; Nor O, 1655–56, p. 26; Nor DWO, 1655–57, ff. 51, 56, 59; Nor DW, 1657–66, pp. 33, 81–82; Coldham, *English Adventurers and Emigrants,* pp. 169–70 (abstracts of High Court of Admiralty examinations).

19. Nor DWO, 1654–55, pp. 75, 82, f. 129; Nor DWO, 1655–57, f. 21, pp. 22, 27, ff. 37, 40, 53, p. 66.

20. Nor O, 1657–64, p. 127; Nor DWO, 1654–55, ff. 46, 98, p. 111, f. 119, p.-f. 127, pp. 128, 129, 139, 145; Nor O, 1655–56, f. 9, pp. 12, 17, f. 17; Nor DWO, 1655–57, f. 68; Nor OW, 1683–89, p. 193.

21. *Statutes at Large,* i. 431; Leonard, *General Assembly,* pp. 34, 39, 46–48.

22. Nor O, 1657–64, f. 12; *Statutes at Large,* i. 431, 502. Kendall became a colonel in 1671. Nor O, 1664–74, f. 109.

23. See Heal and Holmes, *Gentry,* p. 172, and Wyatt-Brown, *Southern*

Honor, p. 354 (discussing symbolic importance of military titles); Shea, *Virginia Militia,* p. 16 (tracing Virginians' fascination with military rank to the military regime imposed by the Virginia Company in the 1610s).

24. Nor DWO, 1655–57, p. 67–f. 68; Nugent, *Cavaliers and Pioneers,* i. 434; Nor D, 1668–80, f. 5.

25. Nor O, 1657–64, p. 192; Nor O, 1664–74, ff. 7, 90; Nor D, 1668–80, ff. 14, 19, p.-f. 20, ff. 23, 36, 38a–39, 40–40a, 43a, pp. 83, 104, 165, 178, 185, 189; Acc OW, 1671–73, p. 114; Nor DW, 1680–92, pp. 8–10, 20–21, 56–58, 96–98, 100, 118–20, 125; Nor OW, 1683–89, pp. 144, 224–32; Nugent, *Cavaliers and Pioneers,* i. 434–35, 507, 533, 551, 553; ii. 3, 9, 48, 66, 80–81, 97, 105, 112, 117, 134–35, 147, 156, 173–74, 183, 192, 259, 295, 296, 322, 332; Whitelaw, *Virginia's Eastern Shore,* i. 64, 149, 151–52, 188, 200, 323, 339, 384–85, 460, 492, 581, 588, 605; ii. 1259; *Minutes of the Council,* pp. 207, 348, 431.

26. Nor DWO, 1655–57, p. 72; Nor DW, 1657–66, pp. 27, 31, 35; Nor O, 1657–64, p. 27, f. 33; Nor DW, 1666–68, p. 5a; Meyer and Dorman, *Adventurers of Purse and Person,* pp. 366–67 n. 2.

27. Meyer and Dorman, *Adventurers of Purse and Person,* p. 695; Nor DW, 1666–68, p. 12a (earliest reference to William II, 1667); Nor OW, 1683–89, pp. 214–16 (JP commission implying that William II was at least 21 in April 1686).

28. John's father was Colonel Kendall's brother Thomas Kendall of Taverham. Nor OW, 1683–89, p. 225; *Norfolk Hearth Tax Assessment Michaelmas 1664,* p.101; *Norfolk and Norwich Hearth Tax Assessment Lady Day 1666,* p. 61. Gaps in the Taverham parish register and other ecclesiastical records prevent us from determining John Kendall's exact date of birth. See *Parish Registers of Norfolk: Taverham 1601–1837,* p. 1.

29. Nor O, 1657–64, f. 138, pp. 176, 198; Nor O, 1664–74, p. 15; Pagan, "Law and Society," pp. 424–26. For an interesting account of the transaction in which Kendall's slave William Harman bought his freedom, see Breen and Innes, *"Myne Owne Ground,"* pp. 76–77.

30. See Sommerville, *Politics and Ideology,* pp. 27–28; Fletcher, *Gender, Sex and Subordination,* pp. 204–5, 212–14, 217–21; Wall, *Fierce Communion,* p. 8.

31. See Norton, "Evolution of White Women's Experience," p. 602; Norton, *Founding Mothers and Fathers,* pp. 8, 10–15, 48–49, 295, 297, 324–26, 336–37, 341–42, 401–4; Taylor, *American Colonies,* p. 141.

32. Allestree (1619–81) was a royalist divine who later served as Regius Professor of Divinity at Oxford and as provost of Eton. Cross and Livingstone, *Oxford Dictionary of the Christian Church,* pp. 38, 1478.

33. Wright, *First Gentlemen,* pp. 133, 143, 148, 180, 198, 237–38.

34. Allestree, *Whole Duty,* pp. 326, 170, 171; see also 38, 298–99 (on fathers' supervisory duties).

35. *Constitutions and Canons Ecclesiasticall* (1604) canon 109.

36. *Statutes at Large,* ii. 52. The oath taken by Eastern Shore church-wardens required them to present people for a variety of "gross misdemeanours," including "common Sweareing and Drunkennesse, Adultery and Whoredom and Fornication, prophaninge Gods holy name and Sabboth, abuseinge and absentinge from Gods word and alsoe malitious backbiteing and slandering." Nor O, 1664–74, unnumbered leaves in front of volume.

37. Nor O, 1657–64, p.-f. 170, f. 179.

38. *Statutes at Large,* i. 433. The law barring testimony by adulterers and fornicators was originally enacted in 1652. "Some Acts," ed. Billings, p. 32. It was repealed in 1662 and never revived. *Statutes at Large,* ii. 43.

39. Landau, *Justices of the Peace,* p. 337.

40. Bishopp arrived on the Eastern Shore sometime between June and November 1663. Nor O, 1657–64, f. 175–p. 176, pp. 196, 198.

41. Ibid., p. 198. In 1664, the first year that Bishopp paid taxes, he had three tithables (including himself) compared to an average of 2.9 for all Northampton taxpayers and 3.3 for Accomack taxpayers. Pagan, "Law and Society," table 8, p. 189.

42. Nor OW, 1674–79, pp. 51–52.

43. Nor OW, 1683–89, pp. 224–32; Nor OW, 1689–98, pp. 499–505.

44. Nor O, 1664–74, f. 37, pp. 50, 67, 93, ff. 106, 265. On the social status of constables, see Kent, *English Village Constable,* chap. 4.

45. Nor O, 1657–64, f. 183.

46. Ibid., f. 196.

Chapter 3

1. Vaughan and Vaughan, *Shakespeare's Caliban,* pp. 38–42. See also Strachey, "True Reportory," pp. 6–16; Culliford, *William Strachey,* pp. 105–7; Craven, *Southern Colonies in the Seventeenth Century,* pp. 93–98.

2. Smith, *Generall Historie,* p. 154; see also pp. 149, 176–77, 181; *Records of Virginia Company,* iii. 571; Meyer and Dorman, *Adventurers of Purse and Person,* pp. 59–60, 651.

3. Nugent, *Cavaliers and Pioneers,* i. 4, 12, 39; *Minutes of the Council,* pp. 22, 62, 87, 89, 95, 106, 129, 130, 134, 159, 173, 183, 186, 187, 193; Meyer and Dorman, *Adventurers of Purse and Person,* pp. 59–60; Smith, *Generall Historie,* p. 149; *Statutes at Large,* i. 125, 131–33; *Journals of the House of Burgesses, 1619–1658/59,* pp. 44, 51; Leonard, *General Assembly,* pp. 6, 7.

4. PRO, Prerogative Court of Canterbury Probate Papers, series 11, PROB 11/158, f. 135–p. 136 (will of Edward Waters).

5. Meyer and Dorman, *Adventurers of Purse and Person,* pp. 461–62;

Billings, "English Legal Literature," p. 406 n. 9; *Minutes of the Council,* pp. 159, 504; Acc-Nor Rec, 1632–40, pp. 1, 18, 20, 22; Nor DWO, 1645–51, p. 62; Nor DWO, 1651–54, f. 59, p. 81; Nor O, 1655–56, f. 25; Nor O, 1657–64, f. 81, p. 122; Nor DW, 1657–66, p. 130; Leonard, *General Assembly,* pp. xxi, 9, 18, 20, 22, 29, 30.

6. Nugent, *Cavaliers and Pioneers,* i. 84, 152, 224–25, 401, 554; Whitelaw, *Virginia's Eastern Shore,* i. 176, 178, 180, 187, 204; Acc-Nor Rec, 1640–45, pp. 14, 39–40, 54–55, 204–5, 241–42, 321–22, 406, 436; *Statutes at Large,* i. 230–36.

7. Acc-Nor Rec, 1640–45, pp. 281–82.

8. In August 1642, for example, the Accomack-Northampton County Court referred to him as "William Waters gentleman Sonn and heyre to Lieutenant Edward Waters deceased" and granted his request to renew his father's 1,000-acre headright certificate for transporting 20 people to the colony. Ibid., p. 198; see also Nor DWO, 1645–51, f. 71.

9. Acc-Nor Rec, 1640–45, pp. 322, 432–33, 436, 440; Nor DWO, 1645–51, f. 14, p. 29, f. 30, p. 36; Perry, *Formation of a Society,* p. 157.

10. Nor DWO, 1645–51, p. 71, 100; Nor DWO, 1651–54, p.-f. 31, f. 37–p. 38, Nor DWO 1654–55, p. 106, f. 115; Nor O, 1655–56, p. 8, f. 17; Nor O, 1657–64, pp. 4, 109, 114, 129, 172, f. 206; Nor DW, 1657–66, pp. 22, 76; Acc DWO, 1663–66, f. 121; Nor O, 1664–74, f. 70; Nugent, *Cavaliers and Pioneers,* i. 260, 417–18, 517, ii. 24, 45, 73, 97, 108; Whitelaw, *Virginia's Eastern Shore,* i. 129, 145–47, 657, ii. 947, 1050, 1333.

11. Nor DWO, 1645–51, f. 7, p. 9, ff. 14, 29, p. 29, f. 30, pp. 31, 36, 49, 54, ff. 59, 68, pp. 100, 114, f. 137, pp. 159, 165, 187; Nor DWO, 1651–54, ff. 25, 37, pp. 38, 52, f. 70, pp. 85, 91, 104, 108; Nor DWO, 1654–55, p. 19; Nor O, 1655–56, f. 17; Nor DWO, 1655–57, f. 62, p. 78; Nor O, 1657–64, ff. 3, 16, pp. 31, 45, 93, ff. 106, 119, 131, 139, pp. 149, 155, 169.

12. Nor DWO, 1645–51, ff. 60, 63, pp. 145, 159, f. 208; Nor DWO, 1654–55, p. 125, f. 145; Nor DWO, 1655–57, p. 27; Nor O, 1657–64, f. 4, p. 49, ff. 113, 153.

13. Nor DWO, 1645–51, ff. 220–21, p. 223, f. 224, p.-f. 227, p. 228, f. 229, p. 236; Nor DWO, 1651–54, pp. 6, 38, f. 56, p. 57, f. 59, p. 61, ff. 70, 107, p.-f. 155, p. 194; Nor DWO, 1654–55, f. 57, pp. 112, 113, ff. 115, 129; Nor O, 1655–56, f. 13; Nor DWO, 1655–57, ff. 6, 16–18, pp. 19, 28, 29, 33; Nor O, 1657–64, pp. 10, 39, 92, 108, f. 115–p. 116, pp. 135, 139.

14. Waters rose to lieutenant colonel in 1663 and retained that rank the rest of his life. Nor DWO, 1651–54, pp. 52, 57; Nor DWO, 1654–55, ff. 60, 98, 105; Nor O, 1657–64, f. 171, p. 172, f. 181; Nor OW, 1683–89, p. 442.

15. Nor DWO, 1645–51, f. 192 (1649 proclamation); *Statutes at Large,* i. 363–68 (Engagement); Nor DWO, 1651–54, f. 188 (1652 surrender).

16. Ames, *Studies,* pp. 5, 198; Ames introductions to Acc-Nor Rec, 1632–40, p. xxvii, and Acc-Nor Rec, 1640–45, p. xii. On Bennett, see Butterfield, "Puritans and Religious Strife," pp. 8, 10, 32; *Dictionary of Virginia Biography,* i. 445–47; Brenner, *Merchants and Revolution,* pp. 143, 595–96.

17. Nor DWO, 1651–54, f. 63, p. 66, f. 220; Nor DWO, 1654–55, p. 1, f. 3.

18. Nor DWO, 1651–54, f. 63.

19. For analyses of the Protest, see Perry, *Formation of a Society,* pp. 214–15; and Haight, "Northampton Protest," pp. 364–75.

20. Nor DWO, 1651–54, pp. 66–68.

21. Ibid., f. 67.

22. Ibid., p. 68; *Statutes at Large,* i. 371; "Some Acts," ed. Billings, p. 27.

23. Nor DWO, 1651–54, p.-f. 117; Nor DWO, 1654–55, f. 4; Nor OW, 1683–89, p. 148; Leonard, *General Assembly,* pp. 32, 36, 39, 46. For examples of the broad scope of the Assembly's work, see, e.g., *Statutes at Large,* i. 391, 410, 413; *Journals of the House of Burgesses, 1619–1658/59,* p. 96.

24. For Charles II's commission to Berkeley, July 31, 1660, see PRO, C. 66/2941, transcribed in *Papers of Sir William Berkeley,* pp. 282–86.

25. "Some Acts," ed. Kukla, pp. 87, 90, 91.

26. See Bliss, *Revolution and Empire,* p. 4.

27. *Statutes at Large,* ii. 24, 25.

28. See, e.g., Nor OW, 1689–98, pp. 266–67.

29. *Lawes of Virginia,* p. 1; see also *Statutes at Large,* ii. 42.

30. Ibid., p. 2; see also *Statutes at Large,* ii. 43.

31. *Statutes at Large,* ii. 74.

32. Ibid., ii. 89, 113.

33. Ibid., ii. 48.

34. *Lawes of Virginia,* p. 2; see also *Statutes at Large,* ii. 43.

35. *Statutes at Large,* ii. 51, 114, 111, 75.

36. See *Records of Virginia Company,* iii. 484; Billings, *Old Dominion,* pp. 51–52.

37. See, e.g., *Statutes at Large,* i. 167, 172, 193–94, 237, 336–37.

38. Nor O, 1657–64, p. 196.

39. See Acc DWO, 1663–66, f. 94, p. 100; *Minutes of the Council,* p. 248; Acc WDO, 1678–82, pp. 330–31; Acc WO, 1682–97, pp. 2a, 30. Many masters voluntarily undertook to hold the parish harmless from their servants' bastards, however. See, e.g., Acc O, 1676–78, pp. 78, 79, 88; Acc WDO, 1678–82, p. 31; Nor O, 1678–83, pp. 35, 97, 108; Nor OW, 1683–89, pp. 76–77, 81. Such an undertaking was often the quid pro quo for a contract or order binding the illegitimate child to serve his mother's master until adulthood. See, e.g., Nor OW, 1683–89, p. 111.

40. Nor O, 1657–64, f. 195, p. 196.

41. Female servants' indentures were worth, on average, about 35 pounds of tobacco for every month of remaining service. See Nor DWO, 1654–55, f. 110 (33 pounds per month in 1656); Nor O, 1657–64, f. 128 (33 pounds per month in 1661); f. 150–p. 152 (42 pounds per month in 1662); Acc DW, 1664–71, f. 28 (27 pounds per month in 1665); f. 41 (33 pounds per month in 1666); ibid., f. 44 (39 pounds per month in 1666). Male servants usually cost more than females. See, e.g., Acc DW, 1664–71, f. 44 (1666 inventory valuing four male servants at 60, 67, 78, and 83 pounds per month, respectively); Bruce, *Economic History,* ii. 51–52.

42. Sheppard, *Whole Office,* p. 125. For cases holding that a master had no right to discharge a servant who got pregnant while in his service, see *Warwick County Records,* ii. 55–56; *Calendar to the Sessions Books of the County of Hertford,* p. 441.

Chapter 4

1. Acc-Nor Rec, 1632–40, pp. 102, 132–33, 145, 147, 155; Acc-Nor Rec, 1640–45, pp. 86, 95, 122, 326, 352; Nor DWO, 1645–51, ff. 177, 230; Nor O, 1655–56, f. 4; Nor DWO, 1655–57, f. 68; Nor OW, 1674–79, p. 239.

2. Acc-Nor Rec, 1640–45, p. 36.

3. Nor DWO, 1651–54, ff. 139, 178, p. 201.

4. Acc-Nor Rec, 1640–45, pp. 62–63, 117.

5. Ibid., p. 257.

6. Ibid., p. 258.

7. Nor O, 1657–64, p. 168; Nor OW, 1689–98, p. 11.

8. Nor DWO, 1645–51, p. 36, f. 38, pp. 105, 142, 172, 177, 178. ff. 178, 187, pp. 214–15; Nor DWO, 1651–54, p. 59, f. 71, p. 216, addendum p. 2; Nor DWO, 1654–55, ff. 41, 49, 58, pp. 120, 127; Nor DWO, 1655–57, p.-f. 16, f. 42; Nor O, 1657–64, p. 90, f. 107, p. 117; Nor O, 1664–74, f. 2, p. 110; Nor O, 1678–83, p. 284; Nugent, *Cavaliers and Pioneers,* i. 418, ii. 9, 112, 116; Whitelaw, *Virginia's Eastern Shore,* i. 229, 237, 366, 593, 595, ii. 1235–36, 1249.

9. Acc-Nor Rec, 1640–45, pp. 21, 380, 387, 419; Nor DWO, 1645–51, p. 13, f./55, pp. 72, 91, f. 134; Nor DWO, 1654–55, p, 80, f. 113; Nor O, 1657–64, p./3, f. 36; Nor OW, 1674–79, f. 332; Nor O, 1678–83, f. 223; *Minutes of the Council,* p. 373.

10. Nor DWO, 1645–51, f. 179, p. 208; Nor DWO, 1651–54, p.-f. 117, f. 188; Nor DWO, 1654–55, f. 136; Nor O, 1657–64, pp. 80, 126, ff. 165, 168; Nor O, 1664–74, p. 37, p.-f. 65, p. 105, f. 125; *Minutes of the Council,* p. 241; Nor OW, 1683–89, pp. 177, 214–16.

11. Leonard, *General Assembly,* pp. 35, 36, 39; Nor DWO, 1651–54, ff. 47, 51; Nor O, 1657–64, f. 12, p. 164.

12. Nor O, 1657–64, p. 108; Nor DW, 1657–66, p. 92.

13. Nor O, 1657–64, f. 159; Nugent, *Cavaliers and Pioneers,* ii. 66; Whitelaw, *Virginia's Eastern Shore,* i. 385.

14. Nor O, 1657–64, ff. 89, 192,195; Nor O, 1664–74, f. 147; Whitelaw, *Virginia's Eastern Shore,* i. 402.

15. Nor O, 1657–64, f. 171.

16. Nor OW, 1674–79, pp. 13–14.

17. Ibid., pp. 301, 307–8, 323.

18. Nor DW, 1680–92, p. 1.

19. Nor O, 1678–83, p. 286. Spencer died in 1688. Nor DW, 1680–92, p. 188.

20. Nor DWO, 1645–51, p. 184; Nor DWO, 1651–54, p. 95.

21. Nor DWO, 1645–51, pp. 91, 188, 200, p.-f. 201, f. 208, p. 219; Nor DWO, 1651–54, ff. 93–95, 121–22, 165, p.-f. 195, f. 202; Nor DWO, 1654–55, f. 127; Nor DWO, 1655–57, f. 51, p. 60, f. 65; Nor O, 1657–64, pp. 45, 50, 87, 92; Nor DW, 1657–66, pp. 175–76. In addition to representing Eastern Shoremen and traders from Amsterdam, Graft, and Manhattan, Michael acted as the attorney for colonial English merchants such as Daniel Sellicke of Boston. Nor DWO, 1651–54, p.-f. 165; Nor DWO, 1654–55, f. 55; Nor DWO, 1655–57, f. 62.

22. Nor DWO, 1651–54, f. 163.

23. Ibid., f. 146, p. 171; Nor DWO, 1654–55, f. 122.

24. Nor DWO, 1651–54, f. 146, pp. 147, 165, f. 175, p.-f. 195; Nor DWO, 1654–55, f. 3; Nor O, 1655–56, p. 6; Nor DWO, 1655–57, p. 62, f. 64; Nor O, 1657–64, f. 75, p. 89, f. 138, p. 176, f. 198, p. 206; Nor O, 1664–74, pp. 15, 42, ff. 54, 114, p. 273; "List of Tithables," pp. 259–60; Nor OW, 1674–79, pp. 75, 149, 190; Nugent, *Cavaliers and Pioneers,* i. 405–6, 482, 551; Whitelaw, *Virginia's Eastern Shore,* i. 117, 133, 148, ii. 591, 1055, 1268, 1334.

25. Nor O, 1657–64, p.-f. 133; Nor DWO, 1645–51, p. 145.

26. Nor O, 1657–64, p.-f. 177, ff. 168, 184, pp. 189, 190; Nor OW, 1674–79, pp. 323, 324. On the naturalization requirement, see Holdsworth, *History of English Law,* ix. 76–77, 89.

27. Lynch, *Custis Chronicles,* pp. 38–47, 157–58, 160–61, 178, 188; Meyer and Dorman, *Adventurers of Purse and Person,* pp. 544–45.

28. Nor DWO, 1651–54, p. 107, ff. 202, 214; Nor DWO, 1654–55, f. 15; Nor DWO, 1655–57, p. 45, f. 59; Nor O, 1657–64, f. 4, p.-f. 6, ff. 10, 14, p. 55.

29. *Minutes of the Council,* p. 584.

30. Nor DWO, 1651–54, ff. 8, 89; Nor DWO, 1654–55, p. 5; Nor

DWO, 1655–57, f. 26, p. 43; Nor O, 1657–64, p. 4, ff. 7, 160; Nor O, 1664–74, p. 82, f. 225; Acc OW, 1671–73, pp. 26, 55; Nugent, *Cavaliers and Pioneers,* i. 251, 346, 353, 419, 434; ii. 69, 207, 230, 237, 242–43, 268, 333, 353, 364.

31. Luccketti, *Archaeology,* pp. 9–10. The other outstanding house was Sir William Berkeley's mansion, Green Spring, near Jamestown.

32. Nor OW, 1683–89, p. 379.

33. Nor DWO, 1651–54, ff. 96, 215, p. 216, p.-f. 221; Nor DWO, 1654–55, f. 39, p. 54, f. 104, p. 113, p.-f. 127; Nor O, 1655–56, f. 17; Nor DWO, 1655–57, p. 49, f. 62; Nor O, 1657–64, pp. 3, 33, 45, f. 56. The post of appraiser offered a useful vantage point from which to scout for wealthy widows. Within six months of his appointment as appraiser of Major Peter Walker's estate, Custis had married Walker's widow, Alicia. Nor DWO, 1654–55, ff. 109–11, 126; Nor DWO, 1655–57, p. 40.

34. *Journals of the House of Burgesses, 1619–1658/59,* p. 112; Nor DW, 1657–66, p. 7.

35. Nor O, 1657–64, f. 43, p. 45, f. 65, p. 70; Nor O, 1664–74, ff. 3, 22; Nor OW, 1674–79, p. 173; Nor OW, 1689–98, pp. 177–78; *Executive Journals,* i. 222–23; Lynch, *Custis Chronicles,* pp. 157–58. Custis's other offices included coroner (1673), burgess (1677), and customs collector (1687–92). Nor OW, 1674–79, p. 66; *Journals of the House of Burgesses, 1659/60 — 1693,* p. vii; Nor OW, 1683–89, p. 279; *Executive Journals,* i. 223. He played a prominent role in the militia, ending his military career as commander-in-chief of all forces on the Eastern Shore. During Bacon's Rebellion, he held the rank of major general in Governor Berkeley's army. *Executive Journals,* i. 263; Washburn, *Governor and the Rebel,* p. 70.

36. Meyer and Dorman, *Adventurers of Purse and Person,* p. 75; Hotten, *Original Lists,* p. 187; Acc-Nor Rec 1632–40, pp. 7–8; Nor DWO, 1651–54, f. 2; Nor DWO, 1654–55, ff. 133, 135; Nor O, 1655–56, pp. 10, 19.

37. Nor DW, 1657–66, p. 156; Nor DWO, 1654–55, f. 52, pp. 79, 103; Nor DWO, 1655–57, f. 14.

38. Nor DWO, 1651–54, f. 190; Nor O, 1664–74, p. 211; Nugent, *Cavaliers and Pioneers,* i. 483. For Andrews's other land transactions, see Nor DWO, 1655–57, f. 71; Nugent, *Cavaliers and Pioneers,* i. 532, 533, 534, 539, ii. 344; Whitelaw, *Virginia's Eastern Shore,* i. 141, 199, 203.

39. Nor DWO, 1654–55, p. 90; Nor O, 1664–74, f. 22, p. 37, f. 176, pp. 202, 212.

40. Nor DWO, 1655–57, f. 18; Nor O, 1657–64, pp. 44, 172; Leonard, *General Assembly,* p. 39.

41. Dorothy was the daughter of Obedience Robins and Grace Waters

Robins, Waters's mother. Andrews married Dorothy around 1662. Nor DWO, 1654–55, p. 47; Nor DW, 1657–66, p. 156; Meyer and Dorman, *Adventurers of Purse and Person,* pp. 76, 271, 463. Dorothy was close to her "Loving Brother" Waters, who acted as her attorney in real estate transactions. Nor DW, 1657–66, p. 233. Andrews and Waters likewise enjoyed a trusting relationship, as reflected in Andrews's designation of Waters as an overseer of his will. Nor O, 1664–74, p. 212.

42. See Billings, "Growth of Political Institutions," pp. 224–32; Wheeler, "County Court," pp. 112–21.

43. Hartwell, Blair, and Chilton, *Present State of Virginia,* p. 44.

44. *Statutes at Large,* ii. 63–64.

45. See, e.g., Nor O, 1657–64, ff. 62–65, 81, 123, p. 124; Acc O, 1666–70, pp. 94, 96, 99–106, 108–12, 114–15, 123–24, 130–31, 137–38, 176; Acc WDO, 1678–82, pp. 159–68, 218, 233–36, 254–57.

46. *Statutes at Large,* ii. 66.

47. Ibid., ii. 72. Single justices adjudicated civil cases below the minimum.

48. Ibid., ii. 65–66. The Assembly repealed this statute in 1677, putting residents of Accomack and Northampton Counties on an equal footing with all other colonists; ii. 397. See also ii. 362, 380 (short-lived appeals act, passed during Bacon's Rebellion).

49. See ibid., ii. 70. In the 1660s, the Northampton County Court held about 9.5 sessions per year, sitting an average of 11.7 days a year. Pagan, "Law and Society," table 2, p. 45.

50. For examples, see Northampton justices to Berkeley, September 28, 1673, and Berkeley's reply, October 25, 1673, Nor O, 1664–74, p. 229; and Accomack justices to Berkeley, December 16, 1673, and Berkeley's reply, January 1674, Acc WDO, 1673–76, f. 19.

51. Nor DWO, 1654–55, f. 136; Nor DWO, 1655–57, p. 69.

52. *Statutes at Large,* ii. 21, 69–70; "Some Acts," ed. Kukla, p. 96.

53. Pagan, "Law and Society," table 4, p. 53 and table 7, p. 74.

54. *Statutes at Large,* ii. 246 (requiring purchase of Dalton, *Countrey Justice;* Dalton, *Officium Vicecomitus;* and Swinburne, *Briefe Treatise of Testaments*).

55. See Acc O, 1666–70, pp. 178–80 (citing Dalton, *Countrey Justice,* and Wingate, *Exact Abridgment*); Acc O, 1697–1703 (citing *Countrey Justice*); Nor OW, 1683–89, p. 54 (inventory listing Malynes, *Consuetudo vel Lex Mercatoria* and Noy, *Compleat Lawyer*); Acc WD, 1676–90, p. 295 (inventory listing Wingate, *Body of the Common Law,* and *Lawes of Virginia*); Butler, "Thomas Teackle's 333 Books," p. 483 (inventory listing Rastall, *Les Termes de la Ley*). On the influence of English law books, see Billings, "En-

glish Legal Literature," pp. 407–15; Billings, "Justices, Books, Laws, and Courts," pp. 283–88.

56. Webb, *Office and Authority of a Justice of Peace,* p. ix.

57. Hartwell, Blair, and Chilton, *Present State of Virginia,* p. 45. Henry Hartwell, an English-trained Virginia lawyer, and Edward Chilton, barrister of the Middle Temple and former attorney general of the colony, also lambasted the General Court for its procedural informality; see pp. 47–48.

58. Nor O, 1657–64, f. 69.

59. Ibid., f. 67, p. 68.

60. Ibid., p. 68.

61. Ibid., f. 68–p. 69. Robins demanded that the court take action against Warren "for the Honnor of Magestracy and sattisfaction of Justice"; p. 69. Warren later apologized for his drunken misconduct, and the court remitted his fine; f. 72.

62. Ibid., p.-f. 70.

63. Ibid., f. 70, p.-f. 71, p. 76.

64. In September 1660, for example, Robert Bayly was fined 100 pounds "for his Insolency and audacious cariage to the Court," and four other men were fined 50 pounds each for "Drinking and Singing and disturbing the Court." Ibid., f. 76, p. 77. In January 1661, the justices fined William Roberts 100 pounds "for his Irreverent behavior and keeping his Hatt on his head in the Court"; p. 88. Recidivists received harsher punishment. In June and December 1663, Thomas Betts was fined 800 pounds for having repeatedly "demeaned himselfe in Insolent and impudent manner in the face of the Court" while intoxicated; pp. 169, 171, ff. 174, 180, 184, 186.

65. Ibid., p.-f. 83.

66. Ibid., p. 128. Mill apologized and the court released him under a good-behavior bond; f. 132, p. 140.

67. Nor DWO, 1651–54, pp. 141–42.

68. Stringer magnanimously forgave the man in response to Mrs. Grace Robins's request that punishment be suspended. Nor O, 1657–64, p. 24.

69. Ibid., p. 195.

70. Ibid., f. 191.

71. Ibid.

72. See Bailyn, "Politics and Social Structure," p. 100.

73. Nor O, 1657–64, pp. 96–99.

74. *Journals of the House of Burgesses, 1659/60 – 1693,* p. 17; *Statutes at Large,* ii. 157–58.

75. Nor O, 1657–64, p. 99.

Chapter 5

1. See *Statutes at Large,* ii. 81, 145. For the clerk's oath, see Nor O, 1657–64, f. 206.

2. Nor O, 1664–74, f. 150; Ames, *Studies,* p. 237; Nor O, 1657–64, f. 90. On hostility to Quakers, see *Statutes at Large,* ii. 180–83; Bond, *Damned Souls in a Tobacco Colony,* pp. 160–74.

3. Nor O, 1657–64, p. 48; see *Statutes at Large,* i. 305, 448.

4. Nor O, 1657–64, f. 206; Acc DWO, 1663–66, ff. 7–10; Acc O, 1666–70, p. 199.

5. See *Statutes at Large,* ii. 60, 71, 145.

6. E.g., Nor O, 1657–64, f. 194 (trespass, assault, and battery); Nor O, 1664–74, pp. 7, 44 (trespass on the case); p. 56 (trespass to chattels); p. 57 (trespass to land); p. 124 (assault and battery); Nor O, 1678–83, p. 231 (detinue); Acc WDO, 1678–82, p. 241 (trover).

7. See Bryson, *Bryson on Virginia Civil Procedure,* p. 201.

8. See Baker, *Introduction to English Legal History,* pp. 73–75, 374–404.

9. See *Statutes at Large,* ii. 79.

10. Webb, *Office and Authority of a Justice of Peace,* p. 354.

11. See *Statutes at Large,* ii. 79–80; Nor O, 1657–64, f. 144, p.-f. 203; Acc O, 1666–70, pp. 14, 154.

12. See Bryson, *Bryson on Virginia Civil Procedure,* pp. 196–97. The petition served the same function in Virginia practice that the declaration performed in English practice.

13. See *Statutes at Large,* ii. 71, 145; Nor O, 1657–64, f. 149, p. 152, f. 201, p. 204, f. 206; Acc O, 1666–70, ff. 23, 61, pp. 146, 171.

14. See Billings, "Pleading," p. 582. For a discussion of procedural informality in the courts of other colonies, see Hoffer, *Law and People,* pp. 35–38.

15. *Statutes at Large,* i. 486–87.

16. Ibid., ii. 43.

17. Ludwell, "Description," p. 57.

18. Beverley, *History and Present State of Virginia,* p. 255.

19. For a good illustration of the relative simplicity of early pleading on the Eastern Shore, compare the brief defamation petition in *Hacke v. Burwell* (1652), Nor DWO, 1651–54, p. 84, f. 105, with the sample defamation declaration in a contemporary English law book, John Herne, *The Pleader,* pp. 239–40.

20. See Nor OW, 1689–98, pp. 88, 119, 314.

21. Nor O, 1657–64, f. 168 (commission from Governor Berkeley to Northampton justices, June 10, 1663).

22. Acc WDO, 1678–82, p. 237.

23. Acc O, 1703–9, p. 6. A similar ruling appears at p. 6a.

24. Baker, *Introduction to English Legal History,* pp. 410–13.

25. Wood, *Institute,* p. 10.

26. Ibid., pp. 9–10. See also Wingate, *Body of the Common Law* (1655), p. 1 ("The Common Law of England is a Law used time out of minde throughout the Realm. . . . In some Counties, Towns, and other places of the Realm, there be speciall Usages time out of mind, differing from the Common Law, which are called Customs.")

27. The historian Warren Billings has argued that seventeenth-century Virginians did not define "common law" in the same way that English lawyers did — that is, as the set of doctrines developed over time by the royal central courts — but simply as "unwritten law," a concept that for the colonists usually meant local law and custom. Billings, "Transfer of English Law to Virginia," p. 221; see also Friedman, *History of American Law,* p. 35 (the colonists "brought with them the law they knew: and this was primarily local law, local customs").

28. In 1662, for instance, the Assembly substantially changed the common law of defamation by restricting the category of actionable words to accusations of criminal conduct. *Statutes at Large,* ii. 72. The governor had the task of trying to justify such deviations from English law. See, e.g., Berkeley to Council for Foreign Plantations, July 21,1662, PRO, C.O. 1/16, transcribed in *Papers of Sir William Berkeley,* pp. 361–64 (explaining rationale for Virginia statutes "deviating from the Lawes of England" and submitting them for the Council's "approbation, admonishment, amendment or rejection").

29. Berkeley to Council for Foreign Plantations, July 21, 1662, in *Papers of Sir William Berkeley,* p. 360.

30. *Statutes at Large,* ii. 71; Nor O, 1678–83, pp. 18, 172 (demurrer); Nor OW, 1683–89, p. 219 (demurrer); Acc DWO, 1678–82, pp. 237, 244 (demurrer); Acc O, 1690–97, p. 83 (res judicata); Acc O, 1678–82, pp. 247, 270 (limitation period); Nor OW, 1689–98, p. 336 (general issue: not guilty); Nor OW, 1683–89, p. 437 (replication); Nor OW, 1689–98, pp. 508 (replication to demurrer), 517 (rejoinder to replication).

31. Nor O, 1657–64, p. 194.

32. See Ibbetson, *Historical Introduction to the Law of Obligations,* pp. 148, 271–73.

33. Cro. Car. 141, 79 Eng. Rep. 725 (K.B. 1628).

34. See *Holmes v. Hall,* 6 Mod. 161, 87 Eng. Rep. 918 (K.B. 1704); Stoljar, "Doctrine of Failure of Consideration," pp. 55–56; Stoljar, *Law of Quasi-Contract,* p. 225.

35. *Anonymous*, 1 Str. 407, 93 Eng. Rep. 600 (K.B. 1721).

36. Stoljar, "Doctrine of Failure of Consideration," p. 55; Stoljar, *Law of Quasi-Contract*, p. 225. On the origins and evolution of the rule, see Hamilton, "Ancient Maxim Caveat Emptor," pp. 1133–87.

37. Baker, *Introduction to English Legal History*, p. 377; Simpson, *History of the Common Law of Contract*, pp. 536–37.

38. Cro. Jac. 4, 79 Eng. Rep. 3 (Ex. Ch. 1604); Baker and Milsom, *Sources of English Legal History*, pp. 518–23.

39. Cro. Jac. 4, 79 Eng. Rep. at 4.

40. Sheppard, *Faithfull Councellor*, pp. 163–64.

41. Nor O, 1657–64, p. 196.

42. Ames, *Lectures*, p. 138; see also Street, *Foundations of Legal Liability*, i. 379–80. There is some evidence in the early modern period of an emerging doctrine that a seller could be held liable in deceit without an express warranty if he made an affirmation of quality he knew to be false. Teeven, *History of the Anglo-American Common Law of Contract*, p. 137; Holdsworth, *History of English Law*, viii. 68–69; Simpson, *History of the Common Law of Contract*, p. 536. S. F. C. Milsom, however, takes a contrary view. He notes that there are no reported seventeenth-century cases in which a non-warranting seller had to pay damages in a deceit action based solely on his knowledge of the falsity of his statements. Therefore, Milsom concludes, "it is likely that *caveat emptor* continued to stand even against actual fraud." Milsom, *Historical Foundations of the Common Law*, p. 365. Milsom's position is consistent with Sheppard's midcentury summary of sellers' liability, which stressed the prerequisite of an express warranty in all transactions save those involving food and beverages. See also Fitzherbert, *New Natura Brevium*, p. 225 (one who buys without a warranty acts at his peril, "and his eies, and his taste ought to be his judges in that Case").

43. See Ibbetson, *Historical Introduction to the Law of Obligations*, p. 86. On the distinction between dependent and independent contract obligations, see Francis, "Structure of Judicial Administration," pp. 37–38, 56–60, 77–82, 102–9, 123–26.

44. See McGovern, "Dependent Promises," p. 674.

45. Nor O, 1657–64, f. 20, f. 21–p. 22.

46. Ibid., f. 20, p. 46, f. 47.

47. Ibid., f. 129–p. 131.

48. Stringer recused himself from judging his wife's case.

49. Nor O, 1657–64, f. 129–p. 131.

50. Ibid., p.-f. 122.

51. Ibid., f. 122.

52. See Fede, "Legal Protection for Slave Buyers," pp. 322–58.

53. Menard, "From Servants to Slaves," p. 381 (comparing price of slaves to cost of white servants with four or more years to serve).

54. Nor O, 1657–64, ff. 197–98. Michael's percentage may be somewhat exaggerated because his "Sloope men," who probably were white, were omitted from the tithables list containing the names of his servants.

55. Deal, *Race and Class,* p. 173.

56. Allestree, *Whole Duty of Man,* p. 243.

57. Ibid., pp. 244, 249 (italics omitted).

58. Ibid., p. 245 (italics omitted).

59. For examples, see Nor DWO, 1645–51, f. 128–p. 229; Nor O, 1657–64, f. 27; Acc DWO, 1663–66, pp. 24, 25; Acc O, 1666–70, p.-f. 17, pp. 71, 92, 145; Nor O, 1664–74, p. 93; Acc OW, 1671–73, pp. 71, 224.

60. Acc DWO, 1663–66, f. 26–p. 27.

61. Acc O, 1666–70, f. 10.

62. Acc O, 1697–1703, p. 144.

63. Nor O, 1657–64, f. 192. Waters disqualified himself from participating in the issuance of the interrogation order. Kendall appears to have been one of the justices who promulgated it, which implies that as of June 28, 1664, he did not yet know about his nephew John's possible involvement in Anne's pregnancy.

Chapter 6

1. Nor O, 1657–64, f. 192.

2. Acc-Nor Rec, 1640–45, p. 350; Nor O, 1657–64, p. 197. For Matthew Gething's economic and political status, see Acc-Nor Rec, 1632–40, p. 68; Acc-Nor Rec, 1640–45, pp. 22–23, 320; Nor DWO, 1654–55, p. 52; Nor DWO, 1655–57, f. 59; Nor O, 1657–64, ff. 127, 134, 138, 167, p. 176, f. 185, p. 191; "List of Tithables," p. 262; Nor O, 1664–74, ff. 5, 7, 12, p. 24, ff. 37, 45, 50, pp. 55, 57; Whitelaw, *Virginia's Eastern Shore,* i. 76.

3. Cressy, *Birth, Marriage, and Death,* pp. 60–62.

4. Nor O, 1657–64, f. 192.

5. Cressy, *Birth, Marriage, and Death,* p. 67 (quoting 1590 visitation article for diocese of Winchester).

6. English JPs usually interrogated women under oath but had discretion to ground child-support orders on unsworn examinations if they saw fit. Sheppard, *New Survey,* pp. 64, 227.

7. On English midwives' interrogations, see Cressy, *Birth, Marriage, and Death,* pp. 78–79; Marchant, *Church under the Law,* p. 221 n. 1; Houlbrooke, *Church Courts,* p. 77; Ingram, *Church Courts,* p. 263; Hair, *Before*

the Bawdy Court, pp. 132–33, 237; Quaife, *Wanton Wenches,* pp. 105, 212; Wrightson, *English Society,* p. 86.

8. Hunt, "Henry Townshend's 'Notes,'" p. 88.

9. Acc-Nor Rec, 1632–40, p. 129.

10. Acc WDO, 1678–82, p. 239.

11. Nor DWO, 1645–51, p. 225.

12. See, e.g., *Warwick County Records,* iii. 96 (parishioners "barbarously carried" a woman out of the parish when she was "ready to travail of a bastard child"); iii. 153–54 (parish taxpayers "uncivilly and unmercifully" drove away a woman on the threshold of labor).

13. 18 Eliz. I, c. 3, s. 1 (1576). The quotation comes from the version in *Statutes of the Realm,* iv. 610. Section 1, the bastardy provision, was continued in force by several subsequent enactments. See 43 Eliz. I, c. 9, s. 1 (1601); 1 Jac. I, c. 25, s. 1 (1603–04); 21 Jac. I, c. 28 (1623–24); 3 Car. I, c. 5 (1627). Ecclesiastical courts continued to issue support orders for a while after 1576, but by the eighteenth century the JPs' remedy was the sole method of compelling maintenance of bastards. See Helmholz, "Support Orders," pp. 446–47.

14. See Mackey, "Operation of English Old Poor Law," pp. 29–37.

15. Bruce, *Institutional History,* ii. 568; Seiler, "Anglican Parish," p. 137; Seiler, "Anglican Church," pp. 147, 158 n. 66; Acc O, 1676–78, p. 6; Nor OW, 1689–98, p. 12.

16. Carr, Menard, and Walsh, *Robert Cole's World,* pp. 37, 39–41; Menard, "Tobacco Industry," p. 145.

17. In 1664, for example, magistrates paid 20.6 percent of the taxes collected in Northampton County. Pagan, "Law and Society," table 6, p. 68.

18. The Eastern Shore constituted a single parish until 1643, when the Assembly divided the peninsula into upper and lower parishes. In 1652, the Assembly established a third parish — called Occahannock until 1663 and Accomack thereafter — covering the northern part of the Shore. The Assembly combined the upper and lower Northampton parishes into a single unit called Hungars Parish in 1691. *Statutes at Large,* i. 249, 374; Ames, "Some Colonial Foundations," i. 114; Nor OW, 1689–98, pp. 117–18.

19. Bernhard, "Poverty and the Social Order," p. 149.

20. Acc O, 1666–70, f. 38, p. 198; Nor O, 1664–74, f. 238; Nor OW, 1674–79, p. 12; Acc O, 1676–78, p. 96; Acc WO, 1682–97, pp. 30, 31a; Acc WDO, 1678–82, p. 276; Nor OW, 1689–98, p. 14; *Vestry Book of Christ Church Parish,* pp. 21, 26, 28, 29, 31, 32, 34, 35, 40, 45; *Vestry Book of Petworth Parish,* pp. 1, 4, 8, 18, 20; *Vestry Book and Register of St. Peter's Parish,* pp. 3, 7, 11, 46, 47, 50, 51.

21. *Statutes at Large,* i. 253, 438–39; "Some Acts," ed. Billings, pp. 37–38. For an example, see Nor O, 1657–64, p. 110 (man who impregnated ser-

vant ordered to pay her master 1,500 pounds of tobacco "according to Act of Assembly for her loss of time").

22. "Some Acts," ed. Kukla, p. 83.

23. *Statutes at Large,* ii. 115. In Accomack County, however, JPs continued to hear suits compensation suits against men under a local bylaw allowing "to the Master of a weoman Servant gott with Child by a free man fifteen hundred pounds of tobacco for damage accruing to the said Master thereby" plus reimbursement of her lying-in expenses. Acc O, 1666–70, p. 79; see also f. 64, p. 188; Acc DWO, 1663–66, p.-f. 55, p. 113.

24. *Statutes at Large,* ii. 114–15. For examples of orders lengthening a woman's term of servitude to compensate her master for the loss of her services due to pregnancy or to reimburse the master for paying her fornication fine, see Acc DWO, 1663–66, p. 100; Acc O, 1666–70, f. 17, pp. 46, 62, 147; Acc OW, 1671–73, p. 84; Nor OW, 1674–79, p. 56; Acc O, 1676–78, p. 132; Acc WDO, 1678–82, p. 158.

25. *Statutes at Large,* ii. 167.

26. For an example, see Nor O, 1664–74, f. 49, p. 53.

27. Nor O, 1657–64, f. 181.

28. Nor O, 1657–64, f. 192.

29. See *Earl of Derby's Case,* 12 Co. Rep. 114, 77 Eng. Rep. 1390 (Chan. 1614).

30. Nor O, 1657–64, p. 194.

31. Ibid., f. 196–p. 197.

32. Eccles, *Obstetrics and Gynaecology in Tudor and Stuart England,* p. 45. On the Greek origins of this belief, see Hanson, "Eight Months' Child," pp. 589–602.

33. "Reckoning," in this context, meant "the calculated period of pregnancy." *Oxford English Dictionary,* xiii. 336.

34. Nor O, 1657–64, p. 197.

35. Ibid., p. 196.

36. Scott, DiSaia, Hammond, and Spellacy, *Danforth's Obstetrics,* p. 394; Eden and Boehm, *Assessment and Care of the Fetus,* p. 652. The mean duration of singleton pregnancies is 266 days from conception; the average length of twin pregnancies is 247 days. Scott, DiSaia, Hammond, and Spellacy, *Danforth's Obstetrics,* pp. 134–35; Iffy and Kaminetzky, *Principles and Practice of Obstetrics,* ii. 1183. Anne's twins were born 243 days after she had sex with John the first time.

37. Leridon, *Human Fertility,* p. 15.

38. Nor O, 1657–64, p. 196.

39. Despite unhygienic conditions, death in childbed was rare. In England, the maternal mortality rate during the second half of the seventeenth

century was just 16 per 1,000 live births. The rate in New England was even lower, but it may have been somewhat higher in the Chesapeake region, where malaria weakened women's resistance to other diseases. On maternal mortality, see Ulrich, *Midwife's Tale*, pp. 169–70, 192; Schofield, "Did the Mothers Really Die?" pp. 248, 250; Wertz and Wertz, *Lying-In*, p. 19.

40. For an example, see Cressy, *Birth, Marriage, and Death*, p. 79 (citing 1630 case in which a midwife purposely increased an expectant mother's pain to induce her to reveal the father's identity).

41. Nor O, 1657–64, p. 197.

42. See, e.g., Nor OW, 1683–89, pp. 30, 38, 40, 222, 239; Acc WDO, 1678–82, p. 239; Acc WO, 1682–97, pp. 3, 30, 50a, 52, 54; Acc O, 1690–97, pp. 138a, 152, 159; see also *Minutes of the Council*, p. 265. Child-support actions occasionally got to court in at least three other ways. (1) Mothers sued fathers to compel support. E.g., Acc-Nor Rec, 1640–45, pp. 236–37; Nor DWO, 1645–51, f. 122, f. 128–p. 129; Acc O, 1666–70, f. 17. (2) Masters of bastard-bearing servants sued fathers to force them to maintain their offspring. E.g., Nor WDO, 1645–51, p. 229; see also Acc DWO, 1678–82, p. 276; Acc WO, 1682–97, pp. 58a–59, 63a (masters' suits against fathers' sureties). (3) JPs issued maintenance orders on their own initiative following fornication prosecutions. E.g., Acc DWO, 1663–66, pp. 20, 23, 25, ff. 54, 64; Acc O, 1666–70, pp. 12, 141, 145; Nor O, 1657–64, ff. 32, 66, 72, 76, 119, p. 124 (maintenance orders after grand jury presentments); p.-f. 170; Nor O, 1664–74, f. 32; Acc O, 1676–78, p. 78 (maintenance orders after churchwardens' presentments).

43. JPs as churchwardens: Nor O, 1657–64, p.-f. 170; Acc O, 1666–70, p. 16; Acc WDO, 1673–76, p. 377; Acc O, 1676–78, p. 48; Nor OW, 1674–79, p. 301; Acc WDO, 1678–82, pp. 154, 191, 239, 240; Nor DW, 1680–92, p. 1; Nor O, 1678–83, pp. 197, 203, 207; Acc WO, 1682–97, pp. 30, 74, 111; Nor OW, 1689–98, pp. 12, 51, 58, 62, 191, 377. Churchwardens were chosen by vestries that often were dominated by magistrates. See Butler, *Awash in a Sea of Faith,* p. 43.

44. Nor O, 1657–64, f. 170, p. 189.

45. For an example of a case in which Custis prosecuted as a churchwarden and recused as a magistrate, see ibid., p. 189.

Chapter 7

1. *Statutes at Large*, ii. 59, 72. On the cultural significance of court day ceremonies, see Roeber, "Authority, Law, and Custom," pp. 29–52; Roeber, *Faithful Magistrates*, pp. 73–95; Isaac, *Transformation of Virginia*, pp. 88–94.

2. Nor O, 1657–64, p. 195.

3. *Lawes of Virginia,* pp. 12, 21; see also *Statutes at Large,* ii. 60, 72.

4. *Lawes of Virginia,* pp. 13, 21; see also *Statutes at Large,* ii. 60, 72.

5. Nor O, 1657–64, p. 195.

6. Murrin and Roeber, "Trial by Jury," p. 115. The first civil (*nisi prius*) trial jury mentioned in the Eastern Shore records was a 12-man panel chosen by the Accomack-Northampton magistrates in 1641. Acc-Nor Rec, 1640–45, p. 121.

7. *Statutes at Large,* i. 273–74.

8. Ibid., i. 303.

9. Ibid., i. 313–14; see also i. 474.

10. Ibid., ii. 73–74, 146. The fee was calculated at 12 pounds of tobacco per cause plus five pounds per juror summoned.

11. "Causes of Discontent," p. 291.

12. For references to Waterson's occupational background, see Nor DWO, 1654–55, f. 67; Nor DW, 1657–66, p. 229; Nor DW, 1666–68, p. 25. Waterson was born in 1629 and died in 1680. Nor O, 1657–64, f. 18; Nor O, 1664–74, p. 120; Nor OW, 1674–79, p. 265; Nor O, 1678–83, pp. 63, 66–67.

13. Nor O, 1657–64, f. 125–p. 126, f. 175, f. 185–p. 186.

14. Nor O, 1657–64, f. 185, p. 196; Nor O, 1664–74, pp. 6, 7, 8, f. 17, pp. 32, 37, 43, f. 44, p. 45, ff. 45, 48, p. 51, ff. 51, 55, 56, pp. 57, 60, 65, ff. 67, 94, 99, 103, p. 113, ff. 118, 119, 124, 125, p. 143, ff. 154, 155, 159, 160, 163, 165, 166, 176, pp. 180, 202, 204, 217, 227, 233, 235, 241, 243, 245, 252, 259, 265; Nor OW, 1674–79, pp. 1, 5, 8, 15, 16, 22, 30, 36, 45, 56, 68, 76, 78, 92, 114, 200, 228, 278, 292, 294, 296–97. Foreman: Nor O, 1657–64, p. 196; Nor O, 1664–74, p. 37, ff. 67, 99, 103, p. 113, ff. 118, 119, 124, 143, 154, 176, p. 259; Nor OW, 1674–79, p. 1.

15. Grand jury: Nor O, 1664–74, p. 37; coroner's jury: Nor O, 1664–74, p. 75; petit jury: Nor O, 1657–64, f. 205–p. 206.

16. Surveyor: Nor O, 1657–64, ff. 127, 167; Nor OW, 1674–79, pp. 42, 256; churchwarden: Nor O, 1664–74, p. 120; appraiser: Nor O, 1657–64, p. 87; Nor O, 1664–74, p. 9, f. 11, p. 19, ff. 24, 31, 87, 97; Nor OW, 1674–79, p. 331.

17. Whitelaw, *Virginia's Eastern Shore,* i. 152. Waterson purchased another 444 acres in 1665. Nor DW, 1666–68, pp. 32–32a.

18. Nor O, 1657–64, ff. 197–98. From 1663–77, Waterson paid taxes on an average of 4.2 people a year, including himself. The average Northampton head of household in that period paid taxes on 2.6 people and the average Northampton JP on 9.4 people. Nor O, 1657–64, f. 175–p. 176, ff. 197–98; Nor O, 1664–74, p. 14–f. 15, ff. 28–29, ff. 41–42, pp. 54–55, ff. 114–15, 272–73; Nor O, 1674–79, pp. 73–75, 148–50, 189–91; "List of Tithables," pp. 194–96, 258–63.

19. Nor O, 1664–74, f. 96. See also Nor DWO, 1651–54, p. 217; Nor DW, 1657–66, p. 129.

20. See Acc O, 1666–70, f. 1.

21. See Baker, *Introduction to English Legal History,* pp. 107–8, 396.

22. Nor O, 1657–64, pp. 196–97.

23. This colloquy is based on the procedure followed in *Rex v. Hayes & Cooke* (1665), ibid., f. 205.

24. Ibid., p. 196.

25. Ibid., p. 131.

26. Ibid., f. 195.

27. For a discussion of a similar line of New York "asymmetric knowledge" cases holding sellers liable for defective horses and slaves, see Scheppele, *Legal Secrets,* p. 285.

28. See Sullivan, "Innovation in the Law of Warranty," p. 348.

29. For post-*Waters* decisions applying *caveat venditor,* see *Randall v. Blacklock* (1667), Nor O, 1664–74, p. 35 (although seller of defective butter did not expressly warrant its quality, court held him liable because he "promised the same to bee good"; buyer granted rescission of sale and restitution of purchase price); *Kelly & Dowell v. Watts* (1667), Acc O, 1666–70, pp. 18, 26 (maidservant whom sellers described as "sound winde and limb" proved so diseased that she could not work; sellers ordered to take her back and give buyer a healthy replacement); *Teackle v. Taylor* (1669), Acc O, 1666–70, pp. 140, 143 (buyer of rotten cloth, which seller had described as "a piece of very good Cloath, the best man in the Country might be seene to ware it," allowed to rescind sale and recover his down payment).

30. See *Milby v. Doe* (1689), Acc WO, 1682–97, p. 165 (buyer negligently mistook seller's mare for a more valuable animal and agreed to pay too much for her; seller knowingly cheated buyer but jurors and justices upheld the sale because buyer could have protected himself by verifying the mare's identity before agreeing to buy her).

31. *Virginia Colonial Decisions,* ii. B45–B50.

32. For an excellent account of the social and economic changes that took place in the Chesapeake between 1660 and 1760, see Greene, *Pursuits of Happiness,* chap. 4.

Chapter 8

1. Nor O, 1657–64, p.-f. 196.

2. Ibid., f. 196.

3. Oath before JPs: *Quarter Sessions Order Book [Sussex],* p. 62; Dalton, *Countrey Justice,* p. 425; Meriton, *Guide for Constables,* p. 187. Oath before

ecclesiastical judges: *Worcestershire County Records,* p. 443, 454. Statement to midwives: *Warwick County Records,* i. 44, 87, 123; ii. 66–67; iii. 337–38; iv. 17, 24, 26, 105, 173, 190. Combination: i. 134–35, 148–49 (woman identified bastard's father during labor and again while testifying before JPs under oath); iv. 276–77 (same); W. T., *Office of the Clerk,* p. 203 (same); *Minutes of Proceedings in Quarter Sessions [Kesteven, Lincoln],* ii. 266, 318 (paternity determined by woman's accusation during labor and "divers other pregnant proofs and circumstances under oath"); Keble, *Assistance to Justices,* p. 201 (same).

4. Dalton, *Countrey Justice,* p. 40.

5. See *Quarter Sessions Records for the County of Somerset,* i. 117, 118–19, 121, 220, 241, 249, 309, 310; ii. 90; *Quarter Sessions Records of the County of Northampton,* p. 193; see also *Warwick County Records,* iv. 10, 24, 142 (man named as father during labor held liable "notwithstanding all the suspicions and probable proof to the contrary").

6. See *Quarter Sessions Records for Somerset,* i. 337; *Quarter Sessions Order Book [Sussex],* pp. 34, 41, 67, 85.

7. Webb, *English Poor Law History, pt. 1,* pp. 311– 12.

8. Dalton, *Countrey Justice,* p. 41.

9. E.g., *Quarter Sessions Records for Somerset,* i. 118–19, 241, 249, 251, 255, 258, 309, 310; ii. 89, 90; iii. 309, 339; *Warwick County Records,* i. 134–35; ii. 46, 176; iii. 213, 232; *Worcestershire County Records,* p. 68; see also Quaife, *Wanton Wenches,* pp. 64, 106–13.

10. W. T., *Office of Clerk,* p. 204. The phrase appears in a model bastardy order approved by the judges of King's Bench. For examples of lump-sum child support payments, see *Quarter Sessions Order Book [Sussex],* pp. 34, 38, 41, 85, 121. Formal maintenance orders were not always necessary. Payments sometimes were fixed by arbitration or private agreement. Fletcher, *Reform in the Provinces,* p. 68; Quaife, *Wanton Wenches,* pp. 203–6, 230.

11. The Poor Law of 1598 authorized churchwardens to bind out bastards who were between the ages of seven and fifteen. 39 Eliz. I, c. 3, s. 4 (1598); 7 Jac. I, c. 3, s. 4 (1610); Meriton, *Guide for Constables,* p. 168. For examples of the standard form used to bind out parish apprentices, see *Guide for Constables* pp. 173–75; Wingate, *Exact Constable,* pp. 133–35; Keble, *Assistance to Justices,* p. 178. I found orders binding out bastards as young as seven and as old as fourteen, but the most common ages were eight to twelve. See *Quarter Sessions Records of the County of Northampton,* pp. 118–19, 165–66, 221 (seven years old); p. xxxi (eight); *Portsmouth Record Series Borough Sessions Papers,* p. 133 (eight); *Quarter Sessions Records for the County of Somerset,* ii. 252–53 (eight); iii. 198, 217 (eight); Dalton, *Countrey Justice,* pp. 425–26 (eight); Willcox, *Gloucestershire,* p. 255 (eight);

Warwick County Records, ii. 110 (nine); *Norfolk Quarter Sessions Order Book,* pp. 25, 59, 70, 76 (ten); *Minutes of Proceedings in Quarter Sessions [Kesteven, Lincoln],* ii. 266, 318 (twelve); Keble, *Assistance to Justices,* p. 201 (twelve); *Hertford County Records,* p. 84 (fourteen).

12. 39 Eliz. I, c. 3, s. 4 (1598); 43 Eliz. I, c. 2, s. 3 (1601). Twenty-four remained the age of emancipation for male parish apprentices until 1778, when Parliament lowered the maximum age to 21 in the hope that "the hardships brought on such parish Apprentices, by the Length of their Apprenticeship, would be avoided, and the good Harmony between Master and Apprentice would be better maintained." 18 Geo. III, c. 47 (1778). Even before Parliament lowered the maximum age, the indenture could provide for early emancipation. Bott, *Collection of Decisions,* pp. 87–88. Most indentures required service until age 24, though, causing considerable friction between masters and servants. Hampson, *Treatment of Poverty in Cambridgeshire,* p. 162.

13. See Keble, *Assistance to Justices,* pp. 200–201.

14. Meriton, *Guide for Constables,* p. 167.

15. See *Somerset Assize Orders,* p. 67 (1633 resolution of the assize judges); *Essex Quarter Sessions Order Book,* p. 32.

16. See, e.g., Nor DWO, 1645–51, p.-f. 155, p. 177, f. 179–p. 180.

17. Order to maintain child: Nor DWO, 1645–51, f. 54, f. 128–p. 129, f. 155, pp. 229, 265; Nor O, 1657–64, f. 163; Acc DWO, 1663–66, p. 23; Acc O, 1666–70, f. 17; Acc OW, 1671–73, p. 204; Nor OW, 1674–79, p. 202; Acc WO, 1682–97, p. 115; Nor OW, 1689–98, p. 426. Order to post security: Nor DWO, 1645–51, ff. 49, 122; Nor O, 1657–64, p. 29, f. 40, p. 175, f. 179; Acc DWO, 1663–66, p. 25, f. 92; Nor O, 1664–74, f. 32, p. 35, f. 38, pp. 76, 124; Acc O, 1666–70, pp. 12, 58, 59, f. 64, pp. 71, 145, 188; Acc OW, 1671–73, pp. 71, 176; Acc WDO, 1673–76, p. 364; Nor OW, 1674–79, p. 135; Acc O, 1676–78, pp. 36, 152; Acc WDO, 1678–82, pp. 3, 37, 108, 109, 202, 252, 282, 283; Acc WO, 1682–97, pp. 3, 10–10a, 105a, 115a, 119, 119a, 125; Nor OW, 1683–89, pp. 40, 112–13, 202, 301, 405; Nor OW, 1689–98, p. 160; Acc O, 1690–97, pp. 128a, 129, 138a, 152, 159, 169a. Primary responsibility for child support fell to the mother if the child was conceived in another county and the father was beyond the court's jurisdiction, or if the father was a slave and thus permanently incapable of guaranteeing maintenance. See Nor OW, 1674–79, p. 50; Nor OW, 1683–89, pp. 59, 442–43; Nor OW, 1689–98, p. 377. If the mother was a slave, the child became her master's property and the father had no support obligation. See *Statutes at Large,* ii. 170 (children of enslaved women inherited their mother's status).

18. See Acc O, 1666–70, f. 17; Nor OW, 1683–89, pp. 112–13; Acc WDO, 1673–76, ff. 77, 112; Nor DWO, 1651–54, p. 205.

19. See Acc-Nor Rec, 1640–45, p. 120; Acc OW, 1671–73, p. 27; Acc WDO, 1678–82, p. 276; Acc WO, 1682–97, pp. 58a-59, 63a; Acc DWO, 1663–66, f. 25; Nor O, 1664–74, p. 53; Acc WDO, 1673–76, f. 23; Nor OW, 1674–79, pp. 12, 26. The sureties or sheriff were entitled to reimbursement from the father.

20. See, e.g., Nor OW, 1689–98, pp. 231, 235, 241; Acc O, 1714–17, pp. 7, 8a, 9. If the mother was a servant, the churchwardens, in essence, rented her child-rearing services from her employer. See Acc O, 1676–78, pp. 48, 96; Acc WDO, 1678–82, pp. 178, 285; Acc O, 1690–97, pp. 2–2a, 27a, 28, 28a.

21. *Statutes at Large,* ii. 168.

22. See, e.g., Acc DWO, 1663–66, p. 87, f. 94, p. 100; Acc OW, 1671–73, pp. 118–19, 121; Nor O, 1678–83, pp. 228–29, 234; Nor OW, 1683–89, pp. 64, 111; Nor 1689–98, pp. 446, 451; Acc O, 1690–97, p. 38; Nor OW, 1698–1710, pp. 320, 352, 379.

23. Acc WO, 1682–97, p. 225. By the early eighteenth century, indenture orders also directed masters to educate illegitimate children in the Christian religion, teach males how to read, write, and practice a trade, and teach females how to knit, sew, spin, and read. See Acc O, 1697–1703, p. 68; Acc O, 1710–14, p. 80; Acc O, 1714–17, p. 21; Acc O, 1717–19, p. 23a.

24. Acc O, 1697–1703, p. 79a.

25. See Nor DWO, 1651–54, f. 214, f. 218–p. 219. If the father previously had been ordered to maintain the child, the court normally sought his consent before binding the child to a third party recruited by the mother. See Acc WO, 1682–97, pp. 111, 119a, 125a.

26. See Acc WO, 1682–97, pp. 119a, 142a.

27. Acc OW, 1671–73, pp. 23, 39–40, 52.

28. My examination of the seventeenth-century records for the Eastern Shore revealed only three instances in which masters required financial inducements to take illegitimate children. Nor DWO, 1651–54, f. 74, p.-f. 77; p. 219; Nor OW, 1689–98, pp. 148–49.

29. Nine days: Acc OW, 1671–73, p. 121. Two months: Nor OW, 1678–83, pp. 101–2. Two and a half months: Acc W, 1692–1715, p. 72a. Six months: Nor OW, 1674–79, pp. 93, 96. Seven and a half months: Acc W, 1692–1715, p. 80a. Ten months: Acc O, 1697–1703, p. 97a. Sixteen months: Nor OW, 1698–1710, pp. 83–84. Under twenty-four months: Acc O, 1690–97, pp. 11a, 15a, 70a. Twenty-five and a half months: Acc O, 1697–1703, pp. 67a–68.

30. Nor O, 1657–64, f. 159 (woman "scandallized and defamed" man by claiming he got her pregnant). See also Nor OW, 1683–89, p. 269 (William Kendall II gave away his maidservant because "hee was afraid of peoples talke").

31. Nor OW, 1698–1710, p. 37 (slave woman "Notoriously Scandalized" her master by accusing him of fathering her mulatto child).

32. I am indebted to Daniel B. Yeager for suggesting that these concepts might be helpful. For his use of them, see Yeager, "Categorical and Individualized Rights-Ordering," pp. 669–715.

33. Nor DWO, 1645–51, p. 225, f. 228.

34. Ibid., f. 128–p. 129; p. 229 (man's culpability established "Not only by the corporall oath of the [woman] But alsoe by sufficient proofe and undeniable circumstance").

35. Acc DWO, 1663–66, p. 25. For a similar statement in another 1663 Accomack case, see p. 24.

36. Nor O, 1664–74, p. 35. For later cases in which a woman's sworn accusation automatically resulted in liability, see Acc O, 1666–70, f. 17, p. 71; Nor O, 1664–74, pp. 93, 124, ff. 219, 238; Acc OW, 1671–73, pp. 71, 176, 204; Acc WDO, 1673–76, p. 364; Acc O, 1676–78, p. 36; Nor OW, 1674–79, pp. 173, 202; Acc WDO, 1678–82, pp. 3, 172, 282, 283; Acc WO, 1682–97, pp. 2a, 10–10a, 30, 119a; Nor OW, 1683–89, pp. 383, 384, 404–5; Acc O, 1690–97, pp. 2a, 27a, 124a, 128a–129, 152, 159, 169a; Nor OW, 1689–98, p. 160.

37. See Acc WDO, 1678–82, p. 202; Acc WO, 1682–97, pp. 3, 115; Nor OW, 1683–89, p. 301; Nor OW, 1689–98, pp. 150, 426. I found one case in which the court ruled in favor of a man who denied paternity, but that decision apparently stemmed from special factors (the possible absence of an oath and the willingness of a third party to support the bastard) rather than from a deliberate revival of the English rebuttable presumption. Acc WDO, 1678–82, pp. 78, 94, 111, 117, 168.

38. Acc O, 1666–70, p. 75.

39. Driggus may have been motivated by a desire for revenge. In 1694, Brewer and his wife reported Driggus's first bastard to the grand jury, which presented the servant for fornication. She was convicted, sentenced to 30 lashes, and ordered to serve Brewer an extra two years. Nor OW, 1689–98, pp. 274, 279. Driggus's 1695 prosecution gave her a chance to turn the tables on her master.

40. Ibid., p. 322.

41. We do not know what advice the governor and Council gave the Northampton justices because the General Court records for this period burned when Confederate forces evacuated Richmond. We do know, however, that a short time later Brewer tried to sell Driggus's indenture to Thomas Mills. Driggus hired a lawyer, Tully Robinson, and sued Brewer and Mills for her freedom in Accomack County Court. In support of her

petition, Driggus alleged that she had completed her term, yet the defendants intended to "transport her to some parts of the world where her free condicon could not be made [to] appear and [she was] thereby indangered to be made a slave." Brewer did not wish to be embarrassed again by the 18-year-old black woman, so he retained the Shore's leading lawyer, John Custis III. Custis produced a purported contract between Driggus's mother and Brewer, binding Driggus for an additional term. The court adjudged the document "invalid in law" and set Driggus free, demonstrating that Eastern Shore judges did not always disregard established legal rules when they decided disputes between blacks and whites. Acc O, 1690–97, pp. 158a, 169a-170.

42. See Acc WO, 1682–97, pp. 2a, 30, 50a, 52, 54 (father required to reimburse churchwardens for the cost of hiring a wet nurse for the bastard of a servant who died in childbed).

43. Acc WDO, 1678–82, pp. 41, 44. See also Acc O, 1697–1703, p. 97a (father arranged for child to be bound to mother's master); Nor OW, 1683–89, pp. 199–200 (father arranged for child to be bound to third party).

44. The two men evidently were fairly close. John Kendall witnessed Richard Patrick's will, and when Patrick died, around January 1676, John authenticated it in court. Nor OW, 1674–79, pp. 102, 113.

45. Acc-Nor Rec, 1640–45, p. 11; Nor O, 1657–64, pp. 138, 176, 187, 198; Nor O, 1664–74, f. 14, p. 40, f. 41, p. 54, ff. 115, 272; "List of Tithables," p. 258; Nor OW, 1674–79, pp. 74, 149. Patrick was literate and sat on several trial and grand juries but never held a major office. Nor DW, 1657–66, p. 123; Nor DW, 1666–68, p.-f. 8; Nor OW, 1674–79, pp. 113–14; Nor O, 1657–64, f. 185; Nor O, 1664–74, f. 23, pp. 122, 124, 127, 176, 189, 217, 224.

46. Nor DW, 1657–66, pp. 122–23; Nor D, 1668–80, ff. 37–38; Nor OW, 1674–79, p. 235. Patrick leased out the northern half of his property in 1666 and sold it in 1672. Nor DW, 1666–68, pp. 8–8a; Nor D, 1668–80, ff. 40a–41; Nor O, 1678–83, p. 35.

47. Nor OW, 1674–79, pp. 110–13, 132–33.

48. Nor O, 1664–74, f. 1.

Chapter 9

1. Nor DWO, 1645–51, pp. 134a, 135, f. 146; Acc OW, 1671–73, p. 60.

2. Nor DWO, 1645–51, p. 165; Nor DWO, 1651–54, p. 199; Nor DWO, 1654–55, p. 83, f. 84; Nor O, 1664–74, f. 14.

3. See *Statutes at Large,* i. 304.

4. Ibid., i., 521; ii. 74.

5. Nor DWO, 1654–55, f. 11.

6. *Statutes at Large,* ii. 52.

7. Nor O, 1657–64, f. 177. See also *Statutes at Large,* ii. 69–70.

8. Acc WDO, 1678–82, pp. 258–59. Had the defendant been male, the case would have been sent to the General Court since "Buggery committed with Mankind or Beast" qualified as a capital crime. Dalton, *Countrey Justice,* chap. 118, p. 319.

9. Acc WDO, 1678–82, p. 51.

10. See, e.g., *Worcestershire County Records,* pp. 139, 336, 453.

11. *Quarter Sessions Records for the County of Somerset,* i. 211.

12. See King, "Punishment for Bastardy," pp. 140–43; Nelson, *Office and Authority of a Justice of Peace,* p. 86.

13. See Keble, *Assistance to Justices,* p. 201.

14. See *Portsmouth Record Series Borough Sessions Papers,* p. 1; *Quarter Sessions Records for Somerset,* i. 19, 52–53, 170.

15. 7 Jac. I, c. 4, s. 7 (1610). In 1650, Parliament augmented the poor laws with an act "for suppressing the detestable sins of Incest, Adultery and Fornication." *Acts and Ordinances of the Interregnum,* ii. 387–89. This harsh measure prescribed death as the penalty for incest or adultery and imprisonment for ordinary fornication. The capital provisions were largely ignored, and juries acquitted many of those who were prosecuted for fornication. The 1650 statute lapsed at the Restoration. See Thomas, "Puritans and Adultery," p. 257; Durston, *Family in the English Revolution,* p. 158; Hirst, "Failure of Godly Rule," p. 61; Roberts, "Fornication and Bastardy in Mid–Seventeenth Century Devon," p. 8.

16. See *Quarter Sessions Records for Somerset,* i. 112–13, 131, 155, 233, 234, 290, 291, 322, 329, 333, 348; ii. 107, 123. Leaving the man's criminal liability to ecclesiastical justice sometimes produced inconsistent results. See, e.g., *Churchwardens' Presentments in the Oxfordshire Peculiars,* pp. 166–67 (putative father cleared himself of fornication charge in ecclesiastical court after JPs held him held liable for child support based on mother's sworn accusation of paternity).

17. For examples of the questions churchwardens were expected to answer, see *Articles to be Enquired of within the Arch-Deaconrie of Middlesex,* pp. 13–14 (requesting names of adulterers, fornicators, and bastardbearers). In addition to receiving biannual archidiaconal visitations, many parishes were subject to episcopal visitations every three years or so.

18. For a more detailed description of ecclesiastical procedure, see Ingram, *Church Courts,* pp. 44–54, 280.

19. See Helmholz, *Marriage Litigation,* pp. 182–83; Woodcock, *Medieval Ecclesiastical Courts,* p. 98; Ingram, *Church Courts,* p. 52; Brinkworth, *Shakespeare and the Bawdy Court,* pp. 15, 74, 75, 142; Marchant, *Church under the Law,* pp. 138–39, 175, 178; Addy, *Sin and Society,* pp. 204, 207.

20. See Marchant, *Church under the Law,* p. 225; Wigmore, *Evidence,* viii. sec. 2250, at 278–91.

21. 16 Car. I, c. 11, s. 4 (1641); *Acts and Ordinances of the Interregnum,* i. 883 (1646 act).

22. Ecclesiastical Causes Act, 13 Car. II, Stat. I, c. 12, s. 4 (1661). The 1661 statute prohibited church officials from tendering an oath whereby a person "may be charged or compelled to confess or accuse, or to purge him or herself of any criminal Matter or Thing, whereby he or she may be liable to any Censure or Punishment."

23. See *Churchwardens' Presentments in the Oxfordshire Peculiars,* p. 167; Wood, *Institute of the Laws of England,* p. 507.

24. *Journals of the House of Burgesses, 1619–1658/59,* pp. 13–14; *Minutes of the Council,* pp. 142, 200. For an overview of bastardy and fornication laws in colonial Virginia, see Lasok, "Virginia Bastardy Laws," pp. 402–21.

25. *Minutes of the Council,* p. 479. Under a 1624 statute, "persons of quality" could be fined or imprisoned but not whipped. *Statutes at Large,* i. 127.

26. *Statutes at Large,* i. 223; see also i. 155, 156, 180, 182 (1632 legislation requiring churchwardens to present adulterers and fornicators to the Quarter Court).

27. See "Acts of the General Assembly, Jan. 6, 1639–40," p. 151 (1640 statute ordering churchwardens to make their presentments to local courts rather than to the Quarter Court).

28. For example, John Holloway, a physician, was ordered to acknowledge his fault before the congregation the next sabbath day and pay a fine of 200 pounds of tobacco; his lover, Catherine Jones, received 30 lashes. Acc-Nor Rec, 1632–40, p. 128. In another 1638 fornication case, the court required John Pope to acknowledge his fault in church and either construct a ferry boat for public use or receive 40 lashes; p. 129. The following year, Pope and his paramour received 40 lashes apiece for living together in fornication; p. 151. Four couples presented for premarital fornication were ordered to "stand in the Church three severall Sundayes doinge penence according to the Cannons of the Church"; p. 151. On county courts' administration of ecclesiastical justice, see Bond, *Damned Souls in a Tobacco Colony,* pp. 125–27, 131–32.

29. *Statutes at Large,* i. 240.

30. Ibid., i. 438–39; "Some Acts," ed. Kukla, p. 83 n. 28.

31. *Statutes at Large,* ii. 114–15.

32. Ibid., ii. 170.

33. Nor O, 1664–74, p. 1.

34. The average number of people prosecuted for sex offenses each year per 1,000 residents was 10.8 in the 1660s, compared to 4.3 in the 1630s, 1.7 in the 1640s, 3.3 in the 1650s, 4.4 in the 1670s, 2.8 in the 1680s, and 2.1 in the 1690s. By "prosecuted," I mean subjected to a judicial proceeding in which some type of punishment was sought, such as a fine, whipping, or penance, as opposed to a wholly civil adjudication dealing with child-support, compensation, or similar financial issues. By "sex offenses," I mean fornication, incontinence, adultery, or bastardy, those relatively minor acts of consensual heterosexual misconduct that fell within county magistrates' summary jurisdiction. For a more detailed analysis, see Pagan, "Law and Society," table 20, p. 391.

35. Council for Foreign Plantations to Governor Sir William Berkeley, February 17, 1661, PRO, C.O. 1/14, transcribed in *Papers of Sir William Berkeley,* p. 322. See also Charles II to Berkeley, September 12, 1662, in "Instructions to Berkeley, 1662," p. 16.

36. Nor O, 1657–64, f. 167; see also p. 172 (releasing Stockley from his good-behavior bond).

37. Acc DWO, 1663–66, f. 23.

38. Nor O, 1664–74, p. 35.

39. *Statutes at Large,* ii. 74.

40. See Nor O, 1664–74, f. 31 (court suspended collection of fornication fine because of grand jurors' mistake in "callinge common fame certain knowledge"). Churchwardens, unlike grand jurors, could present people based on "common fame," but they could not secure a conviction unless the "persons upon whose reports they ground their presentments" appeared in court and gave evidence. *Statutes at Large,* ii. 52.

41. Nor O, 1664–74, f. 17.

42. Berkeley to Accomack justices, May 1667, Acc O, 1666–70, p. 23; see also p. 12. Previously, the Accomack justices had assumed that the 1576 Poor Law required the mother's oath to be corroborated by "circumstances conducing to proofe of the Matter of fact"; p. 23.

43. Beattie, *Crime and the Courts in England,* pp. 341, 348–49. See also Levy, *Origins of the Bill of Rights,* p. 199 (by the early eighteenth century, a defendant was incompetent to testify under oath either for or against himself but still was permitted to tell his story unsworn).

44. Pagan, "Law and Society," table 15, p. 363. From 1633 through 1669, 162 criminal sex cases were initiated on the Eastern Shore against a total of 281 defendants. Males were prosecuted in 144 cases (88.9 percent) and made up 51.25 percent of the defendants; females were charged in 137 cases

(84.6 percent) and constituted 48.75 percent of the defendants. From 1670 through 1699, by contrast, 268 criminal cases were brought against 306 defendants, with males being charged in only 44 cases (16.4 percent) and accounting for just 14.4 percent of the total accused. Females were prosecuted in 262 cases (97.8 percent) and represented 85.6 percent of the defendants. Table 12, p. 356.

45. Ibid., tables 14 and 15, pp. 362–63.

46. Dayton, *Women before the Bar,* pp. 196–97, 225, 246–47, 283. See also Hambleton, "Regulation of Sex," pp. 99–101 (in late seventeenth-century Massachusetts, a man could be held civilly liable for child support on the strength of a woman's accusation during labor but could not be convicted of fornication unless her charge was corroborated or he confessed).

47. Norton, *Founding Mothers and Fathers,* pp. 8, 10–15, 48–49, 295, 297, 324–26, 336–37, 341–42, 401–4.

48. See Rainbolt, "Alteration in the Relationship," pp. 411–34.

49. See Brown, *Good Wives, Nasty Wenches, and Anxious Patriarchs,* pp. 197–201, 207.

50. For a discussion of the cessation of ecclesiastical penance rituals, ibid. pp. 189–92. On the fluctuating fortunes of the Anglican church in seventeenth-century Virginia, see Butler, *Awash in a Sea of Faith,* pp. 38–51, 98–101.

51. See Dayton, *Women before the Bar,* pp. 31–32, 159, 161, 164. See also Norton, "Gender, Crime, and Community," pp. 136–43 (discussing Maryland officials' discrimination against women in criminal cases as a means of enforcing a double standard of sexual conduct).

52. Botein, *Early American Law,* p. 33.

53. Brydon, *Virginia's Mother Church,* p. 282; Flaherty, "Law and the Enforcement of Morals," pp. 222, 226.

54. Jones, *Present State of Virginia,* p. 118.

55. *Statutes at Large,* iii. 72–74; reenacted in 1696, iii. 139. This provision replaced the 1662 fornication statute, which required "proofe . . . by confession or evidence" without specifying the minimum number of witnesses who had to supply the evidence; ii. 114.

56. Ibid., ii. 422 (Assembly's response to an inquiry from Accomack County, October 1677).

Chapter 10

1. "List of Tithables," p. 194. In 1666, the average head of household paid taxes on about two workers plus himself. Pagan, "Law and Society," table 6, p. 68.

2. Meyer and Dorman, *Adventurers of Purse and Person,* pp. 533–35; Perry, *Formation of a Society,* pp. 16, 23, 36 n. 7, 47; Wise, *Ye Kingdome of Accawmacke,* pp. 29–30, 50; Rountree and Davidson, *Eastern Shore Indians,* pp. 50–52.

3. Nugent, *Cavaliers and Pioneers,* i. 30, 524; ii. 140; Acc-Nor Rec, 1640–45, pp. 15, 86; Nor O, 1664–74, f. 265.

4. Savage (1624–1678) served at various times as a juror, vestryman, churchwarden, militia officer, justice of the peace, and burgess. He represented Northampton County in the Assembly from 1665 until 1676. Nor DWO, 1645–51, p. 187; Nor DWO, 1651–54, p. 73, f. 92; Nor O, 1657–64, pp. 17, 66, f. 171; Nor O, 1664–74, f. 46, pp. 78, 84, 223; Nor OW, 1674–79, pp. 235, 309; Leonard, *General Assembly,* p. 39. Politically, Savage led a charmed life. In 1655, the county court fined him 300 pounds of tobacco for permitting a drinking contest at his house during which one of the contestants suffocated on his own vomit. At the same session, the magistrates nominated Savage for sheriff. Nor DWO, 1654–55, pp. 77–78, 79.

5. Tankard (or Tankred) lived in William Kendall's household at the time. Nor O, 1664–74, p. 42.

6. The guests included two of the JPs who adjudicated John Kendall's paternity case, John Stringer and William Andrews II. Nor OW, 1674–79, p. 170.

7. Ibid., pp. 170–71.

8. Nor D, 1668–80, p. 220.

9. See Nor OW, 1683–89, p. 205.

10. Nor O, 1664–74, ff. 67, 111; Nor OW, 1674–79, pp. 56, 296; Nor O, 1678–83, p. 10.

11. Nor O, 1664–74, pp. 56–61, f. 67, p. 105, ff. 124, 166, pp. 180, 204, 217, 233, 252; Nor OW, 1674–79, pp. 16, 56, 68, 200, 228, 296–97.

12. John's taxable work force declined from six servants in 1666 to four in 1667 and 1668, two in 1671, three in 1674 and 1675, two in 1676, and three in 1677. Nor O, 1664–74, f. 41, p. 54, f. 114, p. 272; Nor OW, 1674–79, pp. 74, 148, 189.

13. *Minutes of the Council,* p. 381. The Indians based their claim to part of the land that John occupied on a patent issued to them in 1641 by Governor Sir Francis Wyatt. Whitelaw, *Virginia's Eastern Shore,* i. 281–82. Kendall lived so close to the Gingaskin village that in 1671 a witness described Kendall's house as being "att the Indian Towne." Nor O, 1664–74, f. 111. To avert further friction with the Indians, the General Court instructed John Stringer, John Custis, and two other magistrates to survey the contested property and carve out a tract for the Gingaskins. The dis-

pute was not finally resolved until 1680, when Governor Culpeper granted the Gingaskins a 650-acre tract on the south side of the creek due east of the Kendall property. Nor O, 1678–83, pp. 56–57, 63–64, 69, 97, 108; Nugent, *Cavaliers and Pioneers,* ii. 133; Whitelaw, *Virginia's Eastern Shore,* ii. 1272; Rountree and Thompson, *Eastern Shore Indians,* pp. 63–64.

14. In 1667, following the death of Susannah's mother, Ann Elkington Savage, John Savage married his second wife, Mary Robins, the half-sister of William Waters, with whom he had three sons and two daughters. Nor O, 1664–74, pp. 315–20; Meyer and Dorman, *Adventurers of Purse and Person,* p. 535.

15. Savage died in December 1678. Nor OW, 1674–79, p. 318. Besides the Indiantown Creek property he received in Savage's will, Kendall acquired 200 acres in Northampton County in 1673 and another 200 acres in Northampton in 1674. He bought 700 acres in Accomack County in 1670 and sold it in 1672. *Minutes of the Council,* pp. 227, 349; Nugent, *Cavaliers and Pioneers,* ii. 133, 156; Whitelaw, *Virginia's Eastern Shore,* i. 449, ii. 1272.

16. Fortescue and James gave identical accounts of John's death at a county court hearing where his nuncupative (oral) will was probated. Nor O, 1678–83, pp. 9–10.

17. This type of transaction was necessary to defeat the common-law doctrine of coverture, which automatically transferred a woman's property to her husband at the time of their marriage. See Baker, *Introduction to English Legal History,* pp. 551–54. Warren ratified the trust arrangement after his marriage to Susannah.

18. Nor D, 1668–80, pp. 220–21.

19. Nor OW, 1674–79, pp. 102, 110, 113.

20. Nor DW, 1680–92, pp. 81–82; see also Nottingham, *Virginia Land Causes,* pp. 31–34, 56–57.

21. John Warren was born around 1660 and died in 1725. Nor OW, 1674–79, f. 191; Nor WD, 1725–33, pp. 25–26.

22. Robert Warren was born in 1615; settled on the Eastern Shore in the 1630s; and died in 1673 or 1674. Acc-Nor Rec, 1632–40, p. 74; Nor O, 1655–56, p. 4; Nor O, 1664–74, pp. 189, 273; Nor D, 1668–80, p. 89. He owned a few hundred acres but never prospered sufficiently to afford a servant. Nugent, *Cavaliers and Pioneers,* i. 285; Whitelaw, *Virginia's Eastern Shore,* i. 154; Nor DWO, 1651–54, f. 68; Nor DWO, 1654–55, f. 145; Nor O, 1657–64, f. 138, p. 176, f. 198; Nor O, 1664–74, p. 15, f. 114; Nor DW, 1666–68, pp. 7–7a. Despite his illiteracy, he sat on numerous juries, several times as foreman, and served a two-year stint as constable. Nor DWO, 1645–51, f. 63; Nor O, 1657–64, f. 16, p. 17, ff. 38, 42, 185; Nor O, 1664–74, f. 16, p. 21, f. 22, p. 24, f. 37, pp. 50, 51, ff. 55, 103, 134, 159, 160, p. 189.

23. Nor OW, 1674–79, pp. 310, 324, 330, 348. A jury exonerated the Warren brothers.

24. Argoll Warren sued Carr, but the court found no cause of action and dismissed the suit. Nor OW, 1678–83, pp. 270, 275–78.

25. Nor OW, 1683–89, pp. 198, 210–11, 218.

26. See Games, *Migration,* pp. 89, 92–93; Breen, Lewis, and Schlesinger, "Motive for Murder," pp. 106–20.

27. Nor OW, 1683–89, pp. 49, 52, 55, 61. In April 1684, a jury returned a verdict in Godwin's favor for 400 pounds of tobacco.

28. 43 Eliz. I, c. 2, s. 3 (1601).

29. *Statutes at Large,* ii. 298.

30. Nor O, 1657–64, pp. 191, 192.

31. Nor O, 1664–74, p. 45; Nor OW, 1689–98, pp. 25, 30–32. Holden was sometimes referred to as an "Attorney at law" or as "one of the practiconers of the Law." Nor OW, 1683–89, pp. 112, 273. Those terms distinguished him from a lay attorney, that is, an agent who appeared in court on behalf of a minor or an absent litigant.

32. Nor OW, 1683–89, pp. 286–87. For examples of prosecutions brought by Holden as deputy attorney general, see pp. 300, 327, 445–46.

33. For instance, in 1689 Holden sued on a writ of "ejectione firmae" for an ejectment from land and obtained a writ of "habere facias possessionem" to put the plaintiff back in quiet possession. Ibid., p. 407.

34. Ibid., p. 264 (motion to arrest judgment and abate writ because the plaintiff's declaration "menconed neither time nor place of the Tresspasse done"). See also p. 218 (motion to dismiss action of trespass and battery because the plaintiff's proof varied from his declaration); Nor O, 1678–83, p. 208 (plea that statute of limitations barred presentment).

35. Nor OW, 1683–89, p. 308.

36. See ibid., p. 327 (Holden's charges were dismissed because not "grounded According to Law").

37. Ibid., pp. 202–3.

38. Nor O, 1678–83, p. 208; Nor OW, 1683–89, pp. 254, 265, 266, 300–301, 309. Holden also represented a man accused of fathering a bastard. Ibid., p. 239.

39. Nor OW, 1689–98, p. 67.

40. Nor OW, 1683–89, p. 447.

41. Ibid., p. 459. Holden, Tankard's adversary in countless lawsuits, served as one of the executors for his "lovinge friend" Tankard's estate; p. 463.

42. Nor OW, 1689–98, p. 31.

43. Nor OW, 1683–89, p. 218.

44. See Virginia Rule of Professional Conduct 1.7 and comments 3 and 8 in Virginia State Bar, *2001 Professional Guidelines,* pp. 25–27.

45. The only sure way for a client to prevent his lawyer from representing his opponent in future litigation was to pay the attorney a "Detaineing fee" (in modern parlance, a "retainer") for a right of first refusal to his services. For an example of judicial enforcement of such an agreement, see Nor OW, 1698–1710, p. 431.

46. In *Webb v. Bowman,* decided March 11, 1686, Holden represented the plaintiff, Frances Webb, who brought a freedom petition against her master, Major Edmund Bowman, a JP. In 1670, Webb had been bound to Bowman until she reached 21. In 1672, the Assembly lowered the emancipation age for females to 18. *Statutes at Large,* ii. 298. Declining to apply the statute retroactively, the court held that Webb had to fulfill her original obligation and serve until 21. Acc O, 1666–70, p. 8, f. 10, pp. 43, 52, 62, 188, 190; Acc WO, 1682–97, p. 85a.

47. Leonard, *General Assembly,* pp. 34, 39, 46, 47, 48; *Journals of the House of Burgesses, 1659/60–1693,* pp. 195, 201, 214, 220, 234; *Legislative Journals of the Council,* p. 30.

48. *Journals of the House of Burgesses, 1659/60–1693,* p. 9; *Statutes at Large,* ii. 549.

49. See Trelease, *Indian Affairs in Colonial New York,* p. 239; *Livingston Indian Records,* pp. 48–60.

50. See *Papers of Francis Howard, Baron Howard of Effingham,* pp. 143–45; *Legislative Journals of the Council,* pp. 74, 105.

51. Effingham appointed William Kendall II to the Northampton County Court in April 1686. He served as a magistrate until shortly before his death in 1696. Nor OW, 1683–89, p. 216; Nor OW, 1689–98, pp. 354, 377, 381, 384–87. William II, like his father, sat in the House of Burgesses, serving in 1688 and 1693. Leonard, *General Assembly,* pp. 49, 52. Other family members also inherited some of Colonel Kendall's political power. The colonel's stepson John Eyre (died 1719) sat as a Northampton JP from 1677 to 1691. Nor DW, 1718–25, p. 24; Nor OW, 1674–79, p. 199; Nor OW, 1689–98, p. 88. His posthumous son, William III (1686–1718), served from 1709 through 1715. Nor OW, 1683–89, p. 217; Nor O, 1716–18, pp. 132, 143a; Nor WD, 1711–18, p. 164; Nor W, 1717–25, p. 28a; Nor OW, 1698–1710, p. 469; Nor O, 1710–16, p. 234. His grandson William IV (1687–1720) served from 1708 through 1715. Nor OW, 1698–1710, pp. 76, 411; Nor DW, 1718–25, p. 101; Nor O, 1719–22, p. 85; Nor O, 1710–16, pp. 63, 165, 234.

52. Nor OW, 1683–89, p. 205.

53. Nor DW, 1680–92, pp. 109–10. Sarah was the widow of Walter Mathews, a small farmer who died in 1683. Nor O, 1683–89, pp. 26–27.

54. Nor OW, 1683–89, p. 232. This bequest, which Kendall made on June 16, 1686, augmented the property he had left to Sarah in an earlier version of his will.

55. Ibid., p. 217.

56. Ibid., pp. 224–32.

57. The magistrates who adjudicated Jasper's freedom petition were Major John Robins, Captain John Custis III, Thomas Hunt, Phillip Fisher, Francis Pettit, Adam Michael, and Andrew Andrews. Ibid., p. 217.

58. Ibid., p. 218.

59. Acc WO, 1682–97, pp. 66a, 70a; see also p. 36a (in 1684, a male servant was hired for 1,000 pounds a year plus food, washing, and lodging).

60. Nor O, 1664–74, pp. 219, 228, 238; Nor OW, 1674–79, p. 12; Nor OW, 1689–98, pp. 284–85. If Joseph had been a mulatto, however, he would have been obliged to serve nine years longer. See *Statutes at Large,* iii. 87 (1691 act requiring churchwardens to indenture the illegitimate offspring of white women and black mulatto men until the age of 30).

61. Acc O, 1676–78, p. 36.

62. Acc O, 1697–1703, p. 27a.

63. Ibid., p. 34a.

64. *Essay Upon the Government of the English Plantations,* p. 23.

65. Acc O, 1697–1703, p. 34a.

66. For the view that the Crown's grant of local legislative authority included the power to override general English statutes, see Tucker, *Blackstone's Commentaries,* i. 384.

67. Virtually the entire membership of the Assembly consisted of men who were serving simultaneously as JPs. Billings, "Political Institutions," p. 235; Billings, Selby, and Tate, *Colonial Virginia,* p. 79. On Virginians' preference for changing English law by statute, see Billings, "Law and Culture," pp. 342–43.

68. *Statutes at Large,* ii. 280, 356, 380, 425.

69. Jasper was forbidden to marry without his master's consent while he was a servant. See ibid., ii. 114.

70. Only 9 percent of servants who arrived in Northampton County between 1663 and 1697 acquired land after emancipation, and just 17 percent of those in Accomack County managed to do so. Deal, *Race and Class,* p. 130. For more detailed discussions of the economic difficulties that ex-servants faced, see Breen, *Puritans and Adventurers,* pp. 131–32; Wertenbaker, *Planters of Colonial Virginia,* pp. 71, 96; Morgan, *American Slavery,* pp. 218–21; Walsh, "Servitude and Opportunity," pp. 118–19, 126–27; Menard, Harris, and Carr, "Opportunity and Inequality," pp. 182–83; Menard, "From Servant to Freeholder," pp. 57–64; Taylor, *American Colonies,* pp. 146, 148.

71. Migration by ex-servants occurred throughout the Chesapeake region in the late seventeenth century. See Horn, "Moving on in the New World," p. 185. Many freedmen went to the Middle Colonies, especially Pennsylvania, where diversified agriculture and the availability of fertile land for immigrants gave the region a reputation as "the best poor man's country in the world." Galenson, "Settlement and Growth," pp. 176–77, 188–89.

Conclusion

1. See *Statutes at Large,* ii. 108, 171–72, 441, 512, 527.

2. George Jeffreys, chief justice of the court of King's Bench, in *Rex v. Rosewell* (1684), reported in *Complete Collection of State Trials,* x. 267.

3. Christopher Tomlins labels this preference for just outcomes over formal law "a jurispractice of results." Tomlins, "Introduction: The Many Legalities of Colonization," p.13 n. 28.

4. See Kukla, "Order and Chaos," pp. 296–97.

5. See Breen, "Looking Out for Number One," in Breen, *Puritans and Adventurers,* pp. 106–26.

6. On colonists' selective approach to the reception of English law, see Konig, "Summary View," p. 49.

BIBLIOGRAPHY

Manuscript Sources

Accomack County Circuit Clerk's Office (Accomac, VA)
  Accomack County Court records. For a list of volumes, see the table of abbreviations at the beginning of the notes.
Bristol Record Office (Bristol, England)
  Register of Servants to Foreign Plantations. FC/SFP/1(a), microfiche 20, exposure 30.
Gloucestershire County Library (Gloucester, England)
  St. Mary Le Port, Bristol, Parish Register, 1560–1654. Abstracted in F. S. Hockaday, comp., "Abstracts of Ecclesiastical Records Relating to the Dioceses of Worcester and Gloucester" (compiled 1908–24), vol. 442, Gloucestershire Collection.
Norfolk Record Office (Norwich, England)
  Archdeaconry of Norwich Registers of Wills:
        1612–13. MF/RO 309.
        1632–34. MF/RO 318.
        1638–39. MF/RO 326.
        1648–52. MF/RO 301/4.
        1664–65. MF/RO 330.
  Bradwell Parish Register of Baptisms 1560–1680, Marriages 1565–1677, and Burials 1556–1680. PD 581/1.
  Brinton Parish Register, 1547–1728. PD 504/1.
  Great Yarmouth Parish Register, 1558–1653. PD 28/1.
  "Norwich Consistory Administrations, 1588–1646" (typescript, c. 1900), ch. 1634–46.

Norwich Consistory Court Registers of Wills:

 Vol. 74, 1566–67. MF 59.

 Vol. 143, 1694–98. MF 426.

Thornage Parish Register, 1561–1743. PD 507/1.

Northampton County Circuit Clerk's Office (Eastville, VA)

 Accomack-Northampton and Northampton County court records. For a list of volumes, see the table of abbreviations at the beginning of the notes.

Public Record Office (London)

 Prerogative Court of Canterbury Probate Papers. Series 11.

  Vol.158. PROB 11/158, f. 135–p. 136: Will of Edward Waters, proved September 18, 1630.

Worcestershire Record Office (Worcester, England)

 All Saints, Worcester, Parish Registers, i: 1560–1639; ii: 1639–78. X850/ 2335/4.

 Worcester Consistory Court Papers, 1626–42. 795.02/2302/3/917.

Abbreviations

VMHB	*Virginia Magazine of History and Biography*
WMQ	*William and Mary Quarterly*

Printed Sources—Primary

Acts and Ordinances of the Interregnum, 1642–1660, ed. C. H. Firth and R. S. Rait. 3 vols. London, 1911.

"Acts of the General Assembly, Jan. 6, 1639–40." *WMQ,* 2nd ser., iv (1924): 16–35, 145–62.

Allestree, Richard. *The Whole Duty of Man Necessary for All Families.* London, 1660.

Articles to be Enquired of Within the Arch-Deaconrie of Middlesex, by the Church-Wardens and Sworne-men in Every Parish, and Presentment to be Made Thereof, to the Arch-deacon. London, 1634.

Baker, J. H., and S. F. C. Milsom. *Sources of English Legal History: Private Law to 1750.* London, 1986.

Beverley, Robert. *The History and Present State of Virginia.* Ed. Louis B. Wright. Chapel Hill, NC, 1947; orig. pub. London, 1705.

Billings, Warren M., ed. *The Old Dominion in the Seventeenth Century: A Documentary History of Virginia, 1606–1689.* Chapel Hill, NC, 1975.

Bott, Edmund. *A Collection of Decisions of the Court of King's Bench Upon the Poor's Laws.* London, 1771.

The Bristol Registers of Servants Sent to Foreign Plantations, 1654–1686. Ed. Peter Wilson Coldham. Baltimore, 1988.

Brydall, John. *Lex Spuriorum: or, the Law Relating to Bastardy.* London, 1703.

Bullock, William. *Virginia Impartially Examined, and Left to Publick View, to be Considered by All Judicious and Honest Men.* London, 1649.

Calendar to the Sessions Books and Sessions Minute Books and Other Sessions Records of the County of Hertford, 1619 to 1657. Comp. William LeHardy. Hertfordshire County Records, v (1928).

"Causes of Discontent in Virginia, 1676." *VMHB*, ii (1894–95): 289–92.

The Churchwardens' Presentments in the Oxfordshire Peculiars of Dorchester, Thame and Banbury. Ed. Sidney A. Peyton. Oxfordshire Record Society Publications, x (1928).

Coldham, Peter Wilson, ed. *The Complete Book of Emigrants, 1607–1660.* Baltimore, 1987.

Coldham, Peter Wilson, ed. *The Complete Book of Emigrants, 1661–1699.* Baltimore, 1990.

Coldham, Peter Wilson, ed. *English Adventurers and Emigrants, 1609–1660.* Baltimore, 1984.

A Complete Collection of State Trials and Proceedings for High Treason and Other Crimes and Misdemeanors from the Earliest Period to the Year 1783. Comp. T. B. Howell. 34 vols. London, 1816.

Constitutions and Canons Ecclesiasticall. London, 1604.

County Court Records of Accomack-Northampton, Virginia, 1632–1640. Ed. Susie M. Ames. Washington, DC, 1954.

County Court Records of Accomack-Northampton, Virginia, 1640–1645. Ed. Susie M. Ames. Charlottesville, VA, 1973.

Dalton, Michael. *The Countrey Justice, Containing the Practice of the Justices of the Peace Out of their Sessions.* London, 1661; 1st ed.1618.

Dalton, Michael. *Officium Vicecomitus: The Office and Authoritie of Sherifs.* London, 1662; 1st ed. 1623.

An Essay Upon the Government of the English Plantations on the Continent of America (1701). Ed. Louis B. Wright. New York, 1972.

Essex Quarter Sessions Order Book, 1652–1661. Ed. D. H. Allen. Essex Record Office Publications, lxv (1974).

Executive Journals of the Council of Colonial Virginia. Ed. H. R. McIlwaine. i: 1680–99. Richmond, VA, 1925.

Fitzherbert, Anthony. *The New Natura Brevium.* Ed. William Rastall. London, 1652.

Hair, Paul, ed. *Before the Bawdy Court: Selections from Church Court and Other Records Relating to the Correction of Moral Offences in England, Scotland and New England 1300–1800*. New York, 1972.

Hammond, John. *Leah and Rachel, or, the Two Fruitfull Sisters, Virginia and Maryland* (London, 1656). In *Tracts and Other Papers Relating Principally to the Origin, Settlement, and Progress of the Colonies in North America, From the Discovery of the Country to the Year 1776*, ed. Peter Force, iii, no. 14.Washington, DC, 1844.

Hartwell, Henry, James Blair, and Edward Chilton. *The Present State of Virginia, and the College*. Ed. Hunter D. Farish. Williamsburg, VA, 1940; written 1697; orig. pub. London, 1727.

Herne, John. *The Pleader, Containing Perfect Presidents and Formes of Declarations, Pleadings, Issues, Judgments, and Proceedings in All Kinds of Actions, Reall, Personall, and Mixt; Very Necessary to be Known, and of Excellent Use*. London, 1657.

Hertford County Records. Ed. W. J. Hardy. i: *Notes and Extracts from the Sessions Rolls, 1581 to 1698*. Hertford, England, 1905.

Hotten, John Camden, ed. *The Original Lists of Persons of Quality; . . . and Others Who Went from Great Britain to the American Plantations, 1600–1700*. New York, 1880.

Hunt, R. D., ed. "Henry Townshend's 'Notes of the Office of a Justice of Peace,' 1661–3." In *Miscellany II*, 68–125. Worcestershire Historical Society Publications, new ser., v (1967).

"Instructions to Berkeley, 1662." *VMHB*, iii (1895–96): 15–20.

Jones, Hugh. *The Present State of Virginia*. Ed. Richard L. Morton. Chapel Hill, NC, 1956; orig. pub. London, 1724.

Journals of the House of Burgesses of Virginia, 1619–1658/59. Ed. H. R. McIlwaine. Richmond, VA, 1915.

Journals of the House of Burgesses of Virginia, 1659/60–1693. Ed. H. R. McIlwaine. Richmond, VA, 1914.

Keble, Joseph. *An Assistance to Justices of the Peace, for the Easier Performance of Their Duty*. London, 1683.

The Lawes of Virginia Now in Force. London, 1662.

Legislative Journals of the Council of Colonial Virginia. Ed. H. R. McIlwaine. 2nd ed. Richmond, VA, 1979.

"List of Tithables in Northampton County, Virginia, August, 1666." Comp. Thomas B. Robertson. *VMHB*, x (1902–3): 194–96, 258–63.

The Livingston Indian Records, 1666–1723. Ed. Lawrence H. Leder. Gettysburg, PA, 1956.

Ludwell, Thomas. "A Description of the Government of Virginia." *VMHB*, v (1897–98): 54–59.

Malynes, Gerald. *Consuetudo vel Lex Mercatoria; or, the Ancient Law Merchant*. London, 1656; 1st ed. Islip, England, 1622.

Meriton, George. *A Guide for Constables, Churchwardens, Overseers of the Poor [etc.]*. London, 1669.

Minutes of Proceedings in Quarter Sessions Held for the Parts of Kesteven in the County of Lincoln, 1674–1695. Ed. Sidney A. Peyton. 2 vols. Lincoln Record Society Publications, xxvi and xxvii (1931).

Minutes of the Council and General Court of Colonial Virginia. Ed. H. R. McIlwaine. 2nd ed. Richmond, VA, 1979.

Nelson, William. *The Office and Authority of a Justice of Peace*. 8th ed. London, 1724; 1st ed. 1704.

Norfolk and Norwich Hearth Tax Assessment Lady Day 1666. Ed. P. Seaman. Norfolk and Norwich Genealogical Society Publications, xx (1988).

Norfolk Hearth Tax Assessment Michaelmas 1664. Ed. M. S. Frankel and P. J. Seaman. Norfolk Genealogy, xv (1983).

Norfolk Quarter Sessions Order Book, 1650–1657. Ed. D. E. Howell James. Norfolk Record Society Publications, xxvi (1955).

Nottingham, Stratton, comp. *Virginia Land Causes: Lancaster County, 1795–1848, Northampton County, 1731–1868*. Onancock, VA, 1931; repr. Bowie, MD, 1991.

Noy, William. *Compleat Lawyer, or, Treatise Concerning Tenures and Estates in Lands of Inheritance for Life and Other Hereditaments, and Chattels Real and Personal*. London, 1651.

Nugent, Nell Marion. *Cavaliers and Pioneers: Abstracts of Virginia Land Patents and Grants, 1623–1800*. 3 vols. Richmond, VA, 1934–79.

The Papers of Francis Howard, Baron Howard of Effingham, 1643–1695. Ed. Warren M. Billings. Richmond, VA, 1989.

The Papers of Sir William Berkeley. Ed. Warren M. Billings. Richmond, VA (Library of Virginia), in press.

The Parish Registers of Norfolk: Taverham, 1601–1837. Ed. Judith M. Sims. Norfolk and Norwich Genealogical Society Monograph Series, viii (1986).

Portsmouth Record Series Borough Sessions Papers, 1653–1688. Comp. Arthur J. Willis and ed. Margaret J. Hoad. Chichester, England, 1971.

Quarter Sessions Order Book, 1642–1649. Ed. B. C. Redwood. Sussex Record Society Publications, liv (1954).

Quarter Sessions Records of the County of Northampton, A.D. 1630, 1657, 1657–8. Ed. Joan Wake. Northamptonshire Record Society Publications, i (1924).

Quarter Sessions Records for the County of Somerset. Ed. E. H. Bates Harbin. i: *James I, 1607–1625*; ii: *Charles I, 1625–1639*; iii: *Commonwealth, 1646–*

1660. Somerset Record Society Publications, xxiii–xxiv and xxviii (1907–12).

Rastall, John. *Les Termes de la Ley: or, Certaine Difficult and Obscure Words and Terms of the Common Laws and Statutes of This Realm Now in Use Expounded and Explained.* London, 1641.

The Records of the Virginia Company of London. Ed. Susan Myra Kingsbury. 4 vols. Washington, DC, 1906–35.

Sheppard, William. *The Faithfull Councellor: or the Marrow of the Law in English.* 2nd ed. London, 1653–54; 1st ed. 1651.

Sheppard, William. *A New Survey of the Justice of Peace His Office.* London, 1659.

Sheppard, William. *The Whole Office of the Country Justice of Peace.* 3rd ed. London, 1656; 1st ed. 1650.

Smith, John. *The Generall Historie of Virginia, New-England, and the Summer Isles.* London, 1624.

"Some Acts Not in Hening's *Statutes:* The Acts of Assembly, April 1652, November 1652, and July 1653." Ed. Warren M. Billings. *VMHB,* lxxxiii (1975): 22–76.

"Some Acts Not in Hening's *Statutes:* The Acts of Assembly, October 1660." Ed. Jon Kukla. *VMHB,* lxxxiii (1975): 77–97.

Somerset Assize Orders, 1629–1640. Ed. Thomas G. Barnes. Somerset Record Society Publications, lxv (1959).

Somerset Assize Orders, 1640–1659. Ed. J. S. Cockburn. Somerset Record Society Publications, lxxi (1971).

The Statutes at Large; Being a Collection of All the Laws of Virginia, from the First Session of the Legislature, in the Year 1619. Ed. William Waller Hening. 2nd ed. i: 1619–1660; ii: 1660–1682; iii: 1684–1710. New York and Philadelphia, 1823.

Statutes of the Realm. London, 1819.

Strachey, William. "A True Reportory of the Wreck and Redemption of Sir Thomas Gates, Knight." In *A Voyage to Virginia in 1609: Two Narratives,* ed. Louis B. Wright, 1–101. Charlottesville, VA, 1964.

Swinburne, Henry. *A Briefe Treatise of Testaments and Last Willes.* London, 1640; 1st ed. 1590.

The Vestry Book and Register of St. Peter's Parish, New Kent and James City Counties, Virginia, 1684–1786. Ed. G. C. Chamberlayne. Richmond, VA, 1937.

The Vestry Book of Christ Church Parish, Middlesex County, Virginia, 1663–1767. Ed. G. C. Chamberlayne. Richmond, VA, 1927.

The Vestry Book of Petworth Parish, Gloucester County, Virginia, 1677–1793. Ed. G. C. Chamberlayne. Richmond, VA, 1933.

Virginia Colonial Decisions: The Reports by Sir John Randolph and by Edward Barradall of Decisions of the General Court of Virginia, 1728–1741. Ed. R. T. Barton. 2 vols. Boston, 1909.

Warwick County Records. Ed. S. C. Ratcliff and H. C. Johnson. i: *Quarter Sessions Order Book, Easter, 1625, to Trinity, 1637;* ii: *Quarter Sessions Order Book, Michaelmas, 1637, to Epiphany, 1650;* iii: *Quarter Sessions Order Book, Easter, 1650, to Epiphany, 1657;* iv: *Quarter Sessions Order Book, Easter, 1657, to Epiphany, 1665.* Warwick, 1935–38.

Webb, George. *The Office and Authority of a Justice of Peace.* Williamsburg, VA, 1736.

Wingate, Edmund. *The Body of the Common Law of England.* London, 1655.

Wingate, Edmund. *An Exact Abridgment of All Statutes in Force and Use.* London, 1642.

Wingate, Edmund. *The Exact Constable . . . [and] the Office of Church-Wardens, Overseers of the Poor, [etc.].* 4th ed. London, 1677; 1st ed. 1663.

Wood, Thomas. *An Institute of the Laws of England.* 3rd ed. London, 1724; 1st ed. 1720.

Worcestershire County Records: Calendar of the Quarter Sessions Papers. Comp. J. W. Willis-Bund. i: *1591–1643.* Worcester, England, 1900.

W. T. *The Office of the Clerk of Assize . . . Together with the Office of the Clerk of the Peace.* 2nd ed. London,1682; 1st ed. 1676.

Printed Sources — Secondary

Addy, John. *Sin and Society in the Seventeenth Century.* London, 1989.

Ames, James Barr. *Lectures on Legal History and Miscellaneous Legal Essays.* Cambridge, MA, 1913.

Ames, Susie M. *A Calendar of the Early History of Virginia's Eastern Shore.* Richmond, VA, 1959.

Ames, Susie M. "Law-in-Action: The Court Records of Virginia's Eastern Shore." *WMQ,* 3rd ser., iv (1947): 177–91.

Ames, Susie M. "The Reunion of Two Virginia Counties." *Journal of Southern History,* viii (1942): 536–48.

Ames, Susie M. "Some Colonial Foundations of the Virginia Eastern Shore: Beginnings and Progress." In *The Eastern Shore of Maryland and Virginia,* ed. Charles B. Clark, i: 73–185. New York, 1950.

Ames, Susie M. *Studies of the Virginia Eastern Shore in the Seventeenth Century.* Richmond, VA, 1940.

Amussen, Susan Dwyer. *An Ordered Society: Gender and Class in Early Modern England.* Oxford, 1988.

Anderson, Terry L., and Robert Paul Thomas. "The Growth of Population and Labor Force in the Seventeenth-Century Chesapeake." *Explorations in Economic History,* xv (1978): 290–312.

Bailyn, Bernard. "Politics and Social Structure in Virginia." In *Seventeenth-Century America: Essays in Colonial History,* ed. James Morton Smith, 90–115. Chapel Hill, NC, 1959.

Baker, John H. *An Introduction to English Legal History.* 3rd ed. London, 1990.

Beattie, J. M. *Crime and the Courts in England, 1660–1800.* Oxford, 1986.

Bernhard, Virginia. "Poverty and the Social Order in Seventeenth-Century Virginia." *VMHB,* lxxxv (1977): 141–55.

Billings, Warren M. "English Legal Literature as a Source of Law and Legal Practice for Seventeenth-Century Virginia." *VMHB,* lxxxvii (1979): 403–16.

Billings, Warren M. "The Growth of Political Institutions in Virginia, 1634 to 1676." *WMQ,* 3rd ser., xxxi (1974): 225–42.

Billings, Warren M. "Justices, Books, Laws, and Courts in Seventeenth-Century Virginia." *Law Library Journal,* lxxxv (1993): 277–96.

Billings, Warren M. "Law and Culture in the Colonial Chesapeake Area." *Southern Studies,* xvii (1978): 333–48.

Billings, Warren M. "The Law of Servants and Slaves in Seventeenth-Century Virginia." *VMHB,* xcix (1991): 45–62.

Billings, Warren M. "Pleading, Procedure, and Practice: The Meaning of Due Process of Law in Seventeenth-Century Virginia." *Journal of Southern History,* xlvii (1981): 569–84.

Billings, Warren M. "The Transfer of English Law to Virginia, 1606–50." In *The Westward Enterprise: English Activities in Ireland, the Atlantic, and America 1480–1650,* ed. K. R. Andrews, N. P. Canny, and P. E. H. Hair, 215–44. Detroit, 1979.

Billings, Warren M., John E. Selby, and Thad W. Tate. *Colonial Virginia: A History.* White Plains, NY, 1986.

Bliss, Robert M. *Revolution and Empire: English Politics and the American Colonies in the Seventeenth Century.* Manchester, England, 1990.

Bond, Edward L. *Damned Souls in a Tobacco Colony: Religion in Seventeenth-Century Virginia.* Macon, GA, 2000.

Botein, Stephen. *Early American Law and Society.* Chicago, 1980.

Breen, T. H. *Puritans and Adventurers: Change and Persistence in Early America.* Oxford, 1980.

Breen, T. H., and Stephen Innes. *"Myne Owne Ground": Race and Freedom on Virginia's Eastern Shore, 1640–1676.* New York, 1980.

Breen, T. H., James H. Lewis, and Keith Schlesinger. "Motive for Murder: A Servant's Life in Virginia, 1678." *WMQ*, 3rd ser., xl (1983): 106–20.

Brenner, Robert. *Merchants and Revolution: Commercial Change, Political Conflict, and London's Overseas Traders, 1550–1653*. Princeton, NJ, 1993.

Brinkworth, E. R. C. *Shakespeare and the Bawdy Court of Stratford*. London, 1972.

Brown, Kathleen M. *Good Wives, Nasty Wenches, and Anxious Patriarchs: Gender, Race, and Power in Colonial Virginia*. Chapel Hill, NC, 1996.

Bruce, Philip Alexander. *Economic History of Virginia in the Seventeenth Century*. 2 vols. New York, 1895.

Bruce, Philip Alexander. *Institutional History of Virginia in the Seventeenth Century*. 2 vols. New York, 1910.

Brydon, George Maclaren. *Virginia's Mother Church and the Political Conditions under Which It Grew*. Richmond, VA, 1947.

Bryson, W. Hamilton. *Bryson on Virginia Civil Procedure*. 3rd ed. Charlottesville, VA, 1997.

Butler, Jon. *Awash in a Sea of Faith: Christianizing the American People*. Cambridge, MA, 1990.

Butler, Jon. "Thomas Teackle's 333 Books: A Great Library on Virginia's Eastern Shore, 1697." *WMQ*, 3rd ser., xliv (1992): 449–91.

Butterfield, Kevin. "Puritans and Religious Strife in the Early Chesapeake." *VMHB*, cix (2001): 5–36.

Campbell, Mildred. "Social Orgins of Some Early Americans." In *Seventeenth-Century America: Essays in Colonial History*, ed. James Morton Smith, 63–89. Chapel Hill, NC, 1959.

Canny, Nicholas. "The Origins of Empire: An Introduction." In *The Origins of Empire: British Overseas Enterprise to the Close of the Seventeenth Century*, ed. Nicholas Canny. Oxford History of the British Empire, i: 1–33. Oxford, 1998.

Carr, Lois Green, and Russell R. Menard. "Immigration and Opportunity: The Freedman in Early Colonial Maryland." In *The Chesapeake in the Seventeenth Century: Essays on Anglo-American Society*, ed. Thad W. Tate and David L. Ammerman, 206–42. Chapel Hill, NC, 1979.

Carr, Lois Green, Russell R. Menard, and Lorena S. Walsh. *Robert Cole's World: Agriculture and Society in Early Maryland*. Chapel Hill, NC, 1991.

Carr, Lois Green, and Lorena S. Walsh. "Economic Diversification and Labor Organization in the Chesapeake, 1650–1820." In *Work and Labor in Early America*, ed. Stephen Innes, 144–88. Chapel Hill, NC, 1988.

Carr, Lois Green, and Lorena S. Walsh. "The Planter's Wife: The Experience of White Women in Seventeenth-Century Maryland." *WMQ*, 3rd ser., xxxiv (1977): 542–71.

"Chandelor v. Lopus." *Harvard Law Review*, viii (1894): 282–84.

Clemens, Paul G. E. *The Atlantic Economy of Colonial Maryland's Eastern Shore: From Tobacco to Grain*. Ithaca, NY, 1980.

Craven, Wesley Frank. *The Southern Colonies in the Seventeenth Century, 1607–1689*. Baton Rouge, LA, 1949.

Cressy, David. *Birth, Marriage, and Death: Ritual, Religion, and the Life-Cycle in Tudor and Stuart England*. Oxford, 1997.

Cressy, David. *Coming Over: Migration and Communication Between England and New England in the Seventeenth Century*. Cambridge, England, 1987.

Cross, F. L., and E. A. Livingstone, eds. *The Oxford Dictionary of the Christian Church*. 2nd ed. Oxford, 1974.

Culliford, S. G. *William Strachey, 1572–1621*. Charlottesville, VA, 1965.

Davis, Natalie Zemon. *The Return of Martin Guerre*. Cambridge, MA, 1983.

Dayton, Cornelia Hughes. *Women before the Bar: Gender, Law, and Society in Connecticut, 1639–1789*. Chapel Hill, NC, 1995.

Deal, J. Douglas, *Race and Class in Colonial Virginia: Indians, Englishmen, and Africans on the Eastern Shore During the Seventeenth Century*. New York, 1993.

Dobson, E. J. *English Pronunciation, 1500–1700*. 2 vols. 2nd ed. Oxford, 1968.

Duffy, John. "The Passage to the Colonies." *Mississippi Valley Historical Review*, xxxviii (1951): 21–38.

Durston, Christopher. *The Family in the English Revolution*. Oxford, 1989.

Eccles, Audrey. *Obstetrics and Gynaecology in Tudor and Stuart England*. Kent, OH, 1982.

Eden, Robert D., and Frank H. Boehm, eds. *Assessment and Care of the Fetus: Physiological, Clinical, and Medicolegal Principles*. Norwalk, CT, 1990.

Fede, Andrew. "Legal Protection for Slave Buyers in the U.S. South: A Caveat Concerning *Caveat Emptor*." *American Journal of Legal History*, xxxi (1987): 322–58.

Fischer, David Hackett. "*Albion* and the Critics: Further Evidence and Reflections." *WMQ*, 3rd ser., xlviii (1991): 260–308.

Flaherty, David H. "Law and the Enforcement of Morals in Early America." In *Law in American History*, ed. Donald Fleming and Bernard Bailyn. Perspectives in American History, v: 203–53. Boston, 1971.

Flaherty, David H. "A Select Guide to the Manuscript Records of Colonial Virginia." *American Journal of Legal History*, xix (1975): 112–37.

Fletcher, Anthony. *Gender, Sex and Subordination in England 1500–1800*. New Haven, CT, 1995.

Fletcher, Anthony. *Reform in the Provinces: The Government of Stuart England*. New Haven, CT, 1986.

Francis, Clinton W. "The Structure of Judicial Administration and the Development of Contract Law in Seventeenth-Century England." *Columbia Law Review,* lxxxiii (1983): 35–137.

Friedman, Lawrence J., and Arthur H. Shaffer. "The Conway Robinson Notes and Seventeenth-Century Virginia." *VMHB,* lxxviii (1970): 259–67.

Friedman, Lawrence M. *A History of American Law.* 2nd ed. New York, 1985.

Friedman, Lawrence M. Introduction to *Common Law, Common Values, Common Rights: Essays on Our Common Heritage,* ed. American Bar Association, 11–17. San Francisco, 2000.

Galenson, David W. "'Middling People' or 'Common Sort'? The Social Origins of Some Early Americans Reexamined." *WMQ,* 3rd ser., xxxv (1978): 499–524. "Mildred Campbell's Response," 525–40; Galenson, "The Social Origins of Some Early Americans: Rejoinder," xxxvi (1979): 264–77; "Mildred Campbell Replies," 277–86.

Galenson, David W. "The Settlement and Growth of the Colonies: Population, Labor, and Economic Development." In *The Cambridge Economic History of the United States,* i, *The Colonial Era,* ed. Stanley L. Engerman and Robert E. Gallman, 135–207. Cambridge, England, 1996.

Galenson, David W. *White Servitude in Colonial America: An Economic Analysis.* Cambridge, England, 1981.

Games, Alison. *Migration and the Origins of the English Atlantic World.* Cambridge, MA, 1999.

Gemery, Henry. "Emigration from the British Isles to the New World, 1630–1700: Inferences from Colonial Populations." *Research in Economic History,* v (1980): 179–231.

Gladwin, Lee A. "Tobacco and Sex: Some Factors Affecting Nonmarital Sexual Behavior in Colonial Virginia." *Journal of Social History,* xii (1978–79): 57–75.

Glare, P. G. W., ed. *Oxford Latin Dictionary.* Oxford, 1982.

Godbeer, Richard. *Sexual Revolution in Early America.* Baltimore, 2002.

Greene, Jack P. *Pursuits of Happiness: The Social Development of Early Modern British Colonies and the Formation of American Culture.* Chapel Hill, NC, 1988.

Haight, Elizabeth S. "The Northampton Protest of 1652: A Petition to the General Assembly from the Inhabitants of Virginia's Eastern Shore." *American Journal of Legal History,* xxviii (1984): 364–75.

Hambleton, Else L. "The Regulation of Sex in Seventeenth-Century Massachusetts: *The Quarterly Court of Essex County vs. Priscilla Willson and Mr. Samuel Appleton.*" In *Sex and Sexuality in Early America,* ed. Merrill D. Smith, 89–115. New York, 1998.

Hamilton, Walton H. "The Ancient Maxim Caveat Emptor." *Yale Law Journal,* xl (1931): 1133–87.

Hampson, E. M. *The Treatment of Poverty in Cambridgeshire, 1597–1834.* Cambridge, England, 1934.

Hanson, Ann Ellis. "The Eight Months' Child and the Etiquette of Birth: *Obsit Omen!*" *Bulletin of the History of Medicine,* lxi (1987): 589–602.

Heal, Felicity, and Clive Holmes. *The Gentry in England and Wales, 1500–1700.* London, 1994.

Helmholz, R. H. *Marriage Litigation in Medieval England.* Cambridge, England, 1974.

Helmholz, R. H. "Support Orders, Church Courts, and the Rule of *Filius Nullius:* A Reassessment of the Common Law." *Virginia Law Review,* lxiii (1977): 431–48.

Hirst, Derek. "The Failure of Godly Rule in the English Republic." *Past and Present,* cxxxii (1991): 33–66.

Hoffer, Peter Charles. *Law and People in Colonial America.* Rev. ed. Baltimore, 1998.

Holdsworth, William S. *A History of English Law.* 17 vols. London, 1903–72.

Horn, James. *Adapting to a New World: English Society in the Seventeenth-Century Chesapeake.* Chapel Hill, NC, 1994.

Horn, James. "Moving on in the New World: Migration and Outmigration in the Seventeenth-Century Chesapeake." In *Migration and Society in Early Modern England,* ed. Peter Clark and David Souden, 172–212. London, 1987.

Horn, James. "Servant Emigration to the Chesapeake in the Seventeenth Century." In *The Chesapeake in the Seventeenth Century: Essays on Anglo-American Society,* ed. Thad W. Tate and David L. Ammerman, 51–95. Chapel Hill, NC, 1979.

Horn, James. "Tobacco Colonies: The Shaping of English Society in the Seventeenth-Century Chesapeake." In *The Origins of Empire: British Overseas Enterprise to the Close of the Seventeenth Century,* ed. Nicholas Canny. Oxford History of the British Empire, i: 170–92. Oxford, 1998.

Houlbrooke, Ralph. *Church Courts and the People during the English Reformation, 1520–1570.* Oxford, 1979.

Ibbetson, David J. *A Historical Introduction to the Law of Obligations.* Oxford, 1999.

Iffy, Leslie, and Harold A. Kaminetzky, eds. *Principles and Practice of Obstetrics and Perinatology.* 2 vols. New York, 1981.

Ingram, Martin. *Church Courts, Sex and Marriage in England, 1570–1640.* Cambridge, England, 1987.

Isaac, Rhys. *The Transformation of Virginia, 1740–1790.* Chapel Hill, NC, 1982.

Kent, Joan R. *The English Village Constable, 1580–1642: A Social and Administrative Study.* Oxford, 1986.

King, Walter J. "Punishment for Bastardy in Early Seventeenth-Century England." *Albion,* x (1978–79): 130–51.

Kneebone, John T., J. Jefferson Looney, Brent Tarter, and Sandra Gioia Treadway, eds. *Dictionary of Virginia Biography,* i. Richmond, VA, 1998.

Kökeritz, Helge. *Shakespeare's Pronunciation.* New Haven, CT, 1953.

Konig, David Thomas. "A Summary View of the Law of British America." *WMQ,* 3rd ser., l (1993): 42–50.

Kukla, Jon. "Order and Chaos in Early America: Political and Social Stability in Pre-Restoration Virginia." *American Historical Review,* xc (1985): 275–98.

Kussmaul, Ann. *Servants in Husbandry in Early Modern England.* Cambridge, England, 1981.

Landau, Norma. *The Justices of the Peace, 1679–1760.* Berkeley, CA, 1984.

Laslett, Peter. "Introduction: Comparing Illegitimacy over Time and between Cultures." In *Bastardy and Its Comparative History,* ed. Peter Laslett, Karla Oosterveen, and Richard M. Smith, 1–65. Cambridge, MA, 1980.

Lasok, Dominik. "Virginia Bastardy Laws: A Burdensome Heritage." *William and Mary Law Review,* ix (1967): 402–21.

Leonard, Cynthia Miller, comp. *The General Assembly of Virginia, July 30, 1619-January 11, 1978: A Bicentennial Register of Members.* Richmond, VA, 1978.

Leridon, Henry. *Human Fertility: The Basic Components.* Chicago, 1977.

Levy, Leonard W. *Origins of the Bill of Rights.* New Haven, CT, 1999.

Lewis, Anthony. *Gideon's Trumpet.* New York, 1964.

Luccketti, Nicholas M. *Archaeology at Arlington: Excavations at the Ancestral Custis Plantation, Northampton County, Virginia.* Richmond, VA, 1999.

Lynch, Jr., James B. *The Custis Chronicles: The Years of Migration.* Camden, ME, 1993.

Macfarlane, Alan. "Illegitimacy and Illegitimates in English History." In *Bastardy and Its Comparative History,* ed. Peter Laslett, Karla Oosterveen, and Richard M. Smith, 71–85. Cambridge, MA, 1980.

Macfarlane, Alan. *The Justice and the Mare's Ale: Law and Disorder in Seventeenth-Century England*. Cambridge, England, 1981.

Mackey, Howard. "The Operation of the English Old Poor Law in Colonial Virginia." *VMHB*, lxxiii (1965): 29–40.

Main, Gloria L. *Tobacco Colony: Life in Early Maryland, 1650–1720*. Princeton, NJ, 1982.

Marchant, Ronald A. *The Church under the Law: Justice, Administration and Discipline in the Diocese of York, 1560–1640*. Cambridge, England, 1969.

McCusker, John J. "British Mercantilist Policies and the American Colonies." In *The Cambridge Economic History of the United States*, i, *The Colonial Era*, ed. Stanley L. Engerman and Robert E. Gallman, 337–62. Cambridge, England, 1996.

McCusker, John J., and Russell R. Menard. *The Economy of British America, 1607–1789*. Chapel Hill, NC, 1985.

McGovern, Jr., William M. "Dependent Promises in the History of Leases and Other Contracts." *Tulane Law Review*, lii (1978): 659–705.

McGrath, Patrick. "Bristol and the Civil War." In *The English Civil Wars: Local Aspects*, ed. R. C. Richardson, 91–128. Stroud, England, 1997.

Menard, Russell R. "British Migration to the Chesapeake Colonies in the Seventeenth Century." In *Colonial Chesapeake Society*, ed. Lois Green Carr, Philip D. Morgan, and Jean B. Russo, 99–132. Chapel Hill, NC, 1988.

Menard, Russell R. "Economic and Social Development of the South." In *The Cambridge Economic History of the United States*, i, *The Colonial Era*, ed. Stanley L. Engerman and Robert E. Gallman, 249–95. Cambridge, England, 1996.

Menard, Russell R. "Farm Prices of Maryland Tobacco." *Maryland Historical Magazine*, xlviii (1973): 80–85.

Menard, Russell R. "From Servants to Slaves: The Transformation of the Chesapeake Labor System." *Southern Studies*, xvi (1977): 355–90.

Menard, Russell R. "From Servant to Freeholder: Status Mobility and Property Accumulation in Seventeenth-Century Maryland." *WMQ*, 3rd ser., xxx (1973): 37–64.

Menard, Russell R. "The Growth of Population in the Chesapeake Colonies: A Comment." *Explorations in Economic History*, xviii (1981): 399–410.

Menard, Russell R. "Immigrants and Their Increase: The Process of Population Growth in Early Colonial Maryland." In *Law, Society, and Politics in Early Maryland*, ed. Aubrey C. Land, Lois Green Carr, and Edward C. Papenfuse, 88–109. Baltimore, 1977.

Menard, Russell R. "A Note on Chesapeake Tobacco Prices, 1618–1660." *VMHB*, lxxxiv (1976): 401–10.

Menard, Russell R. "Population, Economy, and Society in Seventeenth-Century Maryland." *Maryland Historical Magazine*, lxxix (1984): 71–92.

Menard, Russell R. "The Tobacco Industry in the Chesapeake Colonies, 1617–1730: An Interpretation." *Research in Economic History*, v (1980): 109–77.

Menard, Russell R., P. M. G. Harris, and Lois Green Carr. "Opportunity and Inequality: The Distribution of Wealth on the Lower Western Shore of Maryland, 1638–1705." *Maryland Historical Magazine*, lxix (1974): 169–84.

Meyer, Virginia M., and John Frederick Dorman, eds. *Adventurers of Purse and Person: Virginia, 1607–1624/5*. 3rd ed. Richmond, VA, 1987.

Milsom, S. F. C. *Historical Foundations of the Common Law*. 2nd ed. London, 1981.

Morgan, Edmund S. *American Slavery, American Freedom: The Ordeal of ColonialVirginia*. New York, 1975.

Morris, Richard B. *Government and Labor in Early America*. New York, 1946.

Morton, Richard L. *Colonial Virginia*. 2 vols. Chapel Hill, NC, 1960.

Murrin, John M., and A. G. Roeber. "Trial by Jury: The Virginia Paradox." In *The Bill of Rights, A Lively Heritage*, ed. Jon Kukla, 109–29. Richmond, VA, 1987.

Norton, Mary Beth. "The Evolution of White Women's Experience in Early America." *American Historical Review*, lxxxix (1984): 593–619.

Norton, Mary Beth. *Founding Mothers and Fathers: Gendered Power and the Forming of American Society*. New York, 1996.

Norton, Mary Beth. "Gender, Crime, and Community in Seventeenth-Century Maryland." In *The Transformation of Early American History: Society, Authority, and Ideology*, ed. James A. Henretta, Michael Kammen, and Stanley N. Katz, 123–50. New York, 1991.

Pagan, John R. "Dutch Maritime and Commercial Activity in Mid-Seventeenth-Century Virginia." *VMHB*, xc (1982): 485–501.

Pagan, John R. "Growth of the Tobacco Trade between London and Virginia, 1614–40." *Guildhall Studies in London History*, iii (1979): 248–62.

Perry, James R. *The Formation of a Society on Virginia's Eastern Shore, 1615–1655*. Chapel Hill, NC, 1990.

Quaife, G. R. *Wanton Wenches and Wayward Wives: Peasants and Illicit Sex in Early Seventeenth Century England*. London, 1979.

Rainbolt, John C. "The Alteration in the Relationship between Leadership and Constituents in Virginia, 1660 to 1720." *WMQ*, 3rd ser., xxvii (1970): 411–34.

Roberts, Stephen K. "Fornication and Bastardy in Mid–Seventeenth Century Devon: How Was the Act of 1650 Enforced?" In *Outside the Law: Studies in Crime and Order*, ed. John Rule, 1–20. Exeter, England, 1982.

Roeber, A. G. "Authority, Law, and Custom: The Rituals of Court Day in Tidewater Virginia, 1720 to 1750." *WMQ*, 3rd ser., xxxvii (1980): 29–52.

Roeber, A. G. *Faithful Magistrates and Republican Lawyers: Creators of Virginia Legal Culture, 1680–1810*. Chapel Hill, NC, 1981.

Rountree, Helen C., and Thomas E. Davidson. *Eastern Shore Indians of Virginia and Maryland*. Charlottesville, VA, 1997.

Rutman, Darrett B., and Anita H. Rutman. "'Now-Wives and Sons-in-Law'": Parental Death in a Seventeenth-Century Virginia County." In *The Chesapeake in the Seventeenth Century: Essays on Anglo-American Society and Politics*, ed. Thad W. Tate and David L. Ammerman, 153–82. Chapel Hill, NC, 1979.

Rutman, Darrett B., and Anita H. Rutman. "Of Agues and Fevers: Malaria in the Early Chesapeake." *WMQ*, 3rd ser., xxxiii (1976): 31–60.

Rutman, Darrett B., and Anita H. Rutman. *A Place in Time: Middlesex County, Virginia, 1650–1750*. New York, 1984.

Sacks, David Harris. *The Widening Gate: Bristol and the Atlantic Economy, 1450–1700*. Berkeley, CA, 1991.

Salerno, Anthony. "The Social Background of Seventeenth-Century Emigration to America." *Journal of British Studies*, xix (1979): 31–52.

Scheppele, Kim Lane. *Legal Secrets: Equality and Efficiency in the Common Law*. Chicago, 1988.

Schofield, Roger. "Did the Mothers Really Die? Three Centuries of Maternal Mortality in 'The World We Have Lost.'" In *The World We Have Gained: Histories of Population and Social Structure*, ed. Lloyd Bonfield, Richard M. Smith, and Keith Wrightson, 231–60. Oxford, 1986.

Scott, James R., Philip J. DiSaia, Charles B. Hammond, and William N. Spellacy, eds. *Danforth's Obstetrics and Gynecology*. 6th ed. Philadelphia, 1990.

Seiler, William H. "The Anglican Church: A Basic Institution of Local Government in Colonial Virginia." In *Town and County: Essays on the Structure of Local Government in the American Colonies*, ed. Bruce C. Daniels, 134–59. Middletown, CT, 1978.

Seiler, William H. "The Anglican Parish in Virginia." In *Seventeenth-*

Century America: Essays in Colonial History, ed. James Morton Smith, 119–42. New York, 1959.

Sharpe, J. A. *Early Modern England: A Social History, 1550–1760.* London, 1987.

Shea, William L. *The Virginia Militia in the Seventeenth Century.* Baton Rouge, LA, 1983.

Simpson, A. W. Brian. *Cannibalism and the Common Law: The Story of the Tragic Last Voyage of the* Mignonette *and the Strange Legal Proceedings to Which It Gave Rise.* Chicago, 1984.

Simpson, A. W. Brian. *A History of the Common Law of Contract: The Rise of Assumpsit.* Oxford, 1975.

Simpson, J. A., and E. S. C. Weiner. *Oxford English Dictionary.* 20 vols. 2nd ed. Oxford, 1989.

Sommerville, J. P. *Politics and Ideology in England, 1603–1640.* London, 1989.

Souden, David. "'Rogues, Whores, and Vagabonds'? Indentured Servant Emigrants to North America, and the Case of Mid-Seventeenth-Century Bristol." *Social History,* iii (1978): 23–39.

Steele, Ian K. *The English Atlantic, 1675–1740: An Exploration of Communication and Community.* New York, 1986.

Steinfeld, Robert J. *The Invention of Free Labor: The Employment Relation in English and American Law and Culture, 1350–1870.* Chapel Hill, NC, 1991.

Stoljar, S. J. "The Doctrine of Failure of Consideration." *Law Quarterly Review,* lxxv (1959): 53–76.

Stoljar, S. J. *The Law of Quasi-Contract.* 2nd ed. Sydney, 1989.

Street, Thomas Atkins. *The Foundations of Legal Liability.* 2 vols. Northport, NY, 1906.

Styles, Philip. "The City of Worcester during the Civil Wars, 1640–60." In *The English Civil Wars: Local Aspects,* ed. R. C. Richardson, 187–238. Stroud, England, 1997.

Sullivan, Timothy J. "Innovation in the Law of Warranty: The Burden of Reform." *Hastings Law Journal,* xxxii (1980): 341–401.

Taylor, Alan. *American Colonies.* New York, 2001.

Teeven, Kevin M. *A History of the Anglo-American Common Law of Contract.* Westport, CT, 1990.

Thomas, Keith. "The Puritans and Adultery: The Act of 1650 Reconsidered." In *Puritans and Revolutionaries: Essays in Seventeenth-Century History Presented to Christopher Hill,* ed. Donald Pennington and Keith Thomas, 257–82. Oxford, 1978.

Tomlins, Christopher. "Introduction: The Many Legalities of Colonization." In *The Many Legalities of Early America,* ed. Christopher L. Tomlins and Bruce H. Mann. Chapel Hill, NC, 2001.

Trelease, Allen W. *Indian Affairs in Colonial New York: The Seventeenth Century.* Ithaca, NY, 1960.

Tucker, St. George. *Blackstone's Commentaries: With Notes of Reference, to the Constitution and Laws, of the Federal Government of the United States; and of the Commonwealth of Virginia.* 5 vols. Philadelphia, 1803.

Ulrich, Laurel Thatcher. *A Midwife's Tale: The Life of Martha Ballard, Based on Her Diary, 1785–1812.* New York, 1990.

Vaughan, Alden T., and Virginia Mason Vaughan. *Shakespeare's Caliban: A Cultural History.* Cambridge, England, 1991.

Virginia State Bar. *2001 Professional Guidelines.* Richmond, VA, 2001.

Wall, Helena M. *Fierce Communion: Family and Community in Early America.* Cambridge, MA, 1990.

Walsh, Lorena S. "Servitude and Opportunity in Charles County, Maryland, 1658–1705." In *Law, Society, and Politics in Early Maryland,* ed. Aubrey C. Land, Lois Green Carr, and Edward C. Papenfuse, 111–33. Baltimore, 1977.

Walsh, Lorena S. "'Till Death Us Do Part': Marriage and Family in Seventeenth-Century Maryland." In *The Chesapeake in the Seventeenth Century: Essays on Anglo-American Society,* ed. Thad W. Tate and David L. Ammerman, 126–52. Chapel Hill, NC, 1979.

Walsh, Lorena S., and Russell R. Menard, "Death in the Chesapeake: Two Life Tables for Men in Early Colonial Maryland," *Maryland Historical Magazine,* lxix (1974): 211–27.

Washburn, Wilcomb E. *The Governor and the Rebel: A History of Bacon's Rebellion in Virginia.* New York, 1957.

Webb, Sidney, and Beatrice Webb. *English Poor Law History.* Pt. 1. *The Old Poor Law.* London, 1927.

Wertenbaker, Thomas J. *The Planters of Colonial Virginia.* New York, 1959; orig. pub. 1922.

Wertz, Richard W., and Dorothy C. Wertz. *Lying-In: A History of Childbirth in America.* Expanded ed. New Haven, CT, 1989.

Wheeler, Robert. "The County Court in Colonial Virginia." In *Town and County: Essays on the Structure of Local Government in the American Colonies,* ed. Bruce C. Daniels, 111–33. Middletown, CT, 1978.

Whitelaw, Ralph T. *Virginia's Eastern Shore: A History of Northampton and Accomack Counties.* 2 vols. Richmond, VA, 1951.

Wigmore, John Henry. *Evidence in Trials at Common Law,* ed. John T. McNaughton. 11 vols. Boston, 1961.

Willcox, William Bradford. *Gloucestershire: A Study in Local Government, 1590–1640*. New Haven, CT, 1940.

Wise, Jennings Cropper. *Ye Kingdome of Accawmacke; or, The Eastern Shore of Virginia in the Seventeenth Century*. Richmond, VA, 1911.

Woodcock, Brian L. *Medieval Ecclesiastical Courts in the Diocese of Canterbury*. Oxford, 1952.

Wright, Louis B. *The First Gentlemen of Virginia: Intellectual Qualities of the Early Colonial Ruling Class*. San Marino, CA, 1940.

Wrightson, Keith. *English Society, 1580–1680*. New Brunswick, NJ, 1982.

Wyatt-Brown, Bertram. *Southern Honor: Ethics and Behavior in the Old South*. New York, 1982.

Yeager, Daniel B. "Categorical and Individualized Rights-Ordering on Federal Habeas Corpus." *Washington and Lee Law Review,* li (1994): 669–715.

Printed Sources — English Cases

Anonymous, 1 Str. 407, 93 Eng. Rep. 600 (K.B. 1721).

Chandelor v. Lopus, Cro. Jac. 4, 79 Eng. Rep. 3 (Ex. Ch. 1604).

Earl of Derby's Case, 12 Co. Rep. 114, 77 Eng. Rep. 1390 (Chan. 1614).

Holmes v. Hall, 6 Mod. 161, 87 Eng. Rep. 918 (K.B. 1704).

Lady Cavendish v. Middleton, Cro. Car. 141, 79 Eng. Rep. 725 (K.B. 1628).

Unpublished Thesis

Pagan, John R. "Law and Society in Restoration Virginia." D.Phil. thesis, Oxford University, 1996.

INDEX

and masters' support obligations, 49, 108, 109–10, 163 n. 39
and parents' duty to provide maintenance, 6–7, 49, 83, 84, 89, 103–4, 105–10, 113–14, 119–20, 127, 175 n. 42, 178 n. 10, 179 n. 17, 182 n. 42
and parishes' rights and responsibilities, 4, 7, 49, 83–84, 85, 89, 107–8, 109–10, 113, 114, 126
punishment for, 83, 84–85, 89, 105–6, 118–20, 185 n. 34
stigma of, 6, 11–13, 16, 145
See also Church of England; churchwardens; fornication; *Ex Parte Kendall*; *Orthwood v. Warren*; paternity; Poor Laws
Bayly, Robert, 168 n. 64
Bennett, Richard, 43, 44, 52, 54
Berkeley, Sir William
  appointments to county court by, 52, 54–55
  and Bacon's Rebellion, 139–40, 166 n. 35
  on following English law, 69, 170 n. 28
  and intercession with the Crown, 46
  on proof required in fornication and bastardy cases, 125–27, 129
  and reappointment as governor, 45
  surrender to parliamentary forces by, 43
Bermuda, 39
Betts, Thomas, 168 n. 64
Beverley, Robert, 68
Billings, Warren, 170 n. 27
Bishopp, Jacob
  as Anne Orthwood's master, 4, 36, 37
  biographical information on, 36, 161 nn. 40, 41
  sale of Anne Orthwood's indenture by, 6, 37, 49–50
  See also Waters v. Bishopp
Bishopp, Jacob, Jr., 36
blacks, free, 33, 59, 112, 181–82 n. 41
Bonwell, James, 49, 96
Boston, Henry, 60
Boston, Massachusetts, 29, 165 n. 21
Bottella, Jaccominta, 79
Bowman, Edmund, 190 n. 46
Brewer, John, 112–13, 181–82 nn. 39, 41
Brinton, England, 27, 158 n. 2
Bristol, England, 16, 54
  description of, 12
  emigration from, 13–14, 19
  as home of Anne Orthwood, 3, 12
Brown, Kathleen, 128
Browne, Tabitha, 82
Brydall, John, 13
Bullock, William, 14–15, 22

Bundocke, Richard, 15
Burdett, William, 23
Burgesses, House of. *See* House of Burgesses
bylaws, 112, 149, 174 n. 23

Canker, Katherine, 119
Cape Charles (point), 20
Cape Charles, Virginia, 42
Carr, Andrew, 135, 189 n. 24
Carter, William, 28
Case, Mary, 79
caveat emptor
  doctrine of, 72–73, 171 nn. 36, 42
  rejection of, 74, 76, 77, 78, 95, 100, 101, 148
caveat venditor
  meaning of, 74, 97, 100
  economic rationale for, 77, 95–96, 148, 177 n. 27
  religious underpinnings of, 77–78
  post-1664 cases applying, 100, 177 nn. 29, 30
Chandelor v. Lopus, 73, 75, 76, 78, 100
Charles I, 46, 119
Charles II
  betrayal of, 43
  contrition toward, 45–46
  newfound loyalty to, 47–48
  punishment of disrespect for, 60
Charlton, Elizabeth, 23
Chaundler, John, 23
Cheriton, Virginia, 3
Cherrystone Inlet, 25, 28, 31, 132
Chesapeake Bay region
  characteristics of, 17, 52
  economy of, 17, 101, 177 n. 32
  family life in, 14–16, 127
  sites in, 28, 31, 55, 131–32
  travel in, 19–20, 54, 141, 145
  See also migration; tobacco
Christina Regina, 30
Church of England
  influence of, 47–48, 128, 186 n. 50
  licensing of midwives by, 81–82
  and regulation of sexuality, 3–4, 5, 7, 11–12, 34, 119–21, 125–22, 128, 184 n. 28
  support orders from, 83, 173 n. 13
Church, Thomas, 15
churchwardens
  enforcement of bastardy and fornication laws by, 7, 34, 89–90, 106, 108, 118, 120, 121, 126, 161 n. 36, 175 nn. 42, 45, 178 n. 11, 180 n. 20, 182 n. 42, 183 n. 17, 184 nn. 26, 27, 185 n. 40, 191 n. 60

law books, 58–59, 137, 167–68 n. 55
Lawes of Virginia Now in Force, The, 47
lawyers
    in county courts, 68, 70
    of Eastern Shore, 132, 137–39, 142–43, 147,
        181–82 n. 41, 187 n. 5, 189 nn. 31–34, 36,
        38, 40, 190 n. 45
    English, 137, 168 n. 57, 170 n. 27
    and procedural rights, 127
Laylor, Nicholas, 79
Leah and Rachel, 18
Leatherberry, Mrs., 24
Leatherberry, Thomas, 23–24
Lex Spuriorum (Brydall), 13
limitations, statute of, 70, 170 n. 30, 189
    n. 34
Little, John, 60–61
local custom, 69, 170 n. 27
London
    bishop of, 129
    businessmen from, 14, 42
    as emigration port, 13
    as seat of empire, 67
    trade of, 12, 17
Long, Elizabeth, 108–9
lower parish of Northampton County, 89,
    173 n. 18
Ludwell, Thomas, 67–68

Macfarlane, Alan, 8
Madeira, 19
magistrates. *See* justices of the peace
Manhattan, 29, 30, 165 n. 21
    See also New Amsterdam; New Nether-
        land
marriage
    duration of, 16
    female servants' prospects of, 14–15
    negotiations, 132–33
    as path to status and wealth, 3, 30–32, 35,
        51, 55, 132, 166 n. 33
    and property transfers, 134, 188 n. 17
    regulation of, 48
    as requiring masters' consent, 191 n. 69
    sex induced by promise of, 4–5, 6, 85, 154
        n. 6
Maryland, 13, 15, 145
Massachusetts, 186 n. 46
    See also Boston, Massachusetts
Mathews, Henry, 135
Mathews, Walter, 190 n. 53
Mellinge, William, 65, 96
Meriton, George, 106
Merrick, Anne, 136
Michael, Adam, 191 n. 57

Michael, John
    as magistrate, 54–55, 91, 92
    origins and mercantile activity of, 30,
        53–54, 165 n. 21
    as slave owner, 77, 172 n. 54
Middle Temple, 168 n. 57
midwives
    harsh treatment by, 89, 175 n. 40
    interrogation by, 6–7, 80–83, 85, 86, 87–88,
        172–73 n. 7, 177–78 n. 3, 178 n. 5, 186
        n. 46
    status of, 81
migration
    to Chesapeake region, 3, 13–16, 19–20, 155
        nn. 11–12, 156 n. 21
    from Eastern Shore, 144–45, 191–92 n. 71
Milby v. Doe, 177 n. 30
militia
    officers in, 27, 31, 40, 41, 42, 53, 56, 162
        n. 14, 166 n. 35, 187 n. 4
    rank as status symbol, 31, 133, 159–60 n. 23
Mill, Alexander, 60, 168 n. 66
Millby, John, 62–63
Mills, Thomas, 181–82 n. 41
miscegenation. *See* race
Mongom, Phillip, 59–60
Morfee, Ann, 125
Morgan, Bridget, 143
Morgan, Joseph, 143
Morgan, Margaret, 112
Morgan, Peter, 114
Morgan v. Bally, 143
Morrish, Edward, 28
mortality rates, 15–16, 174–75 n. 39
Mountford, Thomas, 23–24
Moy, Anne, 52
Moy, Roger, 52

Netherlands, 54
    See also Holland
Nevis, 16
New Amsterdam, 30, 55
    See also Manhattan; New Netherland
New England
    merchants and mariners from, 29, 31, 42,
        55
    mortality rate in, 15, 174–75, n. 39
    regulation of family life in, 33, 129
    See also Boston, Massachusetts;
        Connecticut; Massachusetts; New
        Haven
New Haven, 128
New Netherland, 55
    See also Manhattan; New Amsterdam
Newport, Richard, 52

Newport House Plantation, 3–4, 31, 32
Newport News, Virginia, 40
nihil dicit, 67
Norfolk, England, 3, 33
Norgood, Anne. *See* Orthwood, Anne
North America, 12, 13, 14
Northampton County
   employers of, 54, 77
   grievances of, 93
   location and boundaries of, 2, 3, 20–21,
      157 n. 36
   residents of, 21, 36, 44, 50, 63, 123–24,
      138, 142
   See also county clerk, county courts;
      Eastern Shore of Virginia; *Ex Parte
      Kendall*; grand juries; justices of the
      peace (magistrates); *Orthwood v.
      Warren*; *Rex v. Kendall*; sheriffs;
      Waters v. Bishopp
Northampton Protest of 1652, 44
Northamptonshire, England, 21, 41
Norton, Mary Beth, 127
Norwich, England, 33
novation, 22

Occahannock Parish, 173 n. 18
Old Castle Creek, 31
Onoughton, William, 112
Orthwood, Anne (née Horwood or
      Harwood)
   background and family of, 3, 6, 11–13, 147,
      154–55 n. 1
   death of, 7, 10, 88–89, 90, 99
   emigration to Virginia by, 3, 14–21, 145,
      147
   indentured servitude of, 3, 5, 6, 18–19,
      21, 25, 27, 33, 35–36, 39, 49–50, 147,
      157 n. 38
   marriage hopes of, 5, 6, 85, 88, 147
   pregnancy and delivery of, 3–7, 9–10, 37,
      49–50, 79, 80, 81, 85–89, 91, 97, 98,
      103–5, 147, 149, 174 n. 36
   See also *Ex Parte Kendall*; *Rex v. Kendall*;
      Waters v. Bishopp
Orthwood, Jasper
   birth of, 7, 8, 87–88, 113, 137, 145
   father's obligation to support, 89, 103–4,
      113–14, 123
   headstrong personality of, 136
   servitude and emancipation of, 115, 131,
      133, 135, 136–37, 142, 144–45, 147, 191
      n. 69
   unacknowledged by his father, 133, 134
Orthwood v. Warren (freedom suit), 7–8, 9,
      136–44, 191 n. 57

Parliament
   acts of, 17–18, 47–48, 69, 120, 149, 179
      n. 12, 183 n. 15, 184 n. 22 (*see also* Poor
      Laws)
   victory of, 42, 43, 46, 52
paternity
   ascertainment of, 79–80, 81–83, 172 n. 6,
      177–78 n. 3
   colonial irrebuttable presumption of,
      103–4, 105, 106–7, 110–14, 123–27, 148,
      181 n. 36
   English rebuttable presumption of, 105–6,
      181 n. 37
   See also bastardy; midwives, interrogation
      by
patriarchy, 33–34, 53, 94, 127, 140
Patrick, Eleanor, 115
Patrick, Richard, 115, 131, 135, 182 nn. 44, 45
Patrick, Richard, Jr., 135, 136
Payne, William, 29–30
Pennsylvania, 145, 191 n. 71
Peter and John, 28
petition. *See* pleading and procedure
Pettit, Francis, 191 n. 57
Pleader, The (Herne), 169 n. 19
pleading and procedure, 59, 67–70, 169
      nn. 12, 19, 189 n. 34
   See also forms of action
Pleasance, Robert, Sr., 158 n. 2
Poor Laws, 118–20
   of 1576, 83, 173 n. 13, 185 n. 42
   of 1598, 178 n. 11
   of 1601, 7, 136–37, 139, 142–44, 149
   of 1610, 119
Pope, John, 184 n. 28
Portsmouth, England, 4–5
Pott, Francis, 32
Pott, John, 32
Powell, Thomas, 15
pregnancy
   duration of, 79, 87–88, 97, 104, 174 n. 36
   physical effects of, 6, 37, 49, 50, 74, 76, 77,
      107
Puccini, Giacomo, 147
Puritanism, 43

Quakers, 65, 169 n. 2
Quarter Court, 121, 184 nn. 26, 27
   See also Council of State; General Court

race
   and enhanced penalties for fornication,
      121–22, 128
   as a factor in bastardy cases, 108–9, 112–13,
      191 n. 60